'YOU MUST REMEMBER THIS...'

'YOU MUST REMEMBER THIS...'

Popular Songwriters 1900-1980

Mark White
Foreword by David Jacobs

FREDERICK WARNE

Published 1983 by Frederick Warne (Publishers) Ltd
London, England

© Mark White 1983

ISBN 0 7232 3177 X (Limp Edition)
ISBN 0 7232 3187 7 (Cased Edition)

Typeset by CCC, printed and bound in Great Britain by
William Clowes Limited,
Beccles and London

Contents

Foreword

Mark White has come back into my life at exactly the right time. Our paths have crossed professionally to and fro across the years. It was Mark who employed me as one of the early hosts of the BBC Jazz Club. He encouraged me in the formative years of Radio 2 to make the journey across the musical prairie of *Pick of the Pops* and *Juke Box Jury* to the lusher pastures of the music that now almost fills my life: the kind of music I share with the millions of people who prefer to dance with their partners in their arms than to give solo performances on the floor of a disco. Those millions of discerning folk who hear a melody, catch the tune, then seek out the words and retain them in their memories. The people who then want to know more about the background to the song: who wrote it, when they wrote it, and sometimes even why they did; to know more about the person who made them a present of it—for the gift that a songwriter hands to us is often a great joy to receive. I've been enjoying their talents for over half a century, and earning my living from them for marginally less.

The time is right for this book. That's why Mark White has come back into my life just at the right moment. In fact, if anything the book is long overdue—the last one I could turn to that would help to fill in those empty spaces in my unretentive brain ended with Lionel Bart's *Oliver* and much has happened since then—thank heaven you'll find it between these covers.

David Jacobs

Introduction

I once wrote the sleeve note for an album called *Fifty Years of Popular Hits*, which I was asked to produce. In it I said: 'Those of us who spend our lives making popular music, or who are in any way associated with those who make it, are proud to be part of such a profession'. But it was not simply pride in my years in the music business that made me want to write this book. Having been lucky enough to work with some of the most famous songwriters, both British and American, I know that many of them are fascinating and interesting personalities, and they deserve our attention as individuals every bit as much as the artists who have made their songs famous. The performer is always in the spotlight—the writer seldom is. I hope I have been able to redress the balance a little, and at the same time give you an insight into some of those personalities.

This book is not an encyclopaedia. It is a personal selection of some of those I consider to be among the all-time greats of the songwriting profession. In writing it therefore, I had to lay down some guidelines. I decided to exclude writers who have only written a few songs, with the notable exception of one or two composers whose output, although small, has been truly remarkable. I have also left out composers such as Benny and Stig Anderson, and Bjorn Ulvaeus, who wrote all the Abba hits; Mick Jagger and Keith Richard who wrote the Rolling Stones' hits; and numerous others who have written for famous pop groups, particularly the Bee Gees. The reason is that, in the majority of cases, the hits they wrote have seldom, if ever, been recorded by other artists. They cannot therefore be compared to Lennon and McCartney, whose songs, although originally written for The Beatles, have been recorded literally thousands of times by other performers.

I've also been unfair to lyric writers. After much agonizing, I've left them all out, with just three exceptions—Johnny Mercer and Sammy Cahn from America, and Tommie Connor from Britain. I feel that their contributions to popular music have matched those of the great composers. In justification I can only quote Alan Jay Lerner, without doubt one of the great lyricists of his generation. He once said: 'Lyrics, no less than music, are written to be heard. A lyric without its musical clothes is a scrawny creature and should never be allowed to parade naked across the printed page'. To emphasize the point I would remind you that there have been many instrumental hits, but no set of lyrics ever became a hit without a tune. So, composers had to take pride of place. In compensation, however, I've tried to spare as much space as I could to write about some of the major lyricists in conjunction with the composers with whom they have been most closely associated.

For the unstinting help and advice I received in my researches for this book, I should particularly like to thank Bill Sullivan, former Librarian of the BBC's Popular Music Library; Derek Bromberg of the BBC Gramophone Library; M. B. Wright of Chappell & Co; Laurence Ross and his colleagues at the London office of ASCAP (American Society of Composers, Authors, and Publishers); various contacts at BMI (Broadcast Music Incorporated) the other American collection agency; and George Shepherd of Britain's PRS (Performing Rights Society).

Finally, I hope that this book will help to redress another imbalance that I've been aware of for many years. Popular music and the people who make it have been, and in certain circles still are, thought of as 'not quite nice'. I regret that just occasionally even some members of the profession seem slightly ashamed of what they do. In response to a letter from me asking for information, one contemporary British composer's secretary rang me one day to say: 'I've shown your letter to Mr X, but he feels he's really a man of the theatre, not a popular songwriter, so he doesn't think he should be in your book.' I asked if her boss had ever heard of Richard Rodgers, and hung up. If this book helps to stop that sort of nonsense, I shall be very pleased.

M.W.

A Background to Popular Songwriters

This book is first and foremost about people—the people who have been writing our popular songs since the turn of the century. It is not about the artistic, sociological, cultural, commercial, musical or economic aspects of what has become an industry. Many people more erudite than I have written excellent books about all that. Nevertheless, one cannot launch straight into a series of mini-biographies without a few words on where popular music came from, and why we have it at all.

Folk music has been with us from time immemorial. But folk music implies songs that have been created by the people for the people, and which have obtained their popularity from continual repetition. Nevertheless, it is amazing how much a folk song changes as it is handed down from generation to generation. But there have also been popular songs from the past that were not written by ordinary 'folk'. Henry VIII is said to have written 'Greensleeves', for example. In any event, as the years went by, composers of so-called serious music often came up with a popular song or two, so the success of today's music industry cannot wholly be attributed to the folk songs of previous generations.

Something that is often conveniently overlooked in discussions about music is that composers have usually written things because somebody paid them to do so, rather than because they wanted to. If you're paid to do something, then by definition you're a professional. In earlier days, the person who paid was called a 'patron', perhaps a rather more elegant word than some of those that have been used since to describe somebody who commissions a composer to write something. In European music, for example, Schubert, Handel, Haydn, Mozart, and many other composers who today are regarded as 'classical', were in their day part of a living musical scene and were paid for their work.

In America, popular music dates back to the Pilgrim Fathers. Originally it was based on religious or martial themes inherited from England. Gradually, as it grew, other themes were grafted onto it, particularly French, Italian and Spanish folk tunes. As time went on, the blues songs of the slaves, the chants of the chain gangs and innumerable other indigenous influences, not least that of the vaudeville performers of the late 19th century, became part of America's musical heritage.

European popular song, which, unlike the American, did not have to start on the ground floor, was influenced by composers we now think of as classical, and from them developed the tradition of Viennese operetta—the Strauss family, Franz Lehar, Robert Stolz, and many others. In England, always a land of balladeers, Scottish, Irish and Welsh songs also had their effect, and led to the drawing room ballads of the Victorian era on the one hand, as well as to the more bawdy songs of the variety performers (Britain's equivalent of American vaudeville) on the other. Gilbert and Sullivan of course stood alone, and with a mere nod in the direction of Austrian operetta created the comic opera all on their own.

To start this book at 1900 may have been a completely arbitrary decision, but I believe that popular songs began to take on a new form at the turn of the century. In support of this assumption, Sigmund Spaeth in his *A History of Popular Music in America* says: 'It would be ridiculous to imply that the mere dawn of the year 1900 produced a marked change in the quality of our popular music or in the taste of those who made it their chief aesthetic sustenance. Yet there were signs of an improvement almost immediately, with a higher percentage of literacy than ever before and the first indications of definite musical standards that have progressed and developed ever since'. And certainly British popular music as we know it today stems directly from America. We were into the 1920s before we caught up with what the Americans were doing and stopped writing songs about 'The Bells of St Mary's' or 'Ours Is a Nice 'Ouse Ours Is'.

Popular songs of the last 80 years really started with the invention of Tin Pan Alley. In America I would attribute this to Harry von Tilzer, who was the first songwriter publisher to open up an office on New York's West 28th Street in 1902. And West 28th Street became Tin Pan Alley. Britain followed some nine years later when publisher Lawrence Wright (composer Horatio Nicholls) was the first to open an office in London's Denmark Street, which in turn was to become our Tin Pan Alley. Credit for inventing the name is usually given to an American journalist, Monroe Rosenfeld. One day on a visit to the von Tilzer office in pursuit of a story, he was struck by the awful sounds coming from a beat-up old upright piano in another room. They reminded him, he said, of the noise of a lot of tin pans. In his article he wrote of 'tin pan music', and so it was but a short step to the creation of Tin Pan Alley. England merely followed suit.

What were these developments that after 1900 made popular songs so much better than they had been before? Harry von Tilzer did not seem to be doing anything very different with his first hit of the century, 'A Bird in a Gilded Cage', with lyrics by Arthur Lamb. It was a good tune, but not much different in quality from, say, 'Home, Sweet Home' (1823), 'When You and I Were Young Maggie' (1866), or many of the much loved songs of Stephen Foster (1826–1864).

But look a little closer at the first ten years of the new century and you can see many pointers to the things Sigmund Spaeth was talking about. For instance, the year 1899 also saw the publication of Scott Joplin's 'Maple Leaf Rag'. And what an influence ragtime was to have on popular music. In 1904, a 26-year-old composer called George M Cohan wrote and presented on Broadway a show that made the established impresarios sit up and take notice. It was called *Little Johnny Jones*. Jack Burton, in his *The Blue Book of Broadway Musicals* says of it: '. . . although the critics lambasted the composer-author-star for his flag-waving, audiences loved it, for here was something refreshingly new in the American theatre. His songs packed a punch, his heroes and heroines were American guys and gals you'd meet in Joe's bar and the 5-and-10, and his libretto put New Rochelle NY, Richmond VA, and Boston on the musical comedy map. This "real live nephew of my Uncle Sam" had fired the opening shot in Broadway's war of independence'. To understand the full impact of *Little Johnny Jones,* one must appreciate that the outstanding musicals in New York at the time were shows such as *Florodora* (imported from England), followed a few years later by Franz Lehar's *The Merry Widow* (imported from Austria). But the first of Florenz Ziegfeld's famous series of *Follies* was only four years away.

In 1905 an unknown composer, Porter Steele, published a march called 'High Society', which he had written as early as 1901. Within a few years of publication, this was to be one of the tunes that led the way for a series of jazz-orientated standard to filter out of New Orleans. Syncopation, developed from ragtime by the early jazz pianists, was also beginning to find its way into the structure of popular song. A good early example from 1902 is Hughie Cannon's 'Bill Bailey, Won't You Please Come Home?'.

The arrival from Bremen on the American scene of Irishman Victor Herbert in 1886 was important, because it meant that for almost the first time a really well-trained musician had deliberately associated himself with popular music. Hitherto the skill of the arranger had been responsible for covering up some often pretty shoddy musical workmanship by the composers, although the latter took the credit for any success. So, Victor Herbert's music meant that another change had taken place—'quality' had arrived.

From about 1910 onwards, America went dance crazy, a habit that was to last for some four decades. The first published sheet music 'For Dance Band Instrumentation' appeared in 1911, thus giving rise to the birth of the dance bands, and later of the Big Bands, and Swing. About 1912 the foxtrot was invented (originally it was just one of a number of dances with animal names, such as The Grizzly Bear, The Turkey Trot, and The Bunny Hug), and in 1914 it was swept to universal fame by the talented dance team of Vernon and Irene Castle. But the most significant event of all was (to quote Jack Burton again): 'In 1911 a former singing waiter from the Bowery of New York set a new and faster tempo for our popular music. The ballads that had dominated the music counters since Stephen Foster's day just couldn't keep up with the syncopated pace of Irving Berlin's "Alexander's Ragtime Band"'. By 1911, sheet music was being sold across the counters of every 5-and-10 (Woolworth's to the British). 'Alexander's Ragtime Band' is far from being the best song that Irving Berlin ever wrote, and musically it has nothing to do with ragtime. But it seemed to symbolize a new approach to a new era, and, taken with some of the other developments to which I've already referred, you can seen why Sigmund Spaeth saw 1900 as being the dawn of a new kind of popular music. I would pick 'Alexander's Ragtime Band', coupled with the foxtrot and the progress of dance music, as being the links that took popular music into the frenetic period of The Roaring Twenties.

We have talked about ragtime, about the birth of jazz and syncopation, about increased standards of musical ability and lyrical literacy, about a budding revolution in the Broadway musical, and about dance music's becoming a craze. There was also the musical movie, the 'all-talking, all-singing, all-dancing' celluloid spectacular. But first we should remember that this move towards improvement in the standards of popular music was a slow, slow process. In 1913, songs such as 'The Curse of an Aching Heart' were still being written, but in the same year, too, there was 'Ballin' the Jack'. Twenty years earlier, those two songs could not have co-existed. Similarly, some 20 years later, there was the sentimental and enormously popular ballad

'Little Man You've Had a Busy Day', co-existing with the gorgeous song 'Moonglow'.

Most people are aware that the first ever screen musical was the 1927 Warner Brothers production of *The Jazz Singer*, which starred Al Jolson. Among the songs featured in it were 'Blue Skies', 'Mammy', and 'Toot, Toot, Tootsie Goodbye'. This film produced the same sort of revolution in Hollywood as *Little Johnny Jones* had on Broadway. As quickly as the impresarios on Broadway started to hire songwriters to write stage musicals, so the moguls of Hollywood started draining them away to California to write musical films. It was Hollywood's voracious appetite for music that led to the virtual destruction of Tin Pan Alley as a song factory. Warner Brothers gobbled up the publishing firms of Harms, Witmark, and Remick in one gulp, while MGM retaliated by buying up Leo Feist and Robbins. They also bought all the contract songwriters who went with the companies. In the 1930s, Hollywood could do much for a songwriter. Harry Warren provides a good example. Already a successful writer in New York, he went to Hollywood in 1932, and over the next 20 years his songs graced the soundtracks of more than 60 films. He is the only composer ever to have won three Oscars (see Appendix 1), giving rise to his wisecrack to fellow songwriter Harold Arlen, 'From now on you walk two Oscars behind me!'

In this little historical section I have been writing about the development of popular music in America. This is in no way to denigrate British composers, many of whom are included in this book and who have written songs every bit as good as those of their transatlantic counterparts. But the British did not invent the kind of popular music this book is about. They have, however, been able to exercise a significant influence on popular music from time to time, as we shall see later.

Because of World War II, the 1940s contributed no important changes to the popular music scene. Some of the old hands faded away to be replaced by new names, but the newcomers were composing much in the mould of their predecessors.

As the 1940s gave way to the 1950s, there was still little change in the face of popular music. Be-bop, later to be renamed modern jazz, arrived, but it made no significant mark until 1961, when Dave Brubeck, in the face of all the odds, had an instrumental hit with 'Take Five'. The next development occurred in 1955, with the coming of rock 'n' roll. And it was all started by a bandleader, Bill

Haley, rather than by a songwriter. Haley's hit record 'Rock Around the Clock' set the rock rolling.

Haley himself, talking in 1970 to Robert Hilburn of the *Los Angeles Times* said: 'We started out as a country and western group, then we added a touch of rhythm and blues. It was hard to get bookings for a while. We were something different, something new. We didn't call it that at the time, but we were playing rock 'n' roll'. In that quotation, Bill Haley mentioned two aspects of the music business on which we have not yet touched.

Today's so-called country music is by far the most popular offshoot of mainstream popular music. Unfortunately, it is a term that has been seized on ruthlessly by music publishers, record companies and artists, as a label to promote music that has little or no country roots at all. I have heard everything from a traditional 12-bar blues to a modern pop song described as 'country music', if it suited its promoter to do so. True country music is music that has rural origins. Christopher Wren, who wrote a splendid biography of singer and composer Johnny Cash, summed it up well when he said: 'Country music is really a story told plain, of people trying to get along the best they can. It is music from the ground up, where the lyrics override the melody, and the tune itself is built to a guitar rather than a piano. Country music is traditionally rural southern in its origin, conservative in its politics (but with a stubborn streak of gut liberalism), blue collar in its economics, blatantly patriotic, fundamentalist about God, and nostalgic about Jesus. It distrusts urban wealth and intellect, but tolerates homegrown vices like boozing and philandering, when accompanied by a footnote that they don't come free. If the songs sometimes wallow in self-consciousness, they hold no patent on mediocrity. When the songs are good—and they so often are—something incisive about ourselves as a people shines through. This, like the black soul wail, becomes the real folk music, not what the scholars dissect. The Nashville sound is a misnomer, country music is really the American sound'.

Melvin Shestack, in the introduction to his excellent *The Country Music Encyclopaedia*, describes a conversation with a reporter from a national magazine, sent to interview him about country music. The reporter said: 'I don't know much about country music. What should I concentrate on?' Shestack says: 'I answered almost without thinking. Once when I was in college and I was writing a paper on poetry, I asked my professor the same thing. He answered: "Study the poets themselves, as well as their work, and you'll begin to get an understanding of what poetry is all about".'

As for rhythm and blues, the easiest way to sum up another quite complicated offshoot of mainstream popular music, is to describe it as the development of ethnic black folk music, based on the blues, the chants, the work songs, the music of the slaves, and then urbanized by the influence of jazz. Today it really just means black music. In the 1930s, and even through the 1940s, records by black artists were seldom if ever listed in record companies' general catalogues and supplements. They would be listed separately, frequently described as 'Race Records', 'The Sepia Series', or some other euphemism. By the 1960s, much of this music was being described as 'soul music', a term which has lasted into the 1980s. It has now become something of a promotion man's label, rather like country music.

Jerry Wexler, one of the original producers of this kind of music on records, and one of the pioneers of the Atlantic label, summed it up well in Tony Palmer's book, *The Story of Popular Music*, when he said: 'It was really very simple. We were recording black music performed by black artists to be sold to black people'. He disliked the various euphemisms that the record companies were using, even before his association with Atlantic, when he was working for the magazine *Billboard*. 'We started a little campaign to come up with a new idea. "Rhythm and Blues" was our designation, and it caught on. As a description however, it meant little. The music was not particularly rhythmic, and it was almost never true blues—that had been left behind in the rural southern states of America. Of course, "Rhythm and Blues" was also a euphemism. It meant the music of the black people.'

All of which brings us back to the rock 'n' roll era of the 1950s and 1960s. This was the most startling and far-reaching change that had taken place in popular music since the advent of ragtime and syncopation. It spawned a whole new generation of songwriters, while many of the old generation just gave up the unequal contest and disappeared. In spite of it all, there was still a demand for good ballads throughout the whole period. In 1956, sharing the top spots in the record charts with Elvis Presley's 'Hound Dog', and 'Heartbreak Hotel', were standard ballads such as Pat Boone's 'Friendly Persuasion', and the Bing Crosby/Grace Kelly recording of 'True Love', while Patti Page could still get a million-seller with 'Allegheny Moon'. Five years later, while Jerry Lieber and Mike Stoller were turning out more huge hit songs for Elvis Presley, and Boudleaux and Felice Bryant were doing the same for the Everly Brothers (products of the rock 'n' roll and country music revolutions respectively), the Bert Kaempfert Orchestra could still earn a gold disc with 'Wonderland by Night', and so could Nat King Cole with 'Ramblin' Rose'. And right into the 1980s there has always been room for good ballads to survive alongside the wilder aspects of what was later to be described as the 'pop' revolution. The Bruce Johnston hit 'I Write the Songs', taken high up the lists by Barry Manilow in 1976, shows that good songs, as opposed to pop hits, will continue to be written, and to succeed.

A glance at the appendices to Dave Harker's book *One for the Money* shows that up to the end of 1975, 'White Christmas' topped the list of worldwide sales of individual songs with 135 million. This was followed by 'Rudolph the Red-Nosed Reindeer' (110 million). You have to come down to 8th place before you get to 'Rock Around the Clock' (25 million), and to 10th and 11th places before you find true pop songs. They are 'Twist and Shout' (14 million plus) and 'I Want To Hold Your Hand' (13 million plus). Surprisingly, in the next nine placings, there is only one more pop song, 'Great Balls of Fire'. The rest are made up of titles such as 'I Saw Mommy Kissing Santa Claus' and 'Till the End of Time'.

I said earlier that, while the British had always been in the position of following behind American developments in popular music, there had been occasions when they were able to exercise a decided influence. In the 1930s this was noticeable in Broadway musicals, where the influence of British shows written by composers such as Noël Coward and Vivian Ellis, was often reflected in the New York scene, as was the influence of several British writers who contributed so successfully to the art of revue—Jimmy Kennedy, Michael Carr and Noel Gay, for instance. But it was when The Beatles burst upon an unsuspecting world in 1963 that England exerted her greatest influence.

The Beatles, together with the Lennon and McCartney songs that put them on top, were a phenomenon. One has to be very careful, even 20 years later, about criticizing The Beatles, because they have almost been deified, even by a generation that can hardly remember them. I shall never forget in my BBC days, The Beatles Special that Radio One produced about 1970. We had interviews with the four boys, as well as plenty of their music, and the whole programme was woven together for us by their distinguished record producer, George

Martin. When we had got it all on tape, I thought George ought to come and listen to the completed effort before we broadcast it, and this he gladly agreed to do. When we'd finished listening, I remember saying, 'You know George, it astounds me how old-fashioned some of the big Beatles hits sound, in terms of their construction, and in particular their harmonies. They sound to me like some of those marvellous things the Boswell Sisters used to do in the 1930s.' George smiled at me. 'If you think they sound old-fashioned now', he said, 'you should have heard them when we first got them into the studio!'

The Lennon and McCartney songs as performed by the Beatles were little short of revolutionary. They presented the acceptable face of rock 'n' roll to a generation that didn't understand it, while at the same time attracting the undying worship of their own generation because they represented a whole new image. Somebody was writing for 'the kids' at last. Whatever the explanation, it is interesting to look at some statistics. Again, in *One for the Money*, Dave Harker has a fascinating table of worldwide sales of record units and LPs (he equates 1 LP to 6 units, an EP to 2 units, and a single to 1). Up to the end of 1975, the Beatles topped it with 575 million, Bing Crosby came second with 400 million plus, Elvis Presley third with 350 million plus. James Last has sold more records than the Rolling Stones, Johnny Cash more than Simon and Garfunkel, and Perry Como more than Stevie Wonder.

The last element that I should mention in this brief historical section, is the coming of the singer/songwriter, because he (or she) virtually took over pop music in the 1970s. In the field of country music, artists such as Hank Williams had been writing and successfully recording their own songs since the 1940s. In the wider field of popular music, Paul Anka started doing it in 1957. When the Beatles started, Lennon and McCartney obviously had no thought of anybody else recording their songs. Later in the 1960s, there was Paul Simon with his partner Art Garfunkel, and on into the 1970s with Gilbert O'Sullivan, and many more. All these had the satisfaction of having their songs recorded by many other artists, as well as issuing their own original versions. In addition, there have been many writing members of groups (Abba, the Rolling Stones, the Who, etc.) who have written big hits for themselves, but whose work has seldom if ever been taken up by anyone else. I question whether such composers belong in the same category as those in this book.

The public has, and always has had, a certain 'feel' for a particular song, or a particular performance of it. Even back in the 1950s, when a really good artist's record of a new song would be 'covered' by anything up to half-a-dozen copy versions, the public could sort out the wheat from the chaff, and it can still do it with the singer/ songwriter of today. Certain songs, certain artists singing certain songs, have a magic that is quite inexplicable in terms of music and production. In the 1950s it was by no means always the original recording of a song that became a hit. But the main point about the advent of the singer/songwriter is that it has meant yet another change in the way the music business, and publishing and recording in particular, is run. During the last 20 years we have seen a steady decline in the old way of doing things—composers writing songs to be recorded and performed by established artists looking for something new. Nowadays the majority of popular songs are not only written, but also performed by the composer, who usually, if he's successful, ends up with his own publishing company, and often his own record company as well. This goes for many solo singers as well as pop groups. A case in point is Elton John. However, the real mark of success for these writers is more than just the sales of their own recordings. It lies in whether or not their songs are sufficiently outstanding to be recorded successfully by other singers as well. That is why Stevie Wonder, Neil Diamond, Paul Anka and Neil Sedaka are more important in the context of this book than Mick Jagger and Keith Richard, or Pete Townshend, or the Gibb Brothers. Very few of the songs of the latter group have been recorded by anybody but themselves.

Finally, to the last aspect of this little history, the exploitation of the popular song. Before there was radio, before there were records, music publishers had to do it the hard way. And this meant doing the rounds of every theatre, vaudeville house, club or bar where music was sung, and trying to persuade the performers to include your latest song in their repertoire. Hence the term song-plugging. Before Tin Pan Alley became the mecca of the song business, most of the major publishing houses were located around Union Square in New York. This was because New York was the centre of the entertainment industry. The publishers of the pre-1900 era were quite a dignified lot. To quote David Ewen in his book *Great Men of American Popular Music*: 'They did little to get their songs placed. Frequently (as had been the case with Stephen Foster—1826–1864), the composer himself had to find the place where, and the performer with whom, the song got its hearing'. But the coming together of major publishers in Union Square, and later in Tin Pan Alley, sharply changed the whole approach.

It was from this new generation of publishers that the formula of song-plugging first emerged, and even in those early days it became common practice to give bribes to performers to introduce new songs into their repertoire. Today we call this payola. So, as the publishing houses grew in size and number, the army of pluggers they employed grew proportionately, and so did the tricks and gimmicks they got up to for the sake of a performance. Publishers and composers also began to realize the potential of writing songs for special events and occasions. For instance, 'Get Out and Get Under' (1914), was clearly inspired by the increasing popularity of the motor car; and 25 years later 'Amy, Wonderful Amy', commemorated Amy Johnson's epic flying performance. Campaign songs for politicians were another fruitful source of sheet music sales. W C Handy's 'The Memphis Blues' was originally called 'Mr Crump', and was written for that gentleman's campaign when he stood for mayor of Memphis. Special songs increasingly began to be written for special performers, something which persists to this day, especially in the field of cabaret. As early as 1905, Tin Pan Alley was probably paying out upwards of $500,000 annually to performers in payola of one sort or another, ranging from boxes of cigars to including the performer's name on a song, thus ensuring him a percentage of the copyright royalties.

As the years passed, other techniques began to be employed by the publishing houses. Some of the composers they had under contract were musically fairly illiterate, so they began to take on arrangers who could translate the melodic line, which was often all there was, into a believable song copy. And in the 1920s and 1930s, when dance bands became yet another profitable source for plugging, these arrangers would be required to write complete scores and sets of band parts as an inducement for the bandleader to feature the tune. But not all the early contract songwriters were musical illiterates. One of the best known was George Gershwin, who not only wrote for Remicks, but doubled as staff pianist to demonstrate the company's songs to any artist who happened to be looking for new material. Songs selling a million copies of sheet music were becoming routine, and each million-seller represented a profit to the publisher of maybe $25,000.

Even before World War I, gramophone records were starting to have a big impact on the sales of songs, although they did not take over completely from sheet music until the late 1940s. The first evidence of a million-selling record was Enrico Caruso's 'On With the Motley' in 1903 (this total was cumulative over several years), so it becomes less surprising to recall that in the world of popular music Ben Selvin's Novelty Orchestra had a million-seller with 'Dardanella' in 1919, closely followed by Paul Whiteman with 'Whispering' in 1920. Although it took 25 years or more for the metamorphosis to become complete, from then on the record gradually began to take over from the song sheet as the prime medium for the exploitation of popular music.

Next came commercial radio in 1922. From then on, with every music-plugger in the business exploiting both live performances and gramophone records on the new medium, sales of songs rocketed even higher. By the end of 1924, some 350 million-dollars'-worth of radio sets had been sold in America alone. So important did radio become as a means of exploitation that one band, the Coon-Sanders Nighthawks, who broadcast weekly live from the Blackhawk Hotel in Chicago, claimed to have pioneered the radio request. They had Western Union fix up a ticker tape system between Sanders' piano and Coon's drums, so that there would be no delay in instantly playing requests that were telephoned in by listeners.

I've been telling this story of the exploitation of popular music strictly in terms of America because the Americans invented it. But just as British composers and lyricists mirrored what their American counterparts were doing in terms of the songs they wrote, so also the British publishers of Tin Pan Alley in Denmark Street were not slow to emulate their transatlantic cousins. They, too, started out plugging songs the hard way. Lawrence Wright is a good example: he had an office in London, and annual summer shows in Blackpool, where he was not above going round the streets himself, peddling his song copies to passers by. The British, too, were quick to cash in on the popularity of the gramophone record. Ernest Lough, the boy soprano, sold a million copies of his record 'Oh For the Wings of a Dove' in 1927. Similarly, with the establishment of the BBC as a national broadcasting medium, especially when the dance bands of the 1930s were on the air live almost every night, exploitation of songs and payola followed the same lines as it had in America. One well-known bandleader used to boast that every Tuesday night he would have all the song-pluggers line up in his dressing room, and conduct a sort of Dutch auction to see who was paying out the most money for what songs, so that he could get arrangements done of those on offer from the highest bidders for his broadcast later in the week.

Since records took over from live music on radio, there have been several big payola scandals in America over the years, the last one involving big-name disc jockeys on major stations in the rock 'n' roll era of the late 1950s. And in England too the BBC has not escaped, with at least two well known instances, one in the late 1940s involving dance band broadcasts, and one in the late 1960s involving disc jockeys, producers and record companies.

This book is not an encyclopaedia, nor is it a history of the popular music business. Its task is to give the reader an insight into the lives of some of the fascinating people who have made the business what it is today, and whose songs have brought happiness to millions.

The Songwriters

ADAMSON, Harold, *see* McHugh, Jimmy.

ADLER, Richard, composer/author.

Born New York, 3 August 1921. Best known for his collaboration with Jerry Ross (born New York, 9 March 1926, died New York, 11 November 1955) in the scores of the Broadway musicals *The Pajama Game* (1954) and *Damn Yankees* (1955). Main songs from *The Pajama Game*: 'I'm Not at All in Love', 'Hey, There', 'Once a Year Day', 'Small Talk', 'Steam Heat', 'Hernando's Hideaway'; from *Damn Yankees*: 'Heart', 'A Little Brains—A Little Talent', 'Whatever Lola Wants', 'Who's Got the Pain?', 'Two Lost Souls'. Also wrote 'Rags to Riches' (1953), 'Everybody Loves a Lover' (1958), 'Another Time Another Place' (1961). Has also written musicals for American TV, and many commercials.

AGER, Milton, composer, publisher, pianist, arranger.

Born Chicago, 6 October 1893. Died Los Angeles, 6 May 1979. Educated McKinley High School, Chicago. Self-taught pianist. Early jobs included working as a song-plugger for the publishers Waterson, Berlin and Snyder, moving to their New York office (1913), where he met Irving Berlin, Walter Donaldson and other famous composers, for whom he did arrangements. Also worked as accompanist for vaudeville acts and performed song intermissions at silent movie houses. Drafted into the forces in World War I, where he met lyricist Grant Clarke, with whom he wrote his first smash hit, 'Everything is Peaches Down in Georgia' (1918), popularized by Al Jolson. He was commissioned to write the score of the 1920 Broadway show *What's in a Name?*, in which he had another hit, 'A Young Man's

Fancy'. The show also introduced him to lyricist Jack Yellen, a meeting that produced one of the great songwriting teams of the era.

Later, they founded the publishing firm of Ager, Yellen and Bornstein, a company which, like its writers, was soon destined to occupy a big place in the hit parade. Jack Yellen was born in Poland, 6 July 1892, and his parents emigrated to America in 1897 to live in Buffalo, NY. Yellen went to the University of Michigan, where he started writing songs. If he received $5 per song from a local part-time publisher—he was lucky! He graduated as a BA in 1913 and got a job on the *Buffalo Courier* as a reporter, but continued writing songs in collaboration with a local music teacher, George Cobb, with whom he had two hits, 'All Aboard for Dixieland' and 'Are You From Dixie?'. In 1917 he moved to New York, but soon found himself in the army, where he met composer Abe Olman, and collaborated with him in another hit, 'Down by the Ohio'.

Although it seems Ager and Yellen wrote only one complete movie score, *Honky Tonk* (1929), which marked Sophie Tucker's film debut, the team contributed songs to such films as *Chasing Rainbows*, starring Bessie Love (1930), and *The King of Jazz*, starring Paul Whiteman and His Orchestra (1930). Possibly their greatest hit was 'Happy Days Are Here Again', which assumed the same kind of importance as the theme song of the Depression years as had George M Cohan's 'Over There' in World War I. It was also adopted as Franklin D Roosevelt's campaign song for his nomination at the 1932 National Democratic Convention.

With the upsurge of film musicals in the 1930s, Warner Brothers bought Ager, Yellen and Bornstein, and Jack Yellen took the opportunity of retiring, although he did make odd excursions back into the business, notably to produce a Broadway show called *You Said It* for which he also wrote the lyrics to Harold Arlen's music. He also visited England to write for the London revue *Follow a Star*, featuring Sophie Tucker. His other main production was the 1935 edition of *George White's Scandals*. Once the partnership with Yellen had broken up, Milton Ager continued a successful career with various lyricists, especially Joe Young and Benny Davis, but gradually retired from songwriting after World War II.

Some outstanding Milton Ager songs:

'A Young Man's Fancy' (1920), 'I'm Nobody's Baby' (1921), 'Lovin' Sam' (1922), 'Ain't She Sweet' (1927), 'Crazy Words, Crazy Tune' (1927), 'Hard-Hearted Hannah' (1924), 'Glad-Rag Doll' (1929),

'Happy Feet' (1930), 'A Bench in the Park' (1930), 'The Song of the Dawn' (1930), 'Auf Wiedersehen My Dear' (1932), 'Trust in Me' (1937).

AHLERT, Fred, composer, arranger.

Born New York, 19 September 1892. Died New York, 20 October 1953. Originally trained and qualified as a lawyer, for many years music was only a part-time occupation. First hit song 1921 : 'I'd Love to Fall Asleep and Wake Up in My Mammy's Arms'. Decided to become a full-time composer following the success of 'I'll Get By' in 1928, which became a million seller, and was perhaps his most famous song, since it was revived very succesfully in 1944 in the film *Follow the Boys*, and again in 1961 by Shirley Bassey, whose record was in the UK charts for eight weeks. Roy Turk, who wrote the lyric of 'I'll Get By', was one of Ahlert's main co-writers, and in addition was responsible for 'Mean to Me' (Ahlert), 'Walkin' My Baby Back Home' (with Harry Richman), 'Where the Blue of the Night Meets the Gold of the Day' (with Ahlert and Bing Crosby, whose theme tune it was), 'I Don't Know Why', and 'Love You Funny Thing' (both with Ahlert). Among Ahlert's other main compositions were : 'The Moon Was Yellow' (lyrics Edgar Leslie), 'I'm Gonna Sit Right Down and Write Myself a Letter' (lyrics Joe Young), 'Just You Just Me' (lyrics Jesse Greer), and 'Sing an Old-Fashioned Song' (lyrics Joe Young).

ANKA, Paul, composer, author, singer, producer.

Born Ottawa, Canada, 31 July 1941. Although Paul is Canadian by birth, the family had its origins in Syria. His father ran a restaurant in Ottawa. The young Anka was educated at local schools, and while in the Fisher Park High formed an amateur trio, in which he was the lead singer. It had considerable success, which soon began to extend to engagements in other parts of Canada besides Ottawa. Paul was stage-struck from an early age, spending his spare time hanging round the stage doors of vaudeville houses, seeking opportunities to chat to performers, and it may have been this interest that led him to the belief that his trio would do better if it used different material. It was this desire that led him into trying to write his own songs, and after talks with his father, he was given some money and permitted to go for a vacation to stay with an uncle in Hollywood. The uncle was also a restaurateur who had connections with people in the movie industry.

All this was in 1956, and the result of the visit was one record on a small local label, with total sales of 25,000 copies. Most would have been well satisfied with this, but not Paul Anka. Then in 1957 he borrowed another $100 and went to New York where, much to his astonishment, he passed an audition for ABC Paramount records, and was signed to make a single. The title of the song was 'Diana'. But in spite of the fact that 'Diana' achieved the No 2 slot in both Britain and the US, in spite of the fact that over the years it has won eight golden discs, thus becoming among the top record sellers of all time, in spite of the adulation and the worldwide tours that followed, the Anka story has not been all plain sailing.

In 1958 came the successful follow-up, 'You Are My Destiny' (No 6 in the UK, No 7 in the US), while 1959 brought 'Put Your Head on My Shoulder' (No 7 in the UK, No 2 in the US). By now Anka songs were beginning to be in demand by some, but by no means all, artists for recording. In particular in this category was the last record to be made by Buddy Holly, the prophetic 'It Doesn't Matter Anymore', while country singer Johnny Nash had a hit with a 1957 Anka composition, 'I Lost My Love Last Night'.

Paul had two more big hits in 1960—the million-seller 'Lonely Boy', and the almost equally successful 'Puppy Love'. In 1963 he switched recording labels to RCA, but his first record with them, 'Love Me Warm and Tender' (No 19 in the UK, No 12 in the US) was only a moderate hit. In addition, a year or so before this, he had been profoundly affected by the death of his mother and this, together with various other things, began to dictate a change of emphasis in the Anka career. Throughout the 1960s he concentrated on building up his concert and cabaret appearances, and while continuing to record, he seemed to have lost the initial impetus he had had with records in the late 1950s. In 1963 he married Ann De Zogher, who bore him four daughters. Thus it was that the 1960s were mainly devoted to Anka the performer. But he never stopped writing songs, and towards the end of the decade began to interest himself in record production, particularly when the artist was going to record an Anka composition.

The fact that during the late 1950s and early 1960s Paul found some difficulty in placing his songs with other artists, stemmed, as he soon realized, from the number of his own successes. 'If I offered one of my songs to another singer, they'd say "If it's not good enough for him, who needs it?" So I decided there would be two Paul Ankas'. Thus evolved Paul the performer and Paul the writer, in almost equally successful parts.

It was also during that period that Anka made his first ventures into movies and TV, both as writer and performer. His first appearance was in *Girl's Town*, and he followed this up with *The Private Lives of Adam and Eve*, *Look in Any Window*, and Daryl F Zanuck's *The Longest Day*, in which he was very much a star. But perhaps more importantly from the musical point of view, he wrote all the theme tunes for those films, as well as 'Johnny's Theme', used nightly by the American TV 'Tonight Show'. This alone, it is estimated, brings him in some $20,000 per year in royalties.

That he is now fully accepted as a composer is witnessed by the increasing list of artists who have recorded his songs, from Patti Page, Bobby Rydell, Connie Francis, The Fifth Dimension, Sonny and Cher, and Engelbert Humperdinck in the early days, to Andy Williams, Frank Sinatra, Donny Osmond, Tom Jones, Barbra Streisand and James Last in later years. Of these the best known is the Sinatra recording of 'My Way', originally a French song adapted by Paul Anka in 1969, which achieved No 5 in the UK and No 27 in the US. Equally successful was the Tom Jones recording of 'She's a Lady' in 1971, which reached No 13 in the UK and No 2 in the US, while in 1972 Donny Osmond had a huge hit with his revival of the old song 'Puppy Love', reaching No 1 in the UK and No 3 in the US, and earning a gold disc. In the 1970s, Paul Anka continued to write and record himself, having another gold record in 1974 with the somewhat controversial hit 'You're Having My Baby'. He also specialized more and more on production, but now not only in the recording studio, but also on some of the big Las Vegas spectaculars. Over the years he has spent so much time in the gambling resort, that he now has a home there, as well as in Sun Valley, Idaho, and an apartment in New York, the city from which his multi-million dollar enterprise (publishing, production, etc) is run.

Some other outstanding Paul Anka songs:
'Anytime' (Frank Sinatra, 1975), 'Can't Get You Out of My Mind' (1968), 'Do I Love You?' (1971), 'I Don't Like to Sleep Alone' (1975), 'I'm Not Anyone' (1973), 'Jubilation' (Barbra Streisand,

1972), 'Let Me Try Again' (Frank Sinatra, 1973),* 'Teddy' (1960), 'While We're Still Young' (1975).*

* These are French songs for which he wrote the English words.

ARLEN, Harold (Hyman Arluck), composer, author, pianist, singer.

Born Buffalo, NY, 15 February 1905. Educated at Hutchinson Central High School, which he left after only two years, and studied music privately. His father was cantor in a synagogue, and at the age of 7, Harold Arlen found himself singing in the synagogue choir. His father was already giving him piano lessons, in the hope that one day the boy might become a music teacher, and tuition was then extended to two local teachers. But it was never followed through, and by the time he was 12 he had deserted classical music for ragtime, and had already begun collecting jazz records. As he has said himself: 'My big interest was in the jazz instrumentation of the day. I even ran away from home to hear The Memphis Five'. It was not surprising, therefore, that he soon dropped out of high school, and at 15 began playing piano in local cafés. He formed a jazz outfit, The Snappy Trio, which got quite a few local dates, and did even better when augmented to five and renamed The Southbound Shufflers. In addition to playing piano and singing, Harold also began to do basic arrangements for his little band. With his interest in jazz he had discovered improvisation, but several of his musicians could really only play straight melody from printed parts. Harold would write out jazz solos for them and have them learned by heart, so that when they stood up to play they sounded, hopefully, like a real jazz outfit. Arlen's father regarded all this with considerable doubt, and in an attempt to convince his teenage son that he should go back to studying for a degree, he introduced the boy to the already successful lyricist Jack Yellen, hoping that Yellen would talk him out of jazz. But after hearing Harold play and sing, Yellen reported that the boy was destined to be a musician, if not in the sphere that his father would have wished. By now The Southbound Shufflers had been renamed, this time becoming The Buffalodians, and they were soon extending the scope of their engagements to summer resorts, lake steamers and ballrooms. There they were heard by an agent who gave them the first of a series of bookings, culminating in three separate dates in New York in 1925, including the Palace Theater.

Although he had written two or three songs for his own band, Arlen has repeatedly stated that he had no thought of wanting to be anything but a singer, certainly no thought of becoming a songwriter. This is borne out by the fact that on another visit to New York in 1928, he was heard by bandleader and NBC musical director Arnold Johnson, who offered him a job in his band, then appearing in *George White's Scandals of 1928*. The thing that clinched it for Arlen was that the contract stipulated that he could sing in the pit during the interval. Author Max Wilk, who once interviewed Harold Arlen for his book *They're Playing Our Song*, quotes the composer as saying: 'I wanted to be a singer. Never dreamed of songwriting. I have to be a fatalist and say somebody, something, moved me on the chess board. I was taken by the neck and put there, and put there, and put there—and then things happened to me'.

Nevertheless, by the end of 1928, Arlen had had two of his songs published, one of them, 'The Album of My Dreams', being recorded by Rudy Vallee for RCA-Victor, and in 1929 he was hired by composer Vincent Youmans as rehearsal pianist for the forthcoming Broadway show *Great Day!*, for which Youmans had written the music. A rehearsal pianist's soul-destroying task is to play the show's songs over and over and over again, while the company, from stars to chorus, rehearse interminably as the director makes changes and the artists rehearse the changes. Arlen was also supposed to sing a song in the show, but it was cut out after the first out-of-town performance. Perhaps it was just as well, because during all those boring hours of rehearsal, unknowingly, Harold had given birth to his first hit.

There used to be a standard vamp, or lead-in for singers at rehearsal. Everybody used it, and rhythmically it could be expressed as 'Da-dum, da-dum, DUM DUM'. Bored with this, Harold started improvising round it, changing the pattern and the chords, and before long Will Marion Cook, who was leading the singers in the show, suggested that there was the basis of a tune there, and that Harold should 'get it down on paper before somebody steals it'. With co-operation from lyricist Ted Koehler, the first Arlen-Koehler hit 'Get Happy', was born. To quote Harold again: 'I didn't seek it out, or ask for it—it just happened'. 'Get Happy' was published by Remick, and sung by Ruth Etting, a great star of the times, in a less than successful show, *The 9.15 Revue*. But the song was a hit, both on record and in the sales of sheet music, and Arlen was at last convinced that someone wanted him to be a songwriter. He took a job as a staff composer with Remick, who paid him $55 per week as an advance against royalties for his songs, and with his work as accompanying pianist to such singers as Ethel Merman and Frances Williams, he was soon regularly taking home $100 per week—not bad in 1930.

The Arlen/Koehler partnership next contributed a song to *Earl Carroll's Vanities of 1930* which, while not a hit, was good enough to get their work noticed by the producer of the famous Cotton Club Revue. The Cotton Club had been a sensation since its opening in 1923. Situated in one of the more broken-down areas of Harlem, it specialized in presenting jazz talent—Duke Ellington, Jimmie Lunceford, and Cab Calloway and their bands all appeared there, as well as such singers as Aïda Ward, Ethel Waters, Adelaide Hall and later, Lena Horne. For years people flocked nightly to the Cotton Club shows. Harold Arlen himself, in a radio interview in the late 1960s said: 'Those opening nights were like no other opening nights in the theater, because even though it was a night club, you'd get everyone there from mayor to anybody who was who. It was like a Broadway opening is today'. Indeed it was with those white audiences in mind that lyricist Lorenz Hart, as late as 1940, wrote the line 'Don't go to Harlem in ermine and pearls', for the Richard Rodgers song 'The Lady Is a Tramp'.

The Cotton Club was unique. Prior to 1930, the hit songs for its shows had been written by the very successful team of Jimmy McHugh and Dorothy Fields. In that year, however, they were writing the music for two Broadway revues, so the producer signed the almost unknown Arlen/Koehler team, and another record-breaking songwriting partnership was under way. The 1931 show produced 'Between the Devil and the Deep Blue Sea', sung by Aïda Ward; 1932, 'I've Got the World on a String' and 'Minnie the Moocher's Wedding Day'; 1933, 'Stormy Weather', sung by Ethel Waters; 1934, 'As Long As I Live', introduced by 16½-year-old Lena Horne. These were just a few of the highlights. In her autobiography, *His Eye Is On the Sparrow*, Ethel Waters recalls her introduction of 'Stormy Weather': 'When I got out there in the middle of the Cotton Club floor ... I was singing the story of my misery and confusion ... the story of the wrongs and outrages done to me by people I had loved and trusted ... I sang "Stormy Weather" from the depths of my private hell in which I was being crushed and suffocated.' No matter how well anybody else sings it—and there have been some

superb performances including a notable one by Lena Horne—
'Stormy Weather' will always remain Ethel Waters' song.

But the Arlen/Koehler partnership was writing other hits as well
as those for the Cotton Club Revues. In 1932, the song 'I Gotta Right
to Sing the Blues' found its way into that year's *Earl Carroll's Vanities*.
It was subsequently to be a hit for both Louis Armstrong and Jack
Teagarden, but more importantly at the time it introduced Harold
Arlen to Anya Taranda, a chorus girl in the show. Five years later,
on 8 January 1937, they were married in Harrison, New York.

Arlen had a fear, mentioned by everyone who has written about
him, of being typecast in his songs. He calls himself a blues writer,
although he has only written one genuine 12-bar blues. What he
means is that there is an aura of the blues about much of his work,
and this probably stems partly from his semitic family background,
and the music of his Jewish cantor father; and partly from his never
diminished love of jazz. In his interview with Max Wilk he says: 'I
sang in a night club one night. Just got up and sang. And Bix
Beiderbecke (the legendary jazz cornetist) was there, and when I
finished he said: "Great kid". That meant so much to me'. In spite of
all this, however, the range of Harold Arlen's songs is very wide. You
have only to compare the big ballads, of which 'Stormy Weather' is a
prime example, with the genuine blues song, 'Blues in the Night',
the lively, swinging 'As Long As I Live', and the delicate cadences of
'Let's Fall in Love'. E Y Harburg, the lyricist with whom Arlen
worked after his partnership with Ted Koehler had ended, has said:
'Harold is a very very melancholy person. Inside, deeply religious.
But he's very superstitious. Behind the humour are all sorts of
superstitions and beliefs.'

In 1934 Arlen was in Hollywood for his first contribution to a
movie, *Let's Fall in Love*, starring Ann Sothern. Over the years he
contributed to, or wrote complete scores for some 24 films. Of these
the most important were *Star-Spangled Rhythm* (1942), which starred
Bing Crosby, Bob Hope, Mary Martin, Dick Powell, Dorothy
Lamour, Betty Hutton, and many others; *The Sky's the Limit* (1943),
starring Fred Astaire; *Here Come the Waves* (1944) with Bing Crosby
and Betty Hutton; *A Star Is Born* (1955), with lyrics by Ira Gershwin,
starring Judy Garland; and, of course, the immortal *The Wizard of Oz*
(1939), also starring Judy Garland.

In 1934 Harold Arlen began his close association with those two
other very successful lyric writers, E Y 'Yip' Harburg, and Ira
Gershwin, brother of George. In 1932 Harburg and Johnny Mercer

had collaborated on lyrics for a not very successful Arlen song, 'Satan's L'il Lamb'. But it was quite a surprise when Harburg and Gershwin got together with Arlen, at Harburg's suggestion, to write the Broadway revue, *Life Begins at 8.40*. Of this show, Yip Harburg (incidentally the 'Yip' is a contraction of 'Yipsel', otherwise 'Squirrel') said: 'It was a joyous experience'. Arlen said of it: 'It was a pretty hard job, that show. They collaborated on the lyrics. I did the music alone. And to be asked to do it, and to take it on, took guts. So, I proved that I could come out of the Cotton Club.' The show ran for 247 performances, but times were hard in the Broadway theatre, and Arlen went back to Hollywood with Ted Koehler. Harburg also went, but he worked for a different studio. After two films with Koehler, Arlen teamed up again with Harburg for two more films, and then returned to New York, where he wrote some special songs for two of his first loves, Ethel Waters and Cab Calloway, for yet another Cotton Club Revue.

Then, with Harburg, he wrote the score for another Broadway show, *Hooray for What*. It is a curious fact that perhaps the best Arlen/Harburg Hollywood song of the pre-Oz period, was 'Last Night When We Were Young', a song which never made the screen, being dropped from every movie for which it was suggested. But clearly the partnership's greatest single success was the big hit from *The Wizard of Oz*, 'Over the Rainbow'. As 'Stormy Weather' became Ethel Waters' song, so 'Over the Rainbow' became Judy Garland's. She once said of it: 'I've sung it time and again, and it's still the song that's closest to my heart'. Perhaps Judy's troubled life was due to the fact that all she ever wanted was to be 'Somewhere, Over the Rainbow'.

Nine years after the unsuccessful Arlen/Mercer collaboration on 'Satan's L'il Lamb', the two had a big hit with Arlen's only true 12-bar blues, 'Blues in the Night'. It was to be a highly successful collaboration, for a year later they came up with 'That Old Black Magic' in the film *Star-Spangled Rhythm*, and soon after that with 'One for My Baby' from the Fred Astaire film *The Sky's the Limit*. Perhaps it was because Mercer, like Arlen, was a great jazz devotee, that most of the songs they produced had something unusual about them. 'One for My Baby' has a 48-bar chorus instead of the usual 32, and one of their later hits 'Come Rain or Come Shine' begins in one key and ends in another, which is all highly irregular by the traditional standards of Tin Pan Alley.

Meanwhile, Harold continued to write with both Ted Koehler

and Yip Harburg. In 1944 he was back on Broadway with Harburg's lyrics for the show *Bloomer Girl*. In 1946 he was with Mercer for the all black musical *St Louis Woman*. He was in New York in 1954 for the show *House of Flowers*, based on a book by Truman Capote, starring Pearl Bailey and Diahann Carroll. In 1957 he wrote yet another show, *Jamaica*, starring Lena Horne. Not only the number of hits, but the quality of Harold Arlen's music must put him in the very top echelons of American popular songwriters. And, of course, he is the first to give credit to his lyricists. For details of Ira Gershwin, see GERSHWIN, George; for Johnny Mercer see MERCER, John H (Johnny).

To close the Harold Arlen story, a few words about E Y 'Yip' Harburg might be fitting. He was born in New York on 8 April 1898, and died in a car crash in Hollywood, 5 March 1981. His boyhood was one of extreme poverty. But 'Yip' was also extremely bright, and earned himself admission to Townsend Harris Hall, a school for those with exceptional academic qualifications. Among his school mates was Ira Gershwin, and together they moved on to the College of the City of New York, where Harburg graudated with a BSc. His early pieces in the school magazine had shown a talent for writing, and he later contributed to several publications, including the *New York World*. Later still, on finding himself stranded in Montevideo, he took a job as a journalist. Returning to New York in 1921, he set up his own electrical business, which lasted till the crash of 1929, and all the time he continued to write—not songs, but articles and verse.

His versifying was to stand him in good stead, and it was because he had read some Harburg verse that the composer Jay Gorney picked him to write six lyrics for the show *The Sketch Book*. More songs with Gorney followed, and in 1932 in the show *Americana* (which also introduced him to Harold Arlen over 'Satan's L'il Lamb'), he had his first big hit, 'Brother, Can You Spare a Dime?', also with music by Jay Gorney. Perhaps this was one of the earliest of the so-called protest songs that became the 'in' thing in the 1960s. In 1932, he wrote the lyrics for Vernon Duke's first big hit, 'April in Paris' (although it did not become a hit until much later), and in 1933 had his first major success with Arlen with 'It's Only a Paper Moon', a song written in 1932 for a show that flopped. The rest of the Arlen/ Harburg partnership has already been chronicled, but it should be noted that Harburg also wrote many major lyrics for composers such as Arthur Schwarz, Burton Lane, Jerome Kern and Sammy Fain.

Perhaps the last of his great partnerships was with Burton Lane, which produced the classic Broadway show *Finian's Rainbow* in 1947.

Some other outstanding Harold Arlen songs:
'Kicking the Gong Around' (1932), 'I Love a Parade' (1931), 'I've Got the World on a String' (1932), 'It's Only a Paper Moon' (1933), 'Let's Fall in Love' (1934), 'We're Off to See the Wizard', 'Ding Dong, the Witch Is Dead', and 'If I Only Had a Brain (all from *The Wizard of Oz*, 1939), 'Hit the Road to Dreamland (with Johnny Mercer, 1943), 'Happiness Is Just a Thing Called Joe' (with Yip Harburg, 1943), 'Let's Take the Long Way Home' (with Johnny Mercer, 1944), 'Ac-cent-tchu-ate the Positive' (with Johnny Mercer, 1944), 'Any Place I Hang My Hat Is Home' (1946), 'Come Rain or Come Shine' (with Johnny Mercer, 1946), 'Hooray for Love' (with Leo Robin, 1948), 'Today I Love Everybody' (1953), 'The Man That Got Away' (from *A Star Is Born*, with Ira Gershwin, 1953).

BACHARACH, Burt F, composer, conductor, arranger.

Born Kansas City, Missouri, 12 May 1928. Educated McGraw University, David Mannes School of Music New York, and Music Academy of The West, Santa Barbara, California. His father was a well-known journalist working for the *Journal-American* in New York, where the family moved when Burt was still a schoolboy. His family insisted on music lessons from an early age. Young Burt disliked these intensely, since at that time his desire was to become a professional footballer, which his father had been before becoming a journalist. He kept at it, however, and by the time he was a teenager had attained sufficient talent to become a piano-playing member of a local jazz group, where, since this was the be-bop era, he found himself much influenced by the stars of that school—Dizzy Gillespie and Charlie Parker. Between 1950 and 1952 he served in the US Army, where he organized an army band for local service dates and a tour of the USO camps. It was not until his discharge from the service that he determined to become a professional musician.

He achieved this with some success, playing piano, conducting, and from time to time doing arrangements for such singers as Vic Damone, Steve Lawrence and the Ames Brothers. He also had a spell as accompanist for Marlene Dietrich. It was during his time with the Ames Brothers that he decided to try his hand at songwriting, and up to 1965 had several of his compositions published, although apart from one or two country songs for Gene Pitney, he prefers to forget about them. His first major hit came in 1957, when he wrote 'The Story of My Life', recorded in the US by Marty Robbins, and by the late Michael Holliday in the UK. This was quickly followed by a hit for Perry Como, 'Magic Moments', and it was with these songs that he initiated his successful partnership with lyricist Hal David.

During most of the 1960s he was based in Los Angeles, and the decade saw a string of Bacharach/David hits, with songs such as 'Tower of Strength' (1961), 'Twenty-Four Hours From Tulsa' (1964), 'Walk on By' (1964), 'There's Always Something There to Remind Me' (1964), 'Trains and Boats and Planes' (1965), 'What the World Needs Now' (1966), and 'Close to You' (1970). Among the artists whose recordings contributed in a big way to the success of the songs were The Walker Brothers, Gene McDaniels, Frankie Vaughan, Gene Pitney, Cilla Black, Sandie Shaw, Tom Jones, The Carpenters, and Dionne Warwick. The latter could lay claim by 1970 to have recorded almost every Bacharach/David composition, and certainly her record sales of Bacharach songs are in excess of 15 million.

His first film score, *What's New Pussycat?*, came in 1965. Tom Jones had a big hit with the title song. It was during this picture that he married Angie Dickinson, making her the second Mrs Bacharach. In 1969 he won his first Oscar for 'Raindrops Keep Fallin' on My Head', written for the film *Butch Cassidy and the Sundance Kid*. Prior to that he had received Oscar nominations for 'Alfie' (1967) and 'The Look of Love' (1968). It was during those last two years that Bacharach and David were working on the project dearest to their hearts, a Broadway musical. The result was *Promises, Promises*, which opened in 1968 and ran through 1971.

In addition to his work as a successful songwriter, Burt Bacharach has, along with Henry Mancini, developed into a personality in his own right as a conductor, pianist, and even occasional singer. Thus, for example, in 1970 he sold out not one but two concerts at the 11,000-seat St Louis Auditorium, and he has had equally successful appearances in Los Angeles, Las Vegas, and various European cities. Needless to say, he has not been neglected by TV, often starring in his own spectaculars.

To summarize the success of his songs is not easy. They all have very strong melodies, but the majority break some established rule or other of the traditional songwriting form (which Hoagy Carmichael did a generation before). Bacharach has said: 'I don't like classical music. I never wanted to be a classical composer, or I would have been one. A guy does what he wants to do'. Of record companies he has commented: 'The A & R men used to be omnipotent. They'd say "That's a three-bar phrase. You can't have a three-bar phrase. Make it a four-bar phrase". I ruined some pretty good songs that way, because I believed them' (Irving Stambler, *Encyclopaedia of Pop Rock and Soul*). Of his unusual song formats he has said: 'It just happens. Like we were finishing a song with Dionne [Warwick] the day before a date, and she was counting the 8th note flow. She said "Gee this only comes to 7 notes". I said "You're kidding. Count it again". So we did it as a 7/8 bar. It felt good that way' (*Encyclopaedia of Pop Rock and Soul*). And of his playing and conducting, which has been described as electrifying, he has said: 'I'm not trying to prove anything as a conductor. Or a pianist. Technically, I'm probably rotten at both. But its heartfelt, its honest. Its my music. I've got a feeling you know, I'm not just beating time'. That about sums him up.

Lyricist Hal David is the younger brother of Mack David, and was born in Brooklyn, New York, in 1921. His father was one of those emigrés to New York who had to work in a sweatshop to earn a living. Nevertheless, he saw to it that his three sons all had as good an education as possible, which included some musical training. Young Hal started out as a journalist, but was drafted into the armed forces during World War II. During that time he wrote sketches and material for army shows, and also attempted his first lyrics. After the war he was lucky enough to be hired to write special material by bandleader Sammy Kaye. In 1949 this resulted in a modest hit record, 'Four Winds and Seven Seas' (music by Don Rodney). In 1950, with composers Redd Evans and Arthur Altmann, he had another hit with Frank Sinatra's record of 'American Beauty Rose'. This was followed in 1951 by 'A House is Not a Home' (music by Leon Carr), and, again with Carr, 'Bell Bottom Blues', which was a hit for Teresa Brewer in 1953. There was also 'My Heart Is an Open Book' (music by Lee Pockriss), recorded by several artists in 1957. He also wrote for Henry Mancini ('Baby Elephant Walk'). But once his collaboration with Burt Bacharach was established with 'The Story of My Life', the team joined the ranks of the great songwriting combinations.

Some other outstanding Burt Bacharach songs:
'I'll Never Fall in Love Again' (1968), 'Anyone Who Had a Heart' (1964), 'Message to Michael' (1964), 'The Look of Love' (1968), 'Do

You Know the Way to San Jose?' (1967), 'A House is Not a Home' (film title song 1964), 'Walk on By' (1964), 'What's New Pussycat?' (from the film, 1965), 'Wives and Lovers' (film title song, 1963).

BARRY, John (John Barry Prendergast), trumpet player, pianist, bandleader, composer.

Born York, 3 November 1933. Educated at St Peter's School, York. He achieved considerable success with his group, the John Barry Seven, in radio, records and TV in the late 1950s and early 1960s, but it was his subsequent work as a composer of film themes, many of which have become million-seller world hits, that confirmed his status. Although he had been associated with Leslie Bricusse and Anthony Newley in writing the song 'Goldfinger' for the 1964 James Bond film of the same name, his first solo successes were the theme for the film *The Amorous Prawn* in 1962, and the 007 theme for *From Russia With Love* in the same year. Other successes have been: 'A Man Alone' from the film *The Ipcress File* (1965), 'Thunderball' (1965), 'Born Free' (with Don Black) from the 1966 film of the same name, 'You Only Live Twice' (with Leslie Bricusse) from the 1967 film of the same name, 'The Girl With the Sun in Her Hair' and the theme music for the film *On Her Majesty's Secret Service* (1969), 'The Man With the Golden Gun' (from the film, 1974), and the score for the film *Moonraker* (1979). He has lived and worked in America since 1970, when his British publishing and other companies went into liquidation.

BART, Lionel (Lionel Begleiter), composer, author.

Born London, 1 August 1930. His parents were Jewish immigrants, his father being a tailor in the East End of London. Lionel was the youngest of 12 brothers and sisters. Educated at local schools and St Martin's School of Art, because he hoped to become an artist. His father bought him a violin, but Bart never learned to play it. Not long after leaving school he was conscripted into the RAF, and on release in 1953 tried to put his art school training to use by getting a job as a scene painter at the Unity Theatre in east London. Here he met actor Alfie Bass, who was looking for songs for a revue. He took two unpublished songs from the young Lionel and gave him the encouragement he needed to persevere as a budding songwriter.

In 1956, with friends Mike Pratt (who played a bass made out of a broomstick and a tea chest), and Tommy Hicks (later to become Tommy Steele) who played guitar, he formed a group. Bart played the washboard (these were the days of Skiffle), and because they played in a cellar joint under Waterloo station called The Cave, the group called themselves The Cavemen. Later that year they had a hit record with a Bart song, 'Rock With The Cavemen', Lionel himself having by now given up his washboard to concentrate on writing. The following year he gave Tommy Steele another hit, 'A Handful of Songs', and in 1959 won an Ivor Novello Award for Tommy Steele's next hit, 'Little White Bull' from the film *Tommy the Toreador*.

By now Bart had turned into a successful songwriter. He turned for inspiration to the East End, the area where he had spent his childhood, and was introduced to Joan Littlewood, who was then producing and directing the Theatre Workshop at the Theatre Royal in Stratford East, and who had already acquired the reputation of an *enfant terrible*. Bart was invited to write the music for an adaptation of a play by Frank Norman about life in the underworld of London's Soho—*Fings Ain't Wot They Used t' Be*. The Workshop productions (and *Fings* was no exception) were produced on a shoestring. The West End theatre critics, who were unaccustomed to trailing out to Stratford, were less than kind. 'It is not a good musical, but there are some effective songs', said *The Stage*—a comment that was fairly typical. It ran for only two months, but the following year it was revived in the West End at the Garrick Theatre, by which time the critics were prepared to look on it more favourably, and its title tune has become a standard in the world of humorous songs. By 1960 Lionel Bart had, with Laurie Johnson, written the score for the show *Lock Up Your Daughters* at London's Mermaid Theatre, as well as continuing to write hit songs for recording artists, such as 'D'You Mind' (for Anthony Newley) and 'Living Doll' (for Cliff Richard).

The year 1960 was an epic one for Bart. With *Fings* and *Lock Up Your Daughters* still running, *Oliver!* (based on Charles Dickens' novel) opened to ecstatic revues. It ran for over 2,600 performances, thus beating the long-time record held by *Chu Chin Chow*, and of its 16 songs, four went into the Top Twenty. Of these four, one in particular was to become a standard—'As Long As He Needs Me'—

and it also won two Ivor Novello awards. The title song was an award winner as well.

Bart's next show, *Blitz!*, opened in May 1962, while all three of his previous shows were still running. But the *Daily Express* said it was 'a massive disappointment'. Nevertheless, it ran for 18 months, 14 of them at a profit. But this sudden financial success went to his head. He spent £60,000 on a house in Chelsea; he started a film production company; he had a music publishing business. Somebody told him he was earning £16 per minute. He later said: 'I figured I could spend £8 per minute. Of course, I was wrong; but, with hindsight I wasn't wrong, because I had a great time doing it'. Financial observers of the threatre and music scene thought there were problems ahead. They were right, but not quite yet.

A new show, *Maggie May*, followed *Blitz!* in 1964. Two of its songs crept into the bottom end of the Top Twenty, but the show was a flop. Bart responded by spending more money than ever (his royalties at the time were around £8,000 per week), and refused to accept that his success as a writer of musicals might be at an end. 'Too many people need me', was his response. In 1965 came his undoing—a massive flop with his next show *Twang!*. He'd even put his own money into it after impresario Bernard Delfont pulled out. Bart had forgotten the excellent advice he received from Noel Coward in 1960—'Never invest in your own show, Lionel'. The *Daily Mail* ran the headline, 'Bart's musical booed'. 'I still say it's a hit', responded Bart. But it wasn't. And in its dying it brought the whole Bart empire crashing down with it.

From then on, everything went from bad to worse, ending with a classic bankruptcy. In 1977, with all that behind him, he gave a remarkably optimistic interview to Chris White of the trade journal *Music Week*. He claimed to have unpublished scores for 'at least 5 musicals ... and between 300 and 400 songs ....' He was about to embark on a double album of a rock opera, based on the story of *The Hunchback of Notre Dame*. There was to be a musical based on the life of Golda Meir of Israel, to be written in collaboration with composer/lyricist Roger Cook. Regrettably none of these ideas seem to have borne fruit.

In his book *The Songwriters*, published in 1980, Tony Staveacre says of Lionel Bart: 'Today he lives in the same rented mews flat where he wrote his first song hits. On the piano is a signed photograph of Noel Coward, the Silver Heart of the Variety Club, and his Russian diploma' (it was given to him for *Oliver!*). The final quote must come from the man himself: 'When you want to do it, you do it. And when you *have* to do it, you do it. At the moment I don't have to or want to'.

Some other outstanding Lionel Bart songs:
'Consider Yourself' (*Oliver!*, 1960), 'Food, Glorious Food' (*Oliver!*, 1960), 'I'd Do Anything' (*Oliver!*, 1960), 'Kickin' Up the Leaves' (1960), 'The Day After Tomorrow' (*Blitz!*, 1962), 'It's Yourself' (*Maggie May*, 1964), 'Maggie Maggie May' (*Maggie May*, 1964).

BERLIN, Irving (Israel Baline), composer, author.

Born 11 May 1888, Temun, Siberia. Emigrated to America with his family in 1892. They lived in the slums of Monroe Street, on New York's East Side, later moving to Cherry Street, where young Israel developed a pleasant boy soprano voice in the local synagogue choir. From the age of 14 he tried to earn extra money for his desperately poor family by singing with buskers in the streets, or doing occasional jobs for publishers as a song-plugger. A week of such combined efforts might pay the princely sum of $5.

In 1906 his perseverance was rewarded with a job as a 'singing waiter' at Pelham's Café, Pell Street, in the heart of Chinatown working 8 pm to 6 am. After hours at the café, he soon discovered that, although he couldn't play piano, he could work out little tunes just by using the black notes. Later he said: 'Once you start singing, you start thinking of writing songs—and it's as simple as that'. In 1907 he had his first song published (lyrics only, to music by the café's resident pianist, 'Nick' Nicholson) called 'Marie From Sunny Italy'. It earned total royalties of 75 cents, of which the young Baline got 37. Because of a printer's error on the song copies, 'Baline' became 'Berlin', and he decided to adopt it. Next he offered a song to composer/publisher Ted Snyder, but deciding that his first name 'Israel' didn't sound right for Tin Pan Alley, he changed it to 'Irving'.

By 1910, in partnership with Snyder and other writers, he had become responsible for several songs, including 'Sadie Salome Go Home' (300,000 copies), 'That Mesmerizing Mendelssohn Tune' (500,000), 'My Wife's Gone to the Country—Hurrah! Hurrah!' (with George Whiting, 300,000), and such titles as 'Call Me Up Some

Rainy Afternoon', and 'Doing the Grizzly Bear' (with George Botsford, who was mainly responsible for the 'Grizzly Bear' dance craze). By now Irving was a staff writer at Snyder's, on a salary of $25 per week. That year also saw his first appearance in a show. He sang a medley of his own songs (with Ted Snyder at the piano), in the Shuberts' production of *Up and Down Broadway*.

As a composer, Berlin was hampered by the fact that he was able to play the piano in only one key (F sharp major). Then he discovered that the Weser Company could make him a piano that, by adjusting a lever underneath the keyboard, would enable him to work in different keys, while still fingering the only one he knew. He never did learn to read music or play the piano properly, and in later years always had with him a 'musical secretary', to whom he used to dictate the notes of his tunes so that they could be written down in manuscript form. Soon he was made a partner in the firm of Waterson, Berlin and Snyder, and in 1911 published 'Alexander's Ragtime Band' (without lyrics), but had no success with it at all. He wrote lyrics to it, and tried again, still with no success. Indeed, the song that was destined to change the course of popular music might never have made it if a well-known vaudeville singer called Emma Carus hadn't taken a fancy to it. She put it into a new show of hers in Chicago, and by the end of 1911 the sales figures had topped two million. In the same year the young Berlin wrote 'Everybody's Doin' It', which made a star out of Eddie Cantor, who himself started as a singing waiter.

In 1912 he married Dorothy Goetz, sister of Ray Goetz, with whom he had previously collaborated on some songs. But Dorothy caught typhoid while they were on honeymoon in Cuba, and five months after the wedding she was dead. The tragedy gave birth to another Berlin hit, 'When I Lost You'.

At just the right time for Irving, an offer came from impresario Albert de Courville in England, inviting him to star at the London Hippodrome, singing and playing his own songs. The special key-change piano (now christened 'The Buick') had to go too. On the way over he composed 'The International Rag', to be featured in the show, and arrived to find himself billed as The King of Ragtime. The fact that neither the famous 'Alexander's Ragtime Band', nor any other Berlin song using the word 'rag' had anything to do with ragtime, was quite lost on his adoring public. In the show he simply played whatever they wanted him to play, regardless of whether he had written it or not. The London *Daily Express* of 13 June 1913 said: 'In every London restaurant, park and theatre, you hear his strains. Paris dances to it. Berlin sips golden beer to it. Vienna has forsaken the waltz, Madrid has flung away her castanets, and Venice has forgotten her barcarolles. Ragtime has swept like a whirlwind over the earth, and set civilization humming'. Irving Berlin was then 25 years old.

The songs kept on tumbling out. Not all were instant hits, but those that were not—a tiny proportion—were quietly laid away, and occasionally re-written with success at a later date. In 1914 impresario Charles Dillingham commissioned Berlin to write a musical. It was called *Watch Your Step*, starred Vernon and Irene Castle, and its big hit was 'Play a Simple Melody'. From then on, in addition to maintaining a phenomenal output of hit songs, the music for show after show seemed also to emerge, apparently effortlessly, from The Buick. There was another Dillingham production, *Stop! Look! Listen!*, and then in 1917, Irving was drafted as a private into the US Army. The press headlined: 'Army takes Berlin'! He was stationed at Fort Yaphank, doing the things that privates have to do until, in 1918, the army promoted him to sergeant, and commissioned him to write and produce a forces show for charity. He called it *Yip, Yip, Yaphank*, and filled it with Berlin hits. But one song he cut out prior to the opening on the grounds that in any army show '... it sounds like gilding the lily'. The title? 'God Bless America'.

Following the armistice, Irving again became the darling of Broadway with show after show throughout the 1920s, including three *Ziegfeld Follies* revues, and four *Music Box Revues*. The latter were named after the Music Box Theatre which, in partnership with impresario Sam H Harris, Irving had specially built for future Berlin musicals. In 1923, humorist Robert Benchley wrote of the fourth *Music Box Revue*, in which he also appeared: 'Irving Berlin is so little, and *The Music Box Revue* is so big!' Meanwhile the composer's astute business brain was at work buying back the copyrights of as many of his early songs as possible from other publishers, and assigning them all to his new company, Irving Berlin Inc. About that time, too, his mother, Leah Baline, died and with her went the last vestiges of Israel Baline.

In 1926 Irving Berlin married Ellin MacKay, after a series of stormy exchanges in the press with her father (they had never met), who was very rich, very snobbish, and very Catholic. He threatened to disinherit his daughter, and the wedding took place without his knowledge or consent. As a wedding present for his new bride,

Irving turned over to her all the rights in his song 'Always' (1925). After honeymooning in Atlantic City, they boarded the *Leviathan* en route for London, where a reporter wrote: 'With the arrival of Irving Berlin the American conquest of the English stage is practically complete'.

Later in the year the Berlins' first daughter was born, and in 1927 came another milestone in popular music. Al Jolson took Irving Berlin's song 'Blue Skies' to the top by singing it in the first ever all-talking film, *The Jazz Singer*. In 1928 the Berlins had a son, but he only survived a few days. Whether this tragedy was responsible or not we will never know, but the years 1928 and 1929 were far from vintage ones for Irving as a glance at the list of song titles shows. And in the 1929 Wall Street crash he, along with other investors 'lost his shirt'.

In 1931 Irving and Ellin were at last reconciled to her father and Berlin came out of his personal years of depression thanks to Rudy Vallee's 1932 recording of his song 'Say It Isn't So'. Vallee said later: 'Irving told me I had helped him sort out his career. But he had helped me to save my marriage. That song ... it was all true, and all happening to me'. It was certainly a turning point for Berlin, and gave him the confidence to make a Broadway comeback with the show *Face the Music*. In 1933 *As Thousands Cheer* featured the song 'Easter Parade', originally written under a different title and discarded in 1917.

In 1934, Irving finally succumbed to the lure of Hollywood. The result, a year later, was his magnificent score for *Top Hat*, with the inimitable partnership of Fred Astaire and Ginger Rogers. A year after that came *Follow the Fleet*, then *On the Avenue* in 1937 with Dick Powell, and in 1938 *Carefree* with Fred and Ginger again.

On a visit to London in that year he made some very unprophetic remarks for a man who was both a successful songwriter and an astute businessman. In a *Daily Express* interview he told Paul Holt: 'Swing isn't music. It will die'. And again: 'We don't sing songs today, we listen to them, and they are on top of the radio for 18 hours a day. If I had written "Remember" today it would have been played and forgotten in a month or so, if it clicked at all'. Mr Berlin didn't like radio! But on Armistice Day 1938 when Kate Smith made almost a second national anthem out of the previously rejected but now revived 'God Bless America', broadcasting it from the New York World's Fair, it didn't seem to matter any more—although he always refused to let dance bands play it. All royalties from that song went to a charity—the Boy and Girl Scouts of America.

In 1940 Broadway staged another Berlin musical, *Louisiana Purchase*, and in 1941 he returned to Hollywood to score *Holiday Inn*, which included not only Bing Crosby but also 'White Christmas'. To date, over 70 million song copies and records of 'White Christmas' have been sold, 30 million of them being Bing's recording.

America's entry into World War II brought another Berlin forces show, *This Is the Army* (1942). He wrote music and lyrics, produced it, and starred in it as the only civilian in the cast, wearing his original 1917 *Yip, Yip, Yaphank* uniform. By the time the show reached Britain he had inserted a special extra song, 'My British Buddy', much praised by the Queen at a Royal Performance. *This Is the Army* raised £90,000 for British service charities and $7 million for US service charities.

Meanwhile Ellin Berlin had become a star in her own right as an author with her novel *Land I Have Chosen*, subsequently filmed by Warner Brothers.

In 1945 the death of Jerome Kern, who had been contracted to write *Annie Get Your Gun*, surprisingly produced a partnership between Irving Berlin and Rodgers and Hammerstein. This great songwriting team was producing but not writing the show, and they asked Irving to take over on Kern's death. It went on record as the show with more hit songs than any other before it. In 1948 his songs were featured in the film *Easter Parade*, starring Fred Astaire and Judy Garland. Then came his first flop, *Miss Liberty*. But a year later that flop was followed by another huge success, *Call Me Madam*, starring Ethel Merman.

In 1954 he was awarded a Congressional Medal of Honor by President Eisenhower. The *New York Times* commented: '... there couldn't be a more popular law than the one that gives Mr Berlin his medal. May he wear it for many years to come'. Then for some 10 years or so he went into what he called 'retirement'. In reality it was a fairly miserable period of his life when he just couldn't write hit songs any more, and he didn't want to know about any other kind.

In 1962 he wrote another musical, *Mr President*, but in spite of good advance bookings the critics were unkind to it, and it flopped. Awards for his past successes came in plenty, but alas, no new songs, although in 1966 he did write one, for a revival of *Annie Get Your Gun*—'Old-Fashioned Wedding'.

His 80th birthday was celebrated by a special edition of the Ed

Sullivan TV show. The guests ranged from Bing Crosby to Diana Ross and The Supremes. At 90 (that birthday, too, was marked by an all-star TV tribute), Irving Berlin lives quietly with his wife Ellin and his family, children and grandchildren. He still refuses permission for any film, stage or TV biography.

What Louis Armstrong did for Jazz, and Benny Goodman for the Big Bands, Irving Berlin has achieved in even greater measure for popular music.

Some other outstanding Irving Berlin songs:
'Everybody's Doin' It' (1911), 'When the Midnight Choo-Choo Leaves for Alabam' (1912), 'The Girl on the Magazine Cover' (1916, re-used in *Easter Parade*, 1948), 'Oh, How I Hate to Get Up in the Morning' (from *Yip, Yip, Yaphank*, 1918), 'A Pretty Girl Is Like a Melody' and 'Mandy' (both from *Ziegfeld Follies of 1919*), 'Say It With Music' (from *Music Box Revue*, 1921), 'Everybody Step' (1921), 'What'll I Do?' (1924), 'All Alone' (1924), 'Remember' (1925), 'A Russian Lullaby' (1927), 'The Song Is Ended' (1927), 'Shaking the Blues Away' (from *Ziegfeld Follies of 1927*), 'Marie' (from *The Awakening*, 1929), 'Puttin' on the Ritz' (1930), 'Soft Lights and Sweet Music' (from *Face the Music*, 1932), 'How Deep Is the Ocean?' (1932), 'Heat Wave' (from *As Thousands Cheer*, 1933), 'I Never Had a Chance' (1934), 'Cheek to Cheek', 'Top Hat, White Tie and Tails', 'The Piccolino', and 'Isn't this a Lovely Day?' (from *Top Hat*, 1935), 'I'm Putting All My Eggs in One Basket', 'Let's Face the Music and Dance', 'Let Yourself Go' and 'But Where Are You?' (from *Follow the Fleet*, 1936), 'I've Got My Love to Keep Me Warm', 'Slumming on Park Avenue', 'You're Laughing at Me' and 'This Year's Kisses' (from *On the Avenue*, 1937), 'I Used to Be Color Blind', and 'Change Partners' (from *Carefree*, 1938), 'It's a Lovely Day Tomorrow' (from *Louisiana Purchase*, 1940), 'Be Careful, It's My Heart' and 'Happy Holiday' (from *Holiday Inn*, 1942), 'I Left My Heart at the Stage Door Canteen', 'This Is the Army, Mr Jones', 'With My Head in the Clouds', and 'I'm Getting Tired So I Can Sleep' (from *This Is the Army*, 1942), 'You Keep Coming Back Like a Song' (1946), 'They Say It's Wonderful', 'Who Do You Love, I Hope', 'I Got the Sun in the Morning', 'Doin' What Comes Naturally', 'The Girl That I Marry' and 'There's No Business Like Show Business' (from *Annie Get Your Gun*, 1946), 'It Only Happens When I Dance With You', 'Better Luck Next Time', 'A Fella With an Umbrella', and 'Steppin' Out With My Baby' (from *Easter Parade*, 1948), 'Let's Take an Old-

Fashioned Walk' (from *Miss Liberty*, 1949), 'The Best Thing for You', 'You're Just in Love', 'It's a Lovely Day Today', and 'Hostess With the Mostes' on the Ball' (from *Call Me Madam*, 1950), 'An Old-Fashioned Wedding' (1966).

BERNSTEIN, Leonard, composer, author, pianist, arranger, conductor.

Born Lawrence, Mass, 25 August 1918. Educated at Boston Latin School and Harvard University, where he gained a BA. Subsequently a distinguished classical conductor, especially with New York Philharmonic. Wrote film background score for *On the Waterfront*, and scores for Broadway productions of *On the Town* (1944), *Wonderful Town* (1953), *Candide* (1956), and the TV production of *Peter Pan*. Best known for his music to Stephen Sondheim's lyrics for the score of *West Side Story* (1957), and the songs 'Maria', 'I Feel Pretty', 'A Little Bit of Love', 'America', 'Lonely Town', 'You Got Me', 'Tonight', 'Something's Coming', 'Cool', and 'Gee, Officer Krupke!'. His other best known songs are 'New York, New York' (from *On the Town*, with Betty Comden and Adolph Green), and 'A Quiet Girl' (from *Wonderful Town*, with the same lyricists).

BRICUSSE, Leslie, composer, author, producer.

Born London, 29 January 1931. Educated University College School, London, followed by national service in the army from 1948 to 1950. On discharge, he went to Cambridge University, where he soon became involved in the Footlights Club, writing material for and appearing in their annual revues. In 1954, his last year, he wrote, produced, appeared in, and directed their show *Out of the Blue*. On leaving Cambridge he was fortunate in almost immediately getting the opportunity to appear in the West End show *An Evening With Beatrice Lillie*, in which he performed his own material. Already it had become clear that the young Bricusse was destined for a career in the musical theatre. He married actress Yvonne Romain, and they had a son, Adam, but are now divorced.

His next break was not in the theatre, but was a commission to write the songs for the 1956 Max Bygraves film *Charley Moon*, from which 'Out of Town' became a big enough hit to win an Ivor Novello Award, and the association with Bygraves also resulted in Leslie's writing another hit for Max, 'A Good Idea, Son'. In 1958 he contributed the lyrics to Robin Beaumont's music for the show *Lady at the Wheel*, although interestingly, the only song from that score to be remembered is one called 'Love Is', for which Leslie wrote both words and music.

A more important feature of 1958 for Bricusse was that it was the year of his introduction to Anthony Newley, a meeting that resulted in 1961 in the successful show *Stop the World, I Want to Get Off!*, with such hits as 'Gonna Build a Mountain', 'Once in a Lifetime', and 'What Kind of Fool Am I?'. Prior to this, in 1960, Leslie had a huge hit with a song which, unusually for him, was written merely for the Eurovision song contest (it came second), and was not part of the score for a film or a show. It was 'My Kind of Girl', which Matt Munro took close to the top of the British charts, and Frank Sinatra recorded in the States. It has become a standard.

In 1963 he had another hit, this time co-written with Cyril Ornadel. It was 'If I Ruled the World', which was sung by Harry Secombe in the show *Pickwick*. This was followed by his second close association with Anthony Newley in the score and book of the 1965 production *The Roar of the Greasepaint, the Smell of the Crowd*. The hit songs were 'A Wonderful Day Like Today', and 'Who Can I Turn To?' In addition the team had, with John Barry, a hit the year before, with the title song from the James Bond picture *Goldfinger*.

In 1967 Leslie Bricusse demonstrated that he had not forgotten how to write words without music, by serving as lyricist to composer Henry Mancini for two songs, 'Two for the Road' and 'I Like the Look'. But by far the biggest event in his life in that year was the Rex Harrison film *Doctor Dolittle*, because this was the first time that Leslie had contributed both lyrics and a full score for such a major movie. Of its many good songs, 'Talk to the Animals' was the outstanding one. The following year, *Goodbye Mr Chips* was another major film musical venture, starring Petula Clark and Peter O'Toole. But it was not a success, nor was another Dickensian adventure, *Scrooge* in 1970. All was redeemed later in the same year, however, with Leslie's score for the film *Willie Wonka and the Chocolate Factory*, which produced the song 'Candy Man', for which Sammy Davis Jr won a gold record in 1972.

There was a renewal of the Bricusse/Newley partnership in 1971 with the show *The Good Old Bad Old Days*, from which the song 'The People Tree' will be best remembered. And this association was renewed yet again in 1976 when they wrote 15 songs for the ATV/NBC TV spectacular *Peter Pan*, starring Mia Farrow and Danny Kaye. Other Bricusse musicals in the 1970s included *The Travelling Music Show* (1978) and *Beyond the Rainbow* (1978).

Since the *Doctor Dolittle* days Bricusse has lived in Beverly Hills, California, where he continues to keep his inventive mind busy on future musical projects for both film and stage.

BROWN, Nacio Herb, composer, publisher, pianist.

Born Deming, New Mexico, 22 February 1896. Died San Francisco, 28 September 1964. Educated Musical Arts High School, Los Angeles. He originally started a tailoring business, and later moved into real estate, and it was only at the insistence of the MGM Studios in 1928 that he gave it all up to become a full-time and very successful songwriter. He had shown his talent for writing before 1928 with such songs as 'When Buddha Smiles' (1921, lyrics by Arthur Freed), and an instrumental, 'Doll Dance' (1921) which was widely recorded. His mother, father and sister all played musical instruments, and it was his mother who taught him the piano.

The family moved to Los Angeles in 1904, and the young Brown spent a year as accompanist to a vaudeville singer, Alice Doll, before deciding that this kind of music was not for him. It was following this that he set up his tailoring business, which quickly became successful when he managed to list Rudolph Valentino and Charlie Chaplin among his customers. When he moved into real estate he became successful in that too, and seems to have paid little attention to his songs. These he regarded as a relaxation until persuaded by Irving Thalberg to take three months off work to write the songs for *Broadway Melody* (1929), with Arthur Freed. This was MGM's first musical, and with the newly added feature of sound, the movie became a landmark. The work took him to Hollywood, where he wrote the scores for many successful musical films, including *Going Hollywood* (1933), *Greenwich Village* (1944), *Singin' in the Rain* (1952), and the 1936 and 1937 films of *Broadway Melody*. In addition, his songs were featured in such movies as *A Night at the Opera* with the

Marx Brothers (1935), *San Francisco*, with Jeanette MacDonald, Clark Gable and Spencer Tracy (1936), and *Babes in Arms* with Judy Garland and Mickey Rooney (1939).

He was not continuously in Hollywood during those years however. Although he was encouraged by the success of his first *Broadway Melody* to give up his tailoring and real estate business and become a full-time songwriter, the decline of musical films in 1931 and 1932 left him disillusioned. As a result, he moved back to New York, where he contributed to Broadway revues as well as writing many single hit songs. Irving Thalberg was unable to lure him back to California until 1933 when, with Arthur Freed also bringing pressure to bear, he returned for *Going Hollywood*.

Freed's background and general outlook on songwriting could hardly have been more different from that of Nacio Herb Brown. Born in Charleston, South Carolina, 9 September 1894, he entered the music business immediately after leaving Phillips Exeter Academy. He moved to Chicago and became a song-plugger with a publishing house there, which ultimately led to his becoming a part of the Marx Brothers vaudeville act. He served in the army during World War I, and afterwards lived in New York where he wrote special material for Broadway Revues. His first big hit came in 1923, with 'I Cried for You', to the music of Gus Arnheim and Abe Lyman. He later moved to Hollywood and became managing director of the Orange Grove Theater, where he specialized in presenting Broadway successes. He also put on an obscure show called *The Picklings*, for which he hired two new arrivals in Los Angeles, the then unknown pianist Al Rinker and the equally unknown singing drummer, Bing Crosby.

Arthur Freed became a producer and executive for MGM, and it was under his guidance that we saw such films as *Babes in Arms, Strike Up the Band, Babes on Broadway, For Me and My Gal, Cabin in the Sky, Du Barry Was a Lady, Best Foot Forward, Girl Crazy, Meet Me in St Louis, Ziegfeld Follies, Till the Clouds Roll By, Good News!, The Pirate, Easter Parade, An American in Paris, Brigadoon, Silk Stockings, Gigi, The Bells Are Ringing, Words and Music, The Barkleys of Broadway* and *Annie Get Your Gun*. Among the big names he discovered were Eleanor Powell, Gloria de Haven, June Allyson, Esther Williams, Gene Kelly and Howard Keel. He died 12 April 1973.

Herb Brown preferred to continue as a songwriter, and in addition to his many big hits with Arthur Freed, he also had successful collaborations with lyricists Buddy DeSylva, Gus Kahn, Leo Robin and Gordon Clifford. He retired in 1943, leaving California to live in Mexico, but returned to Hollywood in 1948 to write again for the movies. He continued writing songs until well into the 1960s, although the great days of his partnership with Arthur Freed were sadly never to be repeated.

Some other outstanding songs by Nacio Herb Brown:
'The Wedding of the Painted Doll' (1929), 'Broadway Melody' (1929), 'Singin' in the Rain' (1929), 'You Were Meant for Me' (1929), 'Pagan Love Song' (1929), 'Should I?' (1930), 'You're an Old Smoothie' (with Buddy De Sylva and Richard Whiting, 1933), 'Eadie Was a Lady' (with Buddy De Sylva and Richard Whiting, 1932), 'Temptation' (1933), 'All I Do Is Dream of You' (1934), 'You Are My Lucky Star' (1936), 'I've Gotta Feeling You're Fooling' (1936), 'You Stepped Out of a Dream' (with Gus Kahn, 1941), 'Make 'Em Laugh' (1952).

BROWN, Lew, *see* De Sylva, Brown and Henderson.

BRYANT, Boudleaux, composer, author, musician.

Born Shellman, Georgia, 13 February 1920. **BRYANT, Felice** (Felice Scaduto), author, composer, singer. Born Milwaukee, Wisconsin, 7 August 1925. They married in 1945 in Milwaukee, three days after they first met. They were still married 36 years later, and still writing songs.

Boudleaux Bryant's father was a lawyer. But by instinct he was a musician, playing piano, trombone and violin, while his mother played guitar and mandolin. Boudleaux received musical tuition from an early age on both violin and piano. He later taught himself guitar, bass and sousaphone. The family moved to Moultrie, Ga, where Boudleaux was educated at local schools, and by 1938 he was proficient enough on the violin to join the Atlanta Symphony Orchestra. Chance brought him an introduction to a man from the local radio station WSB, and soon he was doubling the symphony job with playing in a local string band.

An American string band has more guitars, banjos, and percussion instruments than violins, but at least one fiddle is essential. This was Boudleaux's first introduction to the world of country music, and it seems to have fascinated him because he deserted the symphony orchestra and began playing with various country music groups throughout the United States.

On one of these dates in 1945 he was playing with a band in a Milwaukee hotel, where there was a pretty elevator operator called Felice Scaduto. Three days later she became Felice Bryant. Many years afterwards she said in an interview with Lee Rector of *Music City News*: 'When I was 8 years old I dreamed of this man. He and I were dancing to "our song", and I remembered this man's face. So when I saw Boudleaux, I recognized him! I don't know if you call that love at first sight, or "At last, my friend, I was wondering when you'd come along". I just clung on to him. He didn't know who the hell I was, but I somehow knew who he was'. Felice's family were of Italian origin, and all of them were devoted to music, singing and playing various instruments, all by ear. Her personal repertoire was mostly Italian folk songs, but in her spare time she enjoyed writing poetry and lyrics.

Boudleaux, meanwhile, had written some instrumental pieces, but had never attempted popular songs. It is one of the strange things about this fairy-tale couple, that it was not until they had been married for almost a year that they each discovered the other's secret hobby. From then on they decided to try and turn their joint talents to their mutual advantage. When you're writing songs in the deep south, it's even worse than trailing round the publishers offices on foot in a big city such as New York, collecting your rejection slips. You have to do it by post. One song was accepted, thanks to Boudleaux's friend at WSM in Atlanta, but it was never recorded.

By that time they were living in Cincinnati, where they managed to get some songs ('1-2-3-4-5-foot-6', 'Give Me Some Sugar', 'Sugar Baby' and 'I'll Be Your Sweetie Pie') recorded by local artists. But it was 1948 before the breakthrough came. They were given an introduction to Fred Rose, a new publisher operating in Nashville, Tennessee, who later became head of the Acuff-Rose publishing empire. He took their song 'Country Boy', got it recorded by Little Jimmy Dickens, and it made No 10 in the charts.

But one minor hit does not make a successful songwriting team. Fred Rose wanted the Bryants in Nashville, but his struggling young company couldn't afford to pay them on the off-chance of success, so he got them a joint job as song-pluggers in Nashville for publisher

Nat Tannen, while they both kept on playing and singing to earn extra money in the evenings. It is a mark of the faith that both Fred Rose and Nat Tannen had in the Bryants, that there was a special arrangement whereby if Fred Rose commissioned a song, it went into the Acuff-Rose catalogue, but anything the Bryants wrote because they wanted to, went to Tannen Music. The arrangement lasted for four years, during which time a number of their songs were recorded by various top artists, ranging from Tony Bennett and Billy Eckstine (they both recorded 'Have a Good Time'), to Elvis Presley ('How's the World Treating You?') and not forgetting Frankie Laine, who won a gold disc with 'Hey Joe'.

About 1954, Fred Rose died and his son Wesley took over Acuff-Rose, continuing his father's faith in the Bryants by signing a most unusual contract. From 1956 they would write exclusively for Acuff-Rose for 10 years, after which the copyrights reverted to the writers.

The Bryants first started writing for the Everly Brothers in 1957, and their very first song, 'Bye Bye Love', turned into a million-seller. There followed many songs for the Everlys, and no fewer than six of them were also million-sellers: one more in 1957, 'Wake Up Little Susie'; three in 1958 'Bird Dog', 'Problems' and 'All I Have to Do Is Dream'; and 'Take a Message to Mary' in 1959. Based as they were in Nashville, writing for what was in those days very much a country music publishing company, it would be easy but quite wrong to assume that the songwriting talents of the Bryants were or are confined to the country music field. Over the years the term 'country music' has become a convenient peg on which both publishers and record companies have hung certain songs. I mentioned earlier a couple of artists who have had successes with Bryant compositions, artists such as Tony Bennett, who have no connection whatever with country music. There have been many more big names, some, but by no means all, country performers. The list includes Bob Luman, Roy Orbison, Buddy Holly, Leo Sayer, The Osborne Brothers, Lynn Anderson, Bob Dylan, Al Martino, Charley Pride, Herb Alpert, The Grateful Dead, Dean Martin, Dolly Parton, Nazareth, Chet Atkins, The Beach Boys, Glen Campbell, Rosemary Clooney, Alma Cogan, Percy Faith, Arthur Fiedler, Georgia Gibbs, Trini Lopez, Nellie Lutcher, Della Reese, Sarah Vaughan, Lawrence Welk, and many more.

Having said that, the art of being a professional songwriter is that you write for whoever wants your songs, and there is no doubt that the Bryants are rated tops by country artists looking for songs to record. So it was that throughout the 1960s, this was the field for their most notable successes. Bob Luman with 'Let's Think About Living' (1960) and Sonny James with 'Baltimore' (1964) are just a couple that spring to mind from that decade.

By the 1970s, the Bryants could write songs to please themselves. In doing so, they pleased a lot of other people too. Asked how many songs they have written, Boudleaux says: 'We write in 500-page legal ledgers, and right now we're in our 15th ledger'. They have a collection of at least 2,000 songs that as yet no one has ever heard. They have always shied away from appearing in public, claiming that since the 1950s they have been writers, not performers. But fate plays tricks. In the late 1970s they decided to record an album of their songs together—for fun. Almost before they knew it, word got around, and record companies were after it. As Boudleaux said to a *Billboard* reporter in 1980: 'Everything regarding this project has worked out so beautifully that we decided we would put out two albums a year. This is the beginning of a whole new era for us'. 'Will this all create a demand for personal appearances?' he was asked. 'No', was the short answer. 'Personal appearances are not our forte'.

If I believed in fairy stories I should start off the story of the Bryants with the time-honoured words: 'Once upon a time there were these two songwriters . . . .' Thinking it over, you can sum up the Bryants by the title line of one of their most famous songs 'All You Have to Do Is Dream'. For these two, who still hold hands when they walk down the street, this says it all.

Some other outstanding songs by Boudleaux and Felice Bryant:
'Civilization' (1973), 'Come Live With Me' (1970), 'I've Been Thinking' (1955), 'Let's Think About Living' (1960), 'Love Hurts' (1960), 'Poor Jenny' (1959), 'Raining in My Heart' (1959), 'She Wears My Ring' (1960), 'Willie Can' (1956), 'Rocky Top' (1967), 'Devoted to You' (1958), 'When I Stop Loving You' (1981), 'Playing in the Sand' (1980), 'I Can Hear Kentucky Calling Me' (1980).

BURKE, Johnny, *see* Van Heusen, Jimmy.

BURKE, Joseph, composer, pianist.

Born Philadelphia, Pa., 18 March 1884. Died Upper Darby, Pa., 9 June 1950. Educated University of Pennsylvania, where he learned to play the piano. After leaving, he joined the staff of a Philadelphia publisher as an arranger. Although he wrote his first song, 'Down Honolulu Way' in 1916, he had to wait till 1925 for his first hit, and that turned out to be a million-seller, 'Oh, How I Miss You Tonight' with lyrics by Benny Davis. From then on he seemed set for the top, especially when 'Carolina Moon', written in 1928, headed the hit parade for no less than 19 weeks in 1929, the year of the Wall Street crash. That same year he took off for Hollywood, his best known score being for *Gold Diggers of Broadway* (1929), for which Al Dubin wrote the lyrics. He continued to write many hit songs, but his contribution to the musical movies was perhaps less distinguished than that of some other writers. He and Dubin were totally disillusioned when their song 'Dancing With Tears in My Eyes' was cut from a film called *Dancing Sweeties*. But when they released it as a song in its own right it became an instant success, with hit recordings by Ruth Etting and Kate Smith (1930).

Fed up with the moguls, Burke returned to New York, and the 1930s proved to be his most successful years, as hit followed hit, many with lyrics by his new collaborator, Edgar Leslie, who was probably responsible for the lyrics of more Joe Burke hits than any other writer, including Benny Davis and Al Dubin.

Leslie was born in Stamford, Connecticut, 31 December 1885, and was brought up in New York, mostly by his grandparents. One of his earliest attempts at lyric-writing was a successful collaboration with the just starting Irving Berlin, on the song 'Sadie Salome Go Home'. From then on, in addition to his work with Joe Burke, he was lyricist to many famous writers, and references to his work will be found under the names of Fred Ahlert, Jimmy Monaco, Walter Donaldson and Harry Warren. As for Joe Burke, he continued writing successfully until retiring to Upper Darby, Pa in the late 1940s. His last hit, only two years before his death in 1950, was 'Rambling Rose', recorded by many stars of the time including Tony Pastor, Gordon Macrae and Bob Eberly. It was a song not to be confused with the 1962 million-seller of the same title for Nat King Cole, which was written by Noel Sherman.

Some other outstanding Joe Burke songs:
'Tip-Toe Through the Tulips' (with Al Dubin, 1929), 'Moon Over Miami' (with Al Dubin, 1933), 'Carolina Moon' (with Al Dubin, 1928), 'A Little Bit Independent' (with Edgar Leslie, 1936), 'On Treasure Island' (with Edgar Leslie, 1935), 'In a Little Gipsy Tearoom' (with Edgar Leslie, 1935), 'It Looks Like Rain in Cherry Blossom Lane' (with Edgar Leslie, 1937), 'Painting the Clouds With Sunshine' (with Al Dubin, 1930), 'Robins and Roses' (with Edgar Leslie, 1936).

CAHN, Sammy, author, publisher.

Born New York, 18 June 1913. Educated Seward Park High School. As I have explained in the introduction, Sammy Cahn is one of only three lyricists included in this book in his own right. He has been immensely prolific, but has really only worked with three main composers. His work has had an enormous influence on the business of songwriting, and he fully merits this entry. Sammy's rise to fame is the archetypal rags-to-riches story of the poor Jewish boy who was born in the poverty-stricken conditions of a tenement on New York's East Side, but who made it to the very top by his own efforts. His family were first generation immigrants from Galicia, and curiously, in all the books and interviews that have been published about Sammy Cahn, he seldom mentions his father (at one period he owned a small restaurant). It is always of his mother that he talks. His mother insisted that he learn to play the violin. It was of his mother that he said to Max Wilk (*They're Playing Our Song*): 'She was the kind of lady you could do a deal with. I made a deal with her—I'd play the violin until my 13th birthday, the fabled bar mitzvah. Come the bar mitzvah I played the violin solo, and that was the deal. Okay'. His father wanted him to study for one of the professions, but since music was obviously his life, it was inevitable that when he finally left school he should struggle for employment as a violinist in a theatre orchestra. The first job didn't last long, and was followed by a variety of others, from working in a meat-packing plant to operating a freight elevator, a spell as a tinsmith, and a cinema usher.

He started writing songs (mostly lyrics, but sometimes music as well) when he was 16, but nothing happened to them until he met Saul Chaplin, a piano player in one of the orchestras in which Sammy played part-time violin. Even then, they submitted literally dozens of songs to publishers with no success, although one song, 'Shake Your Head From Side to Side' did get published. It took the inevitable stroke of luck to start them off. They began to be asked to write special material for vaudeville acts—singers, comedians, anything. Then in 1935, they were asked to write a speciality number for the Jimmie Lunceford Band. It was called 'Rhythm Is Our Business', and not only was it a hit for Jimmie Lunceford (he adopted it as his signature tune), but it also put the writing team of Chaplin and Cahn on the Tin Pan Alley map.

Other songs followed for Jimmie Lunceford, also for the Casa Loma Orchestra, for Ella Fitzgerald, and for a band called Andy Kirk and His 12 Clouds of Joy. Chaplin and Cahn had, almost without realizing it, stumbled into the very beginning of a new era, when record producers were just starting to get songs specially written for recording purposes. Before that, artist and producer would trail wearily round the publishers' offices looking for new material that nobody else was using. The song Chaplin and Cahn wrote for Andy Kirk was called 'Until the Real Thing Comes Along'. The year was 1936, and it was recorded time and again after that by such artists as The Ink Spots, Fats Waller, and June Christy. That same year they wrote 'Shoe Shine Boy', which was introduced by Louis Armstrong in that year's *Cotton Club Revue*, and this too was taken up by other top artists such as Bing Crosby and The Mills Brothers.

In spite of all this success, the really big one was still around the corner. It arrived in 1937, when Chaplin and Cahn adapted the Yiddish folk song, 'Bei Mir Bist Du Schöen', and it became a million-selling record for The Andrews Sisters. In 1940 the team was in Hollywood, working for Warner Bros and later for Republic Pictures; but as often before, a successful Tin Pan Alley team does not always transfer well to Hollywood movies. Soon the partnership broke up, and Sammy found himself working for 20th Century-Fox with composer Jule Styne, and it was not long before the team of Styne and Cahn were being described as 'Frank Sinatra's personal songwriters'. Within a few years Sinatra had made their 'Saturday Night Is the Loneliest Night of the Week', 'I Fall in Love Too Easily', 'I'll Walk Alone' and 'Five Minutes More' into huge successes. At the same time they were writing hits for Doris Day, Dinah Shore, and Vaughn Monroe. The partnership lasted until the 1950s, culminating in their biggest success, 'Three Coins in the Fountain' (1954).

Sammy Cahn's composer collaborators have really amounted to only three—Saul Chaplin, Jule Styne, and Jimmy Van Heusen. Full details of the last partnership will be found under Jimmy Van Heusen's name, but this is perhaps the place to record that in 1957 they won an Oscar for 'All the Way', and they won a second for 'High Hopes' in 1959, both songs again owing their initial success to records by Frank Sinatra. They won a third Oscar in 1963 with 'Call Me Irresponsible' performed in the movie *Papa's Delicate Condition* by comedian/conductor Jackie Gleason. Within another three years Cahn and Van Heusen were being described as Frank Sinatra's personal songwriters. They did much more, including the title song they wrote for the picture *Star!*. This had Julie Andrews playing the leading role in the biography of Gertrude Lawrence, and the producer of the picture was Sammy's earlier collaborator Saul Chaplin.

In 1945 Sammy Cahn married Gloria Delson, and they had two children, a boy Steven, and a girl Laurie. They were divorced in 1964, and Sammy now divides his time between his home in Beverly Hills and his apartment in New York—when he is not globe-trotting and performing his one-man show somewhere in the world. It is difficult to explain why Sammy Cahn's lyrics have had such a tremendous impact on the songwriting business, but there may be three reasons. First, Sammy Cahn is a 'pro' to his fingertips. Talking to Max Wilk for the book *They're Playing Our Song*, he said: 'Now you ask which comes first, the words or the music? I'll tell you which—the *money*! Or the phone call—or the request!' So, songwriting is his profession, and he will not accept anything but the best. Secondly, he has the natural feel for music and the emotion a tune can create that must be possessed by every top lyricist. And Sammy has that quality in abundance—just listen closely to what he writes, and you will hear. And finally he has the quick-thinking mind of a first-class advocate.

This is perhaps summed up in another quote from his interview with Max Wilk. He talks about the way he and Van Heusen wrote the song 'High Hopes': 'I said, "instead of writing this song from the angle of human beings, why don't we try it from the angle of animals?" And the minute I said it I wanted to tear out my tongue, because I was telling the man who had written the single greatest animal song ever written ("Swinging on a Star"). I said, "forget that, not animals". I'm looking at the bungalow floor at Fox, where we're working, and there are some ants. "*Insects*" I said. "What do you mean insects?" he said. I said, "Well, you just take an ant. An ant has a sense of fulfillment when it moves from one place to another." Jimmy looked at me and he said "Yeah?". The minute you say that, it writes itself; I just happen to be privileged to be there. "Just what makes a little old ant think he'll move a rubber tree plant?". I know ants can't move rubber trees, but it has to be a rubber tree plant, that's what makes the cadence and the syllables fall properly—and the song is home and free, and you just happen to be lucky to be there getting it written.' That's Sammy Cahn, genius lyric-writer.

Some other outstanding Sammy Cahn songs:
'Please Be Kind' (1938, Saul Chaplin), 'I've Heard That Song Before' (1942, Jule Styne), 'It's Been a Long Long Time' (1950, Jule Styne), 'Day by Day' (1946, Stordahl/Weston), 'Let It Snow! Let It Snow! Let It Snow!' (1946, Jule Styne), 'I Should Care' (1945, Stordahl/Weston), 'The Things We Did Last Summer' (1947, Jule Styne), 'Time After Time' (1947, Jule Styne), 'It's Magic' (1948, Jule Styne), 'Be My Love' (1950, N Brodszky), 'Teach Me Tonight' (1955, G de Paul), 'Love and Marriage' (1955, J Van Heusen), 'I'll Never Stop Loving You' (1955, N Brodszky), 'Come Fly With Me' (1958, J Van Heusen), 'My Kind of Town' (1964, J Van Heusen), 'The Second Time Around' (1960, J Van Heusen), 'The Tender Trap' (1957, J Van Heusen), 'Thoroughly Modern Millie' (1967, J Van Heusen).

CALLANDER, Peter, *see* Murray, Mitch.

CARMICHAEL, Howard Hoagland 'Hoagy', composer, author, pianist, singer, actor.

Born Bloomington, Indiana, 22 November 1899. Died Palm Springs, California, 27 December 1981. Educated Bloomington High School and University of Indiana, where he graduated as a Bachelor of Law. Popular music came to him early, for there was a piano at home, and his mother used to play mood music for the silent movies at the local cinema. She would sometimes have to take the youthful Hoagy with her if there was no one at home, and this made him the envy of all the neighbourhood kids, getting to see the films for free. She also had a piano at home, and did other part-time work such as playing for college dances, so it was no surprise that in this atmosphere of popular music Hoagy became a self-taught pianist by the time he was 16. When the family moved to Indianapolis Hoagy was soon looking for kindred spirits, and found one in the shape of a black piano player called Reggie Duval. Reggie worked in one of the city's less salubrious dives, but took Hoagy under his wing, giving him piano lessons at home. 'Never', Reggie told him, 'play anything that ain't right. You may never make any money, but you'll never get mad at yourself'.

Meanwhile Hoagy had been enrolled at an Indianapolis High School, where he was utterly miserable. He finally quit in disgust, taking any job he could find to earn some money, hoping perhaps to get back to Bloomington High under his own steam. He worked on the building of the Indianapolis Union Station, as a 12-hour night shift operator on a cement mixer, and as an entrail cleaner in a slaughterhouse—but he could only stand that for three weeks. He tried to get into the army, but was turned down because he was under weight, although he finally made it on 10 November 1918. The next day was Armistice Day, and Hoagy left. By January 1919 the urge to return to Bloomington was so strong that, armed with only $10, he took himself back to stay with his grandmother, and re-entered the High School. After his studies, there were still pianos. The one in 'The Book Nook', for instance, and another in the Kappa Alpha Phi fraternity room. And thanks to Reggie Duval's training, it was not long before he was earning money as the pianist in a local band.

From then on Hoagy was hooked on music, especially jazz, although he refused to admit it while still studying for his Bachelor of Law degree by entering the University of Indiana in 1922. Soon his music was paying for his studies, and in addition to leading what had now become Bloomington's most popular 5-piece, he also found himself in the band-booking business—arranging visits by out-of-town bands for college and university dances. While his own band was playing out-of-town dates, and while watching the visiting bands he had booked, Hoagy was beginning to meet and talk to many of the early jazz musicians. These included King Oliver and Louis Armstrong, George Johnson (later to find fame with The Wolverines), clarinetist Leon Rapollo, saxophonist Don Murray, and cornetist Bix Beiderbecke, a man who became Hoagy's hero until he died tragically at the age of 28.

During one winter season, when Hoagy's outfit was playing in

Palm Beach, he met Irving Berlin. It was at a private party for which the band had been hired. The hostess asked the great man to play his new song, 'Lady of the Evening'. He did, and the young Carmichael, fascinated, endorsed the words spoken to him by George Johnson: 'Hoagy, if a man that plays that feeble can write a song that good, you can write a song too'. And then The Wolverines, with Bix, came to play a Carmichael booking in Bloomington. It was almost a year since that vow to write a song. Hoagy rushed to the piano in 'The Book Nook'. The result was 'Free Wheelin''. The Wolverines played it for the dance and promised to record it on their next session for the Gennett label. On 6 May 1924 they did just that, throwing out Hoagy's title and calling it 'Riverboat Shuffle'. Hoagy Carmichael, composer, had just been born. In his autobiography, *'Sometimes I Wonder'*, Hoagy describes his reaction to hearing his own music for the first time: 'I listened to it silently, head down, eyes closed. Somehow there was no thrill there (I could have cried). "It's a great arrangement", I said soberly. "Thanks fellows". George (Johnson) was proud of me, and beaming: "That's how you feel?" "I never listened to my own music before. I guess I don't know how to react, George". That has been a major tragedy for me about a lot of things. I either don't react, or I react too much. I sobered up, and experienced a strange detachment from it, maybe setting the pattern of my emotional responses to almost all the tunes that followed. Nothing'.

It was the arrival of yet another band—Curt Hitch and his Happy Harmonists—that effected the commissioning of the next two Carmichael tunes, 'Washboard Blues' and 'Boneyard Shuffle'. Later, Harry Hostetter, another college friend of Hoagy's, took the record of 'Washboard Blues' to a friend and local poet, Fred Callahan (he was a gravestone cutter by trade) and asked if he could write some words. Twenty minutes later, 'Washboard Blues' became a song about an old black woman scrubbing clothes. As Hoagy said many years later: 'That's how things were done in those days'. Hoagy Carmichael tunes seemed to need something to inspire them. 'Rockin' Chair' came about after watching Granny Campbell (an old black lady who supplied many of the impecunious with her special illegal home brew): 'She'd sit in her creaking old rocker, and ask to be handed her own bottle of beer'. It was the first tune for which the composer wrote his own words, and it later became singer Mildred Bailey's theme song. Carmichael songs have never been good at having beginnings, middles and endings, to the strict Tin Pan Alley formula.

Perhaps that is because Carmichael's life has never been good at it either.

In 1926 Hoagy finally graduated, a Bachelor of Law. He was invited by Stuart Gorell, an old friend from Bloomington, then running the city desk of the *Miami Herald*, to move to Miami to set up a practice as an attorney. Jazz and other music were behind him now. A sober life and a career as a distinguished attorney were to be the thing. Strangely, for a man with these intentions, en route from Indiana to Florida he ended up in New York, to see publisher Irving Mills about 'Washboard Blues'. True, after a few days of making the rounds of the clubs, and hearing the jazz talent of people such as Red Nichols, he did actually get to Miami. True, in partnership with another friend, Wilbur Cook, he did get to hanging out his sign, *Hoagland Carmichael Esq., Attorney at Law*. But then one day he heard Red Nichols' latest record of 'Washboard Blues' and 'Boneyard Shuffle' back to back, and it was goodbye to the law books and home again to Bloomington, to 'The Book Nook', and to Bix Beiderbecke and the gang.

'Star Dust', perhaps the world's greatest, and certainly one of the world's top three most played popular songs, was written in 1929, when Hoagy was sitting alone on what was called the spooning wall, on the edge of the college campus. He had just said a final goodbye to Dorothy Kelly, an off-on love of many years' standing. The melody came to him gradually, in his head he says. And after a while he had to rush off to 'The Book Nook' to persuade the proprietor not to close until he had mastered it on the piano. The following day he played it to his friend, Harry Hostetter, who didn't say much. It was quite a while after that that Hoagy one day heard Harry, who had never played anything in his life, knocking out 'Star Dust' with one finger on the piano. Hoagy asked him why. 'Oh,' said Harry, 'just in case you forget it'.

The song had been recorded several times as an instrumental before it acquired Mitchell Parish's now famous lyrics. But from that moment on there was no looking back for Hoagland Carmichael, composer of popular songs, and sometime jazz piano player. 'Georgia on My Mind' had a lyric by Hoagy's friend, Stuart Gorell; 'Lazy River' was written with the aid of jazz clarinetist Sidney Arodin (although composed in 1931, it did not become a hit for another 15 years); 'In the Still of the Night' had lyrics by Jo Trent. Then in 1933 came the first co-operation between Carmichael and another jazz enthusiast, Johnny Mercer, and Carmichael songs in yet another style were born. Unlike many famous popular composers, Hoagy has never had a steady writing partner. The list of big-name lyricists is long: Sammy Lerner (no relation to Alan Jay), Stanley Adams, Paul Francis Webster, Dick Charles, Edward Heyman, Frank Loesser, and there were to be many more songs with his own lyrics, after 'Rockin' Chair'.

Hoagy contributed scores to musicals too. Most of these were Hollywood movies, but some were Broadway shows. The 1936 song 'Little Old Lady' was written for a Broadway revue called *The Show Is On*. Hoagy Carmichael continued to write songs, although his greatest days may perhaps have been from the 1930s through the 1950s. Outstanding songs perhaps are 'Moonburn', which he wrote in 1936 for the picture *Anything Goes* with Bing Crosby and Ethel Merman; 'The Nearness of You', for the 1938 film *Romance in the Dark* with Gladys Swarthout, John Boles and John Barrymore; 'Small Fry' for *Sing You Sinners* (1938) starring Bing Crosby, Fred McMurray and Donald O'Connor; 'Two Sleepy People' (with Frank Loesser) for the 1938 movie *Thanks for the Memory*, starring Bob Hope and Shirley Ross; 'Old Music Master' for the 1943 film *True to Life*, with Mary Martin and Dick Powell; 'How Little We Know' for *To Have and to Have Not*, with Humphrey Bogart and Lauren Bacall (a classic movie, which also marked Hoagy's debut as an actor in the part of Crickett); 'Doctor, Lawyer, Indian Chief' for the 1945 film *The Stork Club* with Betty Hutton and Barry Fitzgerald; 'Memphis in June' for the film *Johnny Angel*, also in 1945, featuring George Raft; and 'Ole Buttermilk Sky' for Dana Andrews's 1946 picture, *Canyon Passage*.

In the first of his two autobiographies, *The Stardust Road* (1946), there is a letter at the end from his great college friend and saxophone player, Wad Allen. It sets out to tell the reader all the important things about Hoagy that he himself left out of the book. He left almost as many details out of his second book *Sometimes I Wonder* (1966). To quote a few items from the Wad Allen letter: '... it leaves out the fact that, each year since you arrived so successfully on the crest of *The Stardust Road*, you have done a wide variety of things, such as being a radio star, becoming a successful movie actor, and having two sons by only one wife. You made your greatest success as a composer by not writing songs about love. You gained popularity on radio and records by singing; yet you have no voice. How do you do that? It worries us. It was not long after your return to these parts, when a good-looking girl named Ruth Meinardi was introduced to you in your apartment. You plied her with her first drink of straight liquor, and quickly got about your then customary business of being boldly progressive. No wonder she said you were crude, and no wonder I choked on my drink when she also said "Nevertheless, I'm going to marry him some day". You were married to Ruth in New York's 5th Avenue Presbyterian Church, where Ruth's father used to preach. And I forgot to pay the preacher, remember? Then that eldest boy of yours, Hoagy Bix was born. This almost took place on the hospital steps due to your insistence that you take movies of the whole blessed event. That was almost as trying for us as was the night your second son, Randy Bob was born. You had your ears so plastered to the radio that you didn't hear the nurse tell you that you were the father of a fine baby son. Who would guess from all this that you were to become a better than average father? Honestly Carmichael, we couldn't. What did Howard Hawks do for you? He decided you ought to be a motion picture actor. And what did you do? You took it seriously. It should (all) have been in the book. Great world, ain't it Hoagmichael? Wad Allen'.

Some other outstanding Hoagy Carmichael songs:
'Hong Kong Blues' (1939), 'I Get Along Without You Very Well' (1939), 'Small Fry' (with Frank Loesser, 1938), 'Lamplighter's Serenade' (with Paul Francis Webster, 1942), 'My Resistance Is Low' (with Harold Adamson, 1941), 'Judy' (1934), 'Old Man Harlem' (1933), 'Moon Country' (1934), 'Lazybones' (with Johnny Mercer, 1933), 'One Morning in May' (with Mitchell Parish, 1934), 'Skylark' (with Johnny Mercer, 1942), 'In the Cool Cool Cool of the Evening' (with Johnny Mercer, an Academy Award Winner, 1951), 'Thanksgiving' (with Johnny Mercer, 1951), 'Baltimore Oriole' (1945).

CARR, Michael, composer, author.

Born Leeds, England, 1904. Died London, England, 16 September 1968. **KENNEDY, James (Jimmy),** composer, author, pianist. Born Omagh, Co Tyrone, Northern Ireland, 20 July 1902.

Michael Carr was one of those slightly larger-than-life characters who belonged to what is now regarded as the golden age of Tin Pan Alley. The son of a featherweight boxer, 'Cockney' Cohen, he spent his early years in Dublin. It was there that he acquired more than just a touch of Irish blarney, because he featured in more apocryphal stories than probably any other songwriter of the time. It was in 1924 that he became a bit of a rebel, jumped a windjammer and sailed to Boston.

For six years he did a variety of jobs in America including that of stage hand, newspaper reporter and bit-part actor. He also spent nine months as a cowhand in Montana where he acquired a first-hand knowledge of the cowboy songs he was to write so successfully later. In Las Vegas he played piano in a gambling joint called the Golden Bar where they called him 'The Rhyming Limey', an early indication of his ability to juggle with words.

Soon after his return to Dublin in 1930, Michael wrote a tune for a song contest that so impressed a local bandleader he advised him to try his luck in London. He also gave him a letter of introduction to a fellow Irishman, Jimmy Kennedy, who was already a well established songwriter in London. This was to lead eventually to one of the most productive partnerships in Tin Pan Alley. Before he teamed up with Kennedy, however, he collaborated with several other writers, including Leo Towers and Will Haines. In 1930 he wrote with them the big Gracie Fields hit of the year "Fonso My Hot Spanish (K)Night'.

Michael was soon put under contract to a major music publisher and shortly afterwards, in 1934, came up with his first really big hit. He was astute enough to appreciate the current craze for cowboy songs (hillbilly songs they were called then). With his earlier experiences in Montana he reckoned he could write one as good as those that were being churned out at the time. He did just that, called it 'Ole Faithful' and it sold over two-and-a-half million records and tens of thousands of copies of sheet music.

He followed it with a whole series of cowboy songs over the years including 'The Wheel of the Wagon Is Broken' (1935), 'The Sunset Trail' (1936), 'There's a Cowboy Ridin' Thru the Sky' (1942), and 'Cowboy' (1936). This last one he wrote with Jimmy Kennedy, with whom he'd teamed up the previous year. Together they were to write a long string of memorable hits that included not only popular single numbers but also show tunes and film songs. It would be true to say that the Michael Carr/Jimmy Kennedy partnership was on the same level as some of the famous American author/composer teams.

Jimmy Kennedy was educated at Trinity College, Dublin. On completing his studies, he spent some time at his university as a graduate teacher before branching out into the Colonial Service, as a

Political Officer. None of this appealed to him very much, however, and in the late 1920s he decided to try his luck at songwriting. He began his onslaught as every beginner does, in the publishing houses of London's Tin Pan Alley. He had his first song, 'Hear the Ukeleles', published in 1929. It was not a great success, and he did better the following year with 'The Barmaid's Song' (otherwise known as 'Time Gentlemen Please'), designed for and much appreciated by, the holiday crowds in Blackpool. The song was published by Feldman's, whose proprietor, Bert Feldman, felt sufficient enthusiasm for the young Irishman to offer him a writing contract with his firm, and the job of 'lyric editor'. In the latter capacity Jimmy wrote the English words for such continental songs as 'Oh Donna Clara' (1930), 'Play To Me Gypsy' (1934), 'The Isle of Capri' (1934), and 'My Song Goes Round the World' (1934). He also wrote in 1933 the words to a melody that had been composed in 1904 by John W Bratton. During the American presidential election of that year Theodore (Teddy) Roosevelt took time out to go on a bear-hunting picnic. The event caused some amusement and was quickly commemorated with a characteristic musical take-off—'Teddy's Bear Picnic' which Bratton called *The Teddy Bear's Picnic*. Almost 30 years later, now with Jimmy's words, the recording by Henry Hall and the BBC Dance Orchestra sold over four million copies.

Long after his lyric-writing contract with Feldman had expired, Jimmy Kennedy continued to turn out successful lyrics, including 'Harbour Lights' (1937, with Hugh Williams), 'My Prayer' (1939, with Georges Boulanger), 'Red Sails in the Sunset' (1935, with Hugh Williams), 'The Cokey-Cokey' (1942, frequently called 'The Hokey Cokey'—the tune is traditional), 'Poor Little Angeline', and 'Serenade in the Night' (both 1936, with Will Grosz and C A Bixio respectively). As late as 1953 he was still turning out first-class lyrics such as 'April in Portugal', for Raoul Ferrao's melody.

Although we may think of Jimmy primarily for his lyrics in collaboration with other composers, he has also written some enduring melodies of his own. There was 'Roll Along Covered Wagon' (1934), 'The Coronation Waltz' (1937), 'There's a Boy Coming Home on Leave' (1940), 'I'll Just Close My Eyes' (1942), 'My Serenade' (1943), and 'A House Never Passes' (1944). And he was still writing lyrics in 1960—'Love Is Like a Violin'.

During World War II he served in the army, and after his discharge lived in America for some years, where his writing was much in demand, particularly by the growing band of country singers. His

'The Red We Want Is the Red We've Got', a Korean war song, became a best-seller for singer Eddie Fisher and bandleader Hugo Winterhalter. In the 1960s he went into semi-retirement in Switzerland, convinced, like so many writers of his generation, that the modern rock 'n' rollers did not want his talents. But he soon moved back home to Ireland, where he found himself much in demand again.

Jimmy received an Ivor Novello Award in 1971 for his services to British popular music, and during that decade began to compose a number of instrumental pieces, one of which, 'The St John March' was adopted by the St John Ambulance Brigade. He has also written music for plays performed in Dublin and elsewhere.

In 1976 he received an ASCAP Award (an unusual honour for a British writer), because 'Red Sails in the Sunset' was the most played record on America's country music radio stations in that year, and he gained a similar award in 1977 for the song 'My Prayer'. In 1978 the University of Ulster recognized 'his outstanding services to light music' with an honorary D Litt. In 1980 he won yet another Ivor Novello Award for his services to British popular music.

The great Kennedy/Carr partnership lasted a mere five years, yet during that period they turned out some of the most successful British songs of the time. Among their many hits were 'Why Did She Fall for the Leader of the Band?' (1935) for the Jack Hylton film *She Shall Have Music*, but which George Elrick made famous when he was singing with Henry Hall's BBC Dance Orchestra; 'Misty Islands of the Highlands' (1935), another big hit for Henry Hall; 'Did Your Mother Come From Ireland' (1936), a natural from two Irishmen; and 'There's a New World' (1937), for the London Palladium show *Okay for Sound*. They also found time in the same year to compose an orchestral piece they called 'The Spice of Life', which became the signature tune for the BBC's Saturday night *Music Hall* programme for many years; 'Home Town' (1937), which they wrote for the London Palladium show *London Rhapsody* and which became an enormous hit for Flanagan and Allen; 'Stay in My Arms Cinderella' (1938), the biggest waltz song of the year; and 'South of the Border' (1939), probably their biggest international hit, a 'standard' that has been recorded by well over a hundred different singers, including Crosby, Sinatra, and Como as well as the original hit recording by Gene Autry. Jimmy Kennedy called this one 'a songwriter's dream'.

Together they also dreamed up the biggest hit song of World War II. It began when Jimmy saw a cartoon that depicted a young British soldier writing home from France and saying, 'Dear Mum, I'm sending you the Siegfried Line to hang your washing on'. The Siegfried Line was Germany's vast, allegedly impregnable, fortification. Jimmy, like a true professional, immediately saw the song possibilities of the young soldier's cheeky remark.

Jimmy was by then in the army and stationed a few miles out of London. When Michael went to visit him he found Jimmy marching up and down on guard inside the perimeter of a water-pumping station. Michael couldn't get inside and neither could Jimmy get outside. He did, however, tell Michael about the cartoon he'd seen and there and then, with both of them marching up and down in the pouring rain, was laid the foundation for what was to become one of the biggest morale-boosting songs of the war. It was called 'We're Gonna Hang Out the Washing on the Siegfried Line' and was the last big hit they composed together. Both being prolific writers, they had continued to write songs independently during their partnership. Among Michael's hits were 'The Girl With the Dreamy Eyes' (1935, with Eddie Pola), 'Dinner for One Please, James' (1935, a solo effort which became one of Nat King Cole's biggest hits as well as a hit for the French star Jean Sablon), 'The Little Boy That Santa Claus Forgot' (1937, with Tommy Connor and Jimmy Leach), 'Somewhere in France With You' (1939), and 'A Pair of Silver Wings' (1941, with words by Eric Maschwitz, which Frances Day sang in *Black Vanities*).

In 1941 Michael joined the army on what was called 'special entertainment duties' and became closely associated with a production called *Stars in Battledress*. This led to his promotion to sergeant, which he naturally celebrated by writing a song about it. It was called 'How Did You Ever Become a Sergeant?' and was clearly autobiographical.

After the war Michael, like so many of the old school of songwriters, found himself somewhat baffled by the postwar pop scene. He continued to write but never seemed able to find the same magic touch with his later songs, except for a brief period in the early 1960s. 'Countin' Colours in a Rainbow' became a fair-sized hit for Nina and Frederick; and on the theory that if you can't beat 'em, join 'em, he wrote two big hits for the pop group The Shadows. The first was 'Man of Mystery', the theme from an Edgar Wallace TV series, which reached the No 2 spot in the British charts in 1960; and in the following year The Shadows took Michael Carr's 'Kon-Tiki' to the top of the British charts.

The most famous songs by Michael Carr and Jimmy Kennedy have been referred to in the text. But the following, which they wrote together or in association with others, should not be overlooked.

Carr and Kennedy: 'The General's Fast Asleep' (1935), 'Waltz of the Gypsies' (1937), 'Sing a Song of London' (1937), 'On Linger Longer Island' (1938), 'There's Danger in the Waltz' (1939).

Michael Carr: 'Old Timer' (1935, with Lewis Ilda), 'That's How a Love Song Is Born' (1951), 'Lonely Ballerina' (1954, with Paul Lamprecht).

Jimmy Kennedy: 'Café in Vienna' (1934, with Karel Vacek), 'At the Café Continental' (1936, with Will Grosz), 'Ten Pretty Girls' (1938, with Will Grosz), 'The French Can Can Polka' (1950, adapted from Offenbach), 'Istanbul, Not Constantinople' (1954, with Nat Simon).

CASH, Johnny, composer, author, singer.

Born Kingsland, Arkansas, 26 February 1932. There were seven children in the family of farmer Ray Cash when in 1935, his farm ruined by the Depression, he decided to take his whole family to Dyess, Arkansas. There the government offered him a new piece of land to develop. It was barren, the living was hard, and the family extremely poor, and Johnny, like the rest of them, did his daily share of picking cotton, ploughing, or whatever other farm chores had to be done. His education was minimal but even then there was music in the home, for somehow they acquired a piano, and Johnny was always singing (frequently hymns), and listening to country music on the radio. Even as a schoolboy he sang his own song over the local station and later won first prize in an amateur song contest.

In 1950, he joined the air force and served in Germany, where he acquired his first guitar, and where there was an opportunity for him to perform with his own songs at various service clubs. He also began to write poetry, some of which was published in the service paper *Stars and Stripes.* He was discharged in 1954, and married Vivian Liberto, going to live in Memphis. Times in Memphis were hard, and the budding writer/singer became a door-to-door salesman by day, while continuing to write at night, and studying radio presentation, in the hope of getting a job as a disc jockey.

It was in 1955 that he was heard by Sam Phillips of Sun Records, based in Memphis (the Company that was responsible for discovering

Elvis Presley), and it was for Phillips that he made his first record of his own songs—'Hey Porter' and 'Cry, Cry, Cry', the latter making the charts. This was soon followed up by 'Folsom Prison Blues', and that was Johnny Cash's first million-seller. After that, hits followed each other in quick succession, and Johnny earned the distinction of having every record he released during the period 1956–1959 reach the top ten in the charts of country and western music.

It was during that period that he produced such songs as 'So Doggone Lonesome', 'There You Go', 'Train of Love', 'Orange Blossom Special', 'I Walk the Line', 'Five Feet High and Rising', 'The Man on the Hill', 'Ballad of a Teen-Age Queen', and 'Don't Take Your Guns to Town' (his first hit for the Columbia label to which he switched in 1959).

By the early 1960s all this success began to take its toll. The result of the record sales inevitably made him a most sought after figure in the entertainment business, starting as a star of Nashville's Grand Ole Opry, and going on to concert tours, featured TV specials, and parts in movies. To cope with it all, Johnny resorted to pills and alcohol, and although his fans remained loyal to his music, his career nose-dived. He divorced his wife in 1968 and brought himself close to death. Perhaps the thing that pulled him round was that by then he had co-written a song called 'Ring of Fire' with the noted country singer June Carter, an association that developed into marriage, and Johnny found he wanted to live again. At the same time Cash found a revival of interest in the religious training he had received as a boy, and this added another new dimension to his life. During the 1960s he had many successful albums out on the Columbia label, including the particularly well known ones such as 'Johnny Cash at Folsom Prison' (where he once spent one night on a drug charge), and 'Johnny Cash at San Quentin'. By the early 1970s his Columbia album sales totalled some 15 million copies. His autobiography, *Man in Black*, was also published in the 1970s.

There were also more single successes, including 'A Boy Named Sue', 'Cotton Pickin' Man' and 'If I Were a Carpenter'. His annual income is reckoned to be in excess of $2 million. Yet Johnny Cash is a simple man at heart. He opens his shows just with the words 'Hello—I'm Johnny Cash'. And he told journalist Peter McCabe in 1973: 'I see myself on stage, if God lets me live 20 or 30 more years. It's what I feed on, the performance, and the audience reaction. It's what I love, and that's all I want to do. I want to try to write and record better country songs'.

In the 1980s Johnny Cash became increasingly involved with gospel music (he financed, produced, and appeared in the documentary film *Gospel Road* in 1973), in addition to his traditional country idiom. He signed a new contract with CBS and continued to draw large audiences for his concerts and TV spectaculars. He also continued to be a prolific recording artist, with six albums released in 1979. And although sales of singles may not have reached previous heights, they continued to be very successful.

CHAPLIN, Saul, *see* Cahn, Sammy.

CHAPMAN, Michael, composer, author, producer.

Born Brisbane, Australia, 16 May 1947. **CHINN, Nicholas B,** author, composer. Born Bristol, England, 13 April 1946. Mike Chapman was educated at local schools in Brisbane, and went to England at 20 hoping to make it as a pop singer. Instead, he got a job as a waiter at Tramps nightclub. Nicky Chinn was educated at Clifton College, Bristol, and his first job was in his father's extensive car hire firm, although from his school days he enjoyed writing lyrics as a hobby.

Luck gave Nicky Chinn an introduction to Michael D'Abo, the ex-Manfred Mann singer, and together they were commissioned to write the songs for the Goldie Hawn/Peter Sellers film, *There's a Girl in My Soup* (1970). He also met Mike Chapman in 1970 when Mike was a waiter at Tramps, and he (Nicky) was a customer. Mike once said: 'Until I heard the songs from *Girl in My Soup* I just thought Nicky was a rich playboy. Then I realized he was writing the same sort of thing as I was, and took it from there'. At first it was music by Chapman, words by Chinn, but it very quickly developed into a complete fifty/fifty collaboration. Their first major hit was 'Funny Funny' for the group Sweet in 1970, and this brought them to the attention of Mickie Most of RAK Records, who became their adviser and guru. 'I can't emphasise too much how Mickie Most has influenced and helped us. But we didn't make the mistake of relying on him completely', said Mike in an early interview. By 1975 the team had 16 major hits to their credit, including eight with Sweet, three with Mud, and three with Suzi Quatro. Eleven of their songs have become million-sellers. Since 1975 they have both lived in Los Angeles, where Mike has become a distinguished record-producer.

Some other outstanding Chapman/Chinn songs:
'Co-Co' (1971, Sweet), 'Poppa Joe' (1972, Sweet), 'Little Willy' (1972, Sweet), 'Wim Wam Bam' (1972, Sweet), 'Block Buster' (1973, Sweet), 'Hell Raiser' (1973, Sweet), 'The Ballroom Blitz' (1973, Sweet), 'Can the Can' (1973, Suzi Quatro), '48 Crash' (1973, Suzi Quatro), 'Tiger Feet' (1974, Mud), 'Teenage Rampage' (1974, Sweet), 'Devil Gate Drive' (1974, Suzi Quatro).

COHAN, George M, composer, author, producer, actor.

Born Providence, Rhode Island, 3 July 1878 (he always claimed to have been born on 4 July, Independence Day), died New York, 4 November 1942. He was the youngest of the three children of Jeremiah and Helen Cohan, who were vaudeville artists. George M (Michael) was almost literally born in a trunk, for his parents were on tour at the time of his birth.

George M Cohan finds his place here for two reasons, the most important being the revolution he created in the musical theatre with the presentation of his show *Little Johnny Jones* in 1903. Although it was not an immediate success on Broadway, it toured the US to packed houses, and returned to triumph on the Great White Way in 1905, and came back yet again in 1906. It was probably the first real American musical in an age when most Broadway successes were imported from England, Austria or elsewhere in Europe. The second reason is that although many of George's songs were written prior to 1900, a few of his greatest hits do fall within our scope, and these are listed below.

By the 1920s, George M Cohan had become better known as a producer and actor than as a songwriter, and his career continued in that direction up to his death. By the 1930s, critics who had been busy slamming his musicals a decade earlier, were saying of his acting such things as: 'Mr Cohan has never been in better form. The audience was his, and lovingly his, all last evening'. Belatedly, a statue was erected in his honour in 1959, in Duffy Square on Broadway, the street he loved so much. But this was for his contribution to acting, rather than for his songwriting, although it is his songs that will live on.

He paid only one visit to Hollywood, in 1932 to star in *The Phantom President* with Claudette Colbert and Jimmy Durante. The visit was a disaster. The studios refused to recognize him as a star, and would not allow him to contribute any suggestions to the making of the picture. The ultimate humiliation came when they refused to allow him to tell them how to produce a flag-waving routine that he himself had created in one of his Broadway shows. After it was all over he was reported as saying: 'I'd rather go to Leavenworth Prison than work in Hollywood again'. It was not until 1942, the year of his death, that Hollywood finally recognized what they had missed, by making the film *Yankee Doodle Dandy* based on Cohan's life, with Jimmy Cagney in the leading role. Cohan was well enough to attend a private showing, and was seen to be visibly moved at the tribute that had been paid to him.

Some outstanding George M Cohan songs:
'The Yankee Doodle Boy' (*Little Johnny Jones*, 1904), 'Give My Regards to Broadway' (*Little Johnny Jones*, 1904), 'Forty-Five Minutes From Broadway', and 'Mary's a Grand Old Name' (both from *Forty-Five Minutes From Broadway*, 1906), 'You're a Grand Old Flag' (*George Washington, Jr*, 1906), 'Over There' (1917; won a belated Congressional Medal of Honour in 1941), 'Nellie Kelly, I Love You' (*Little Nellie Kelly*, 1922), 'Born and Bred in Brooklyn' (*The Rise of Rosie O'Reilly*, 1923), 'We Must Be Ready' (1941, his last song, written six months before the Japanese attacked Pearl Harbor).

COLEMAN (Kaufman) Cy, composer, pianist.

Born New York, 14 June 1929. Educated High School of Music and Art and New York College of Music. Best known for his score for the 1966 musical *Sweet Charity*, which contained the following hits: 'Hey Big Spender', 'I Love to Cry at Weddings', 'I'm a Brass Band', 'Where Am I Going?', 'Rhythm of Life', and 'If My Friends Could See Me Now'. He also wrote the 1957 Frank Sinatra hit, 'Witchcraft', and will be remembered for 'Hey, Look Me Over' from *Wildcat* (1960), 'Real Live Girl' from *Little Me* (1962), and 'Nobody Does It Like Me' from *See-Saw* (1973). He also wrote the song 'The Best Is

Yet to Come' (1959), and has been responsible for the scores of *I Love My Wife* (1976) and *Barnum* (1980). But however good these scores may be musically, they have not produced any memorable hits. Lyrically, his main collaborator has been Carolyn Leigh (born New York, 21 August 1926), and from the start of *Sweet Charity* it was Dorothy Fields (see McHugh, Jimmy).

CONNOR, Thomas P (Tommie), author, composer.

Born Bloomsbury, London, 16 November 1904. Educated Macklin Street RC School, Holborn, London. Tommie Connor is first and foremost a lyricist, but in the same way that Johnny Mercer and Sammy Cahn have been included on the grounds that each has made a very special contribution to the art of popular songwriting, I feel that Tommie's inclusion is justified for the same reason.

Tommie Connor's first job, at 14, was that of call boy at the Kingsway Theatre. Two years later he had progressed to being call boy at the Theatre Royal, Drury Lane, where he found himself calling for the great stars of the day, from Ivor Novello to Gladys Cooper. He was there during the run of *Rose-Marie*, and used to amuse himself by writing his own words to its famous tunes. This was how he met composer Herbert Stothart, who had contributed one of his songs to the Rudolf Friml score. The composer was sufficiently impressed with young Tommie's efforts to advise him quite seriously to take up songwriting. 'But first, go round the world', he said. So, a year or two later, Tommie became a steward on the *Empress of France*, which did almost take him round the world over the next two years.

He then returned to London, took a job in the theatre, started writing songs in earnest, and spent his days on the dreary trail up and down Denmark Street (London's Tin Pan Alley), having his material constantly rejected. Connor himself said of this period: 'The hard part was the five-year fight to be accepted in the Alley by a publisher's editor. Turned down by every publisher in London, I was later to be begged for songs by all the same people who at one time had slammed their doors (via secretaries) in my face. The knack was to keep going back for more. Songwriters also wrote at least two or three songs per week to enable their "bag" to contain anything from a waltz to a comic song at the drop of a hat. I personally wrote a song a day. Then the well stocked bag starts to pay off, because among the glut is just that song that cannot be found anywhere else, and finally one day you happen to have what no other writer in the country can supply at that given moment!' His first published song came, at long last, in 1932. It was called 'My Home Town', and he was even lucky enough to get it recorded—on Decca by Little Mary Hagan. His first hit came two years later and was called 'Jump on the Wagon'. It was described as a 'number one radio hit'. Just a year later he topped the hit parade for the first time with 'When the Guardsman Started Crooning on Parade'.

By 1935 Tommie Connor had started writing with composer Eddie Lisbona, and that same year they came up with 'It's My Mother's Birthday Today'—a song that not only reached number one in the hit parade but was also to become a standard, destined to find its way into the repertoire of many famous artists. Even in 1935 it had a best-selling record by Arthur Tracy, 'The Street Singer'. During the next 15 years Tommie had at least 10 chart-topping songs, of which two, 'Lilli Marlene' (English lyric 1944) and 'I Saw Mommy Kissing Santa Claus' (1952, for which he also wrote the music), were also international hits. Jimmy Boyd's recording of the latter was a million-seller.

A writer of Tommie Connor's talent was much in demand in the theatre, in movies, and as a writer of special material for the famous. Between 1933 and 1977 he contributed lyrics for songs to more than 50 film musicals, his last commission being for *The Good the Bad and the Ugly*. He also wrote for many West End revues, for such impresarios as Firth Shepherd and George Black. As for special material, his list of artists runs from Gertie Gitana to Vera Lynn, and Maurice Chevalier to Richard Tauber.

In some respects Tommie Connor is a sort of British Sammy Cahn—a complete professional. When somebody wants a song written, Tommie will oblige. Eddie Rogers, in his book *Tin Pan Alley* quotes Tommie as follows: 'Bert Hyson rang us' (Tommie and Eddie Lisbona) 'one Friday night and said that the following Monday he had an all-French show opening at the Café Anglais. He wanted 20 numbers, covering the whole gamut of the French musical scene—from the nostalgic Montmartre ballad to the rousing Can-Can type number. A completely mixed bag, and all with French lyrics. Eddie and I knew about five French words between us. So we bought a 2s 6d French textbook from Foyles and worked all Friday night on the score. Hyson had his songs the next day. Of course, the lyrics were in the most fractured French imaginable, but Eddie and I worked it out this way. Those in the audience who knew French would be too discreet to comment on the torture of the language; and those who didn't know would try to impress their friends by telling them how clever the lyrics were'.

He also has that natural feeling for the emotion a tune can create, which is essential to a top-class lyricist. Just listen to the words of his three Christmas songs. The first was 'The Little Boy That Santa Claus Forgot' (1937). The second was 'I'm Sending a Letter to Santa' (1939), which Gracie Fields first performed at a troop concert in France. It's the story of a little boy who wrote to Santa and asked for the safe return of his soldier daddy for a Christmas present. The papers headlined: 'Gracie makes the troops cry'. And the third was the delightfully sentimental 'I Saw Mommy Kissing Santa Claus' (1952), with its delightfully humorous undertones. To quote Eddie Rogers again: '... Tommie has the gift of being able to translate the wishes, hopes and dreams of ordinary people into simple, singable lyrics'. Yet the same Tommie Connor could contribute lyrics as hilarious as those of the immortal Gracie Fields number 'The Biggest Aspidistra in the World'.

His most famous composer collaborators have been Eddie Lisbona, Horatio Nicholls, Jimmy Kennedy, Michael Carr, and Robert Stolz, not forgetting Spencer Williams of 'Basin Street Blues' fame, who wrote the music for 'I'm Sending a Letter to Santa'. Perhaps the last word should be with the master lyricist himself: 'I thank God for being my partner. He gave me my talent, and He has provided my inspiration'.

Some other outstanding Tommie Connor songs:
'The Spreading Chestnut Tree' (1938), 'Till the Lights of London Shine Again' (1940), 'Who's Taking You Home Tonight?' (1940), 'Be Like the Kettle and Sing' (1943), 'Down in the Glen' (1949), 'Hang on the Bell Nellie' (1949), 'Boys and Girls Love Saturday Night' (1949), 'The Wedding of Lilli Marlene' (1949), 'The Homing Waltz' (1952), 'Never Do a Tango With an Eskimo' (1956).

COOK, Roger, *see* Greenaway, Roger.

COSLOW, Sam, *see* Johnston, Arthur James.

COWARD, Sir Noël, Pierce, composer, author, pianist, actor, playwright, producer.

Born Teddington, 16 December 1899. Died Port Maria, Jamaica, 26 March 1973. Of all the composers' names that appear in this book, that of Sir Noël Coward must surely be the most distinguished, so much has been written about him, about his life, his times, his plays and the stars who performed in them. But in a book on songwriters we must inevitably confine ourselves strictly to that particular talent of this multi-talented man. Although music was much in evidence in the families of both his father and mother (his father was a piano salesman), Noël never received any musical training, although he could pick out tunes on the piano from the age of seven. In his introduction to *The Noel Coward Songbook* he says: 'To this day my piano playing is limited to three keys—E flat, B flat and A flat. The sight of two sharps frightens me to death. Oddly enough C major, the key most favoured by the inept leaves me cold. I can firmly but not boastfully claim that I am a better pianist than Irving Berlin, but as that superlative genius of light music is well known not to be able to play at all except in C major, I will not press the point'.

He was educated at private schools, if somewhat spasmodically, to quote himself, the family moving from Teddington to Sutton in Surrey, and then to a flat in Battersea in London. During schooldays he appeared in school concerts, took ballet lessons, and was bitterly disappointed at being rejected as 'not good enough' to sing in the choir. Maybe it was as a result that, as Noël Coward himself once wrote: 'My further education stopped when I was 10, and I began to learn my job, which was theatre'. This seems to have been accepted, if somewhat reluctantly, by his parents, and his first professional acting engagement came in 1911 in: A Fairy Play in Three Acts with a STAR CAST OF WONDER CHILDREN. It was called *The Goldfish*, and by the standards of the time it was a success, running for a week of matinées at the Little Theatre in London over Christmas. It was widely reviewed, young master Coward getting a mention in every notice. From then on the theatre became his life. Noël Coward's first song was written when he was 16 and called 'Forbidden Fruit', but his first published song was 'Parisian Pierrot', written in 1923 for the show *London Calling*, which starred Gertrude Lawrence (who sang the song), and Maisie Gay. Coward himself was also in the show. Music was by Philip Braham, who wrote a number of songs with Coward, and whose efforts have perhaps been overshadowed. Braham is best remembered as the composer of 'Limehouse Blues', which he wrote in 1922 with lyrics by Douglas Furber.

From then on the history of Coward songs became also the history of the musical productions he wrote, and in which he later starred. Thus 1925 saw his first real hit, 'Poor Little Rich Girl' from the Charles Cochran production *On With the Dance*, for which Coward wrote both book and lyrics, and Philip Braham the music. Among the stars were Alice Delysia, Ernest Thesiger, Léonide Massine, and Hermione Baddeley. This, incidentally, was a show in which Coward did not appear, as he was in his play *The Vortex* at the time. His next musical was *This Year of Grace* (1928) but before that he had been as busy as ever, receiving more and more acclaim for his plays and for his own performances in them. *This Year of Grace* starred, among others, Sonnie Hale, Douglas Byng, Maisie Gay, Tillie Losch and Jessie Matthews in the London production, and it was also Coward's first big Broadway success, in which he starred with Beatrice Lillie. It was also the first time that he had written both words and music for a complete revue. 'A Room With a View' and 'Dance Little Lady' were the two big hits, and it was while he was in New York that he conceived the idea for his next musical. Fully supported by C B Cochran, who presented it, this turned out to be a Coward-style operetta, based on the Viennese tradition of Lehár and Strauss. The title was *Bitter Sweet*, and it opened in London in 1929 with a cast that included George Metaxa, Peggy Wood, Ivy St Hellier, Billy Milton and Betty Huntley-Wright. Later the same year, the equally successful Broadway cast included Evelyn Laye. It included two hits, 'Zigeuner', and 'I'll See You Again' of which Coward himself said: 'It is one of my own favourite compositions. I'm happy to say it has been sung incessantly by everybody. It has proved over the years to be the greatest song hit I have ever had, or am ever likely to have'.

In 1930, while recovering from a bout of 'flu, Noël Coward wrote the play *Private Lives* ('in four days, and not a word of it was changed'). It had only one song, enchantingly sung by Gertrude Lawrence, for whom it had been written, but it turned out to be Coward's second biggest hit ever, 'Someday I'll Find You'. It was at that time that another Coward song appeared, perhaps the first not to have been created for a specific show. It was 'Mad Dogs and Englishmen', which was used by Beatrice Lillie in an American revue before Coward included it is his 1932 C B Cochran show *Words and Music*. In between, in 1931, came *Cavalcade*, a production so complicated that Drury Lane was the only theatre capable of staging it. It was also unusual in that it contained many non-Coward tunes, especially popular refrains from World War I, from vaudeville, and even included Irving Berlin's 'Alexander's Ragtime Band', and Ivor Novello's 'Keep the Home Fires Burning'. Among the cast were John Mills and Binnie Barnes, who sang one of the only two Coward songs in the show, 'Twentieth Century Blues'. *Cavalcade* was an enormous success. Hollywood paid $100,000 for the film rights, in which Clive Brook and Diana Wynyard starred.

Coward's London revue, *Words and Music* (1932) starred Romney Brent, John Mills, Ivy St Hellier and Doris Hare, and among the songs were 'Mad About the Boy', and 'The Party's Over Now'. Noël Coward wrote of it: 'It ran for about eight months. Notices were terrible. They always were!'

In 1934 Coward wrote *Conversation Piece*. Described as a romantic comedy, we would nowadays probably call it a play with music rather than a musical. Coward himself starred with Yvonne Printemps, and also in the cast were George Sanders and Heather Thatcher. Valerie Hobson was in the chorus. This was the show that produced another Coward hit, 'I'll Follow My Secret Heart', which he claimed came to him in a rare burst of inspiration as opposed to hard work. Having achieved nothing all day, he was about to go to bed, when he saw he had left a light on by his piano. 'I walked automatically to turn it off, sat down and played "I'll Follow My Secret Heart" straight through in G flat, a key I had never played in before'. During the next five years there were to be three more musical productions—*Tonight at 8.30* (1936), *Operette* (1938), and *Set to Music* (1939). Probably the two best known songs to come out of these productions were 'The Stately Homes of England' and 'I Went to a Marvellous Party'.

The early 1940s once again produced some songs that were just written as songs. The enchanting 'London Pride' (1941) was inspired by hanging about in a blitzed railway station, while 'Don't Let's Be Beastly to the Germans' was intended simply as a satirical song. Coward said that Winston Churchill once made him sing it seven times in one evening, but that the BBC refused to broadcast it and HMV refused to issue the record, on the grounds that it was pro-German. Coward's comment was, 'After all, "Let's help the dirty swine again, to occupy the Rhine again", and "Let's give them full air-parity, and treat the rats with charity", are not, as phrases, exactly oozing with brotherly love'.

The end of the war brought a new show, *Sigh No More*, with Graham Payn and Joyce Grenfell in the cast, the best song probably being 'I Wonder What's Happened to Him', although high in Coward's own affection was 'Matelot'. This show was followed in 1946 by *Pacific 1860*, in which the main song, 'Bright Was the Day', was sung by Graham Payn and Mary Martin. The cast list included Mantovani and his orchestra. But this paucity of musical output during the decade must be regarded in the context of Noël Coward's other activities of those years. During the war period he was out of the country more than he was in it, entertaining troops wherever troops were to be found. He was also responsible for films such as *Blithe Spirit, This Happy Breed, Brief Encounter* and *In Which We Serve.*

Only two musicals graced the 1950s. In *Ace of Clubs*, which starred Pat Kirkwood and Graham Payn, the main songs were 'Sail Away', and 'Chase Me, Charlie', but sadly the show flopped. So did *The Lyric Revue* (1951), for which he wrote 'Don't Make Fun of the Fair'. And in 1954, despite a cast that included Irene Brown, Vanessa Lee, and Mary Ellis, *After the Ball*, Coward's musical adaptation of Wilde's *Lady Windermere's Fan*, became just another flop. As writer and actor, the 1950s were not good years for Sir Noël, and were mainly redeemed by his hugely successful appearances in cabaret (four visits to the Café de Paris in London, and a $40,000-per-week engagement at the Desert Inn in Las Vegas). These somewhat restored his flagging financial fortunes. In the 1960s, although his only successful musical was *Sail Away*, he found yet another outlet for his talents by writing books and by appearing in films as a straight actor (*Our Man in Havana* and *The Italian Job* were good examples). There was also *The Girl Who Came to Supper*, based on Terence Rattigan's play *The Prince and the Showgirl* which, although it had some pleasant music and good notices, did not run for long. More film and personal appearances followed, but sadly, no more music. Somewhere along the road he found time to write the highly amusing composition, 'Alice Is at It Again'. He called his autobiography *A Talent to Amuse*. How right he was.

Although there are many more Noël Coward songs, almost all of them from his shows, the best have already been referred to in the text.

DAVID, Hal, *see* Bacharach, Burt.

DESYLVA, BROWN and HENDERSON.

Ray Henderson composer, pianist, publisher, producer. Born Buffalo, New York, 1 December 1896. Died Greenwich, Connecticut, 31 December 1970. Educated Chicago Conservatory of Music. His father was a musician, and Ray became a pianist in the early dance bands, and did arrangements for New York publishers. He also worked as an accompanist for vaudeville acts. His first hit was 'That Old Gang of Mine' (1923), which had lyrics by Billy Rose and Mort Dixon. In 1925 he had three hits in a row, one of which, 'Alabamy Bound' is of particular significance, because not only was it a million-seller, but also it marked his first collaboration with Buddy DeSylva.

Lew Brown (Louis Brownstein) author, producer. Born in Odessa, Russia, 10 December 1893. He died in New York, 5 February 1958.

Buddy DeSylva (George Gard DeSylva) author, producer, director. Born in New York, 27 January 1895, and died in Los Angeles, California, 11 July 1950.

These three widely divergent personalities, who came together so successfully for the last half of the 1920s to form the most famous three-way songwriting partnership of all time, were all born within three years of each other. Although Henderson was always the composer, and the other two always the lyricists, their collaboration often overlapped, rather in the same way that many of the successful songwriting teams of the 1960s and 1970s did. David Ewen, in his book *Great Men of American Popular Song*, says: '... they functioned with a unanimity of thought, feeling and style, as if they were a single person'. Lew Brown was first introduced to Ray Henderson by music publisher Louis Bernstein in 1922, and their first collaboration resulted in a song called 'Georgette', in that same year.

When Lew Brown's family emigrated from Russia, they first settled in New Haven, Connecticut, before moving to New York, where he was educated at the De Witt Clinton High School. On leaving, he worked at various jobs, including that of life guard at Rockaway Beach, although he had always been interested in writing verse, and soon turned this talent to songwriting. He sold his first song for the princely sum of $7. His first success, however, came after an introduction to Albert von Tilzer, with whom he wrote five songs as early as 1912. But the big break came in 1917 with 'Give Me the Moonlight, Give Me the Girl', followed in 1919 with 'Oh, by Jingo'. 'Dapper Dan' was a von Tilzer/Brown hit of 1920, so by the time he met Ray Henderson in 1922, he had considerably more experience of the ways of Tin Pan Alley than had the budding composer.

Unlike Brown and Henderson, Buddy DeSylva had been brought up in an atmosphere of popular song because his father was a vaudeville performer. Although born in New York, his family moved to Los Angeles when he was a child, and it was there he was educated at public schools, and at the University of Southern California. He was already making child prodigy appearances, and was clearly developing the stage bug, when family pressure insisted that he pay more attention to his education. It was all in vain, however, for while at college he continued to appear with local dance bands and to perform in college shows, all of which led him to try his hand at writing lyrics. Al Jolson read some of his efforts and liked them so much that he had music written for them, and used them in his shows. Thus it was that the first DeSylva hit, 'I'll Say She Does', was introduced in the show *Sinbad* in 1918. His collaborator with these lyrics was the established writer Gus Kahn.

By 1919 Buddy DeSylva realized that he could make it as a professional lyricist and moved to New York, where he was lucky enough to start working for the publishing house of Remick. One of his first commissions was to write a set of lyrics for the young George Gershwin. The show was called *La La Lucille*, and the Gershwin/ DeSylva song was 'Nobody but You'. By 1920 he was sufficiently well thought of to be assigned to write with the great Jerome Kern, and in that year they had a big hit with 'Look for the Silver Lining'. DeSylva followed this in 1921 with 'April Showers' with Louis Silvers—the song that was made into a gigantic hit by Al Jolson. From 1922 to 1924 he worked yet again successfully with George Gershwin ('Stairway to Paradise'), with Victor Herbert ('A Kiss in the Dark'), and with Joseph Meyer ('California, Here I Come'), another huge Jolson hit.

While DeSylva and Brown had been pursuing their successful ways until 1925, the young Ray Henderson was also in New York, working as a song-plugger and as a staff pianist with various publishers, and had achieved some success in his collaboration with various lyricists. Apart from 'Georgette' and 'Alabamy Bound', already mentioned, his other big hits of that period were 'Don't Bring Lulu' with Billy Rose and Lew Brown, 'Five Foot Two, Eyes of Blue' with Sam Lewis and Joe Young, and 'I'm Sitting on Top of the World' with the same lyricists.

It was 1925 that saw the beginning of the DeSylva, Brown and Henderson partnership, and their first commission was to write the songs for *George White's Scandals of 1925*. Surprisingly, although the songs were competent, none was memorable, yet George White had sufficient faith in his protegés to give them the same commission for his 1926 show, and this time they made no mistake. Among the hits were 'Lucky Day', 'Black Bottom', and 'The Birth of the Blues'. The last-named, as a critic of the time observed, 'swept Broadway like a tornado', while 'Black Bottom' sparked off a dance craze to rival the previous year's 'Charleston'. In 1926 the publishing house of DeSylva, Brown and Henderson was formed. From now on, nobody else was going to collect their royalties!

With the success of their 1926 songs still echoing, the team moved for the first time into a real Broadway musical in 1927, with the show *Good News!*. This ran for some 500 performances, and among its hits were the title song, as well as a new dance routine, 'Varsity Drag', and 'The Best Things in Life Are Free'. The latter was used as the title of the 1956 movie that was based on the lives of DeSylva, Brown and Henderson. The following year, 1928, saw the trio writing for the show *Hold Everything!* from which came one particularly big hit, 'You're the Cream in My Coffee'. Other successful Broadway shows followed: *Follow Thru* in 1929, and *Flying High* in 1930, the former giving us the song 'Button Up Your Overcoat'. While all this was going on, the team also turned its attention to movies. For Al Jolson's *The Singing Fool*, they produced the never-to-be-forgotten 'Sonny Boy', and for the Charles Farrell/Janet Gaynor classic *Sunny Side Up* they produced not only the title song, but also 'If I Had a Talking Picture of You', and 'I'm a Dreamer'. The year was still 1929. David Ewen, in his book *Great Men of American Popular Song* quotes film star Eddie Cantor as the author of a hilarious story concerning 'Sonny Boy'. Jolson, filming in Hollywood, rang the songwriters one evening and demanded a song by the following morning, a song '... about a kid—a boy supposed to be my son—a ballad to make people cry'. They sat down to write, not a beautiful ballad, but the corniest song they could dream up—a real practical joke. The following morning they sang it into the telephone to Jolson. He loved it. 'It'll be the biggest ballad I've ever sung', he told them. They could hardly believe it, and could hardly stop laughing, either. The song sold more than a million copies of the sheet music, and the 1929 Jolson recording, re-issued in 1946, sold a million records.

As the 1920s became the 1930s, the most successful three-way songwriting partnership of all time broke up. Hollywood called Buddy DeSylva, leading him to a distinguished second career as a motion picture producer, particularly of several of the classic Shirley Temple films. He also produced *Panama Hattie*, *Du Barry Was a Lady* and *Louisiana Purchase* for Broadway. He had one last big hit song, for which he wrote both words and music, 'Wishing', immortalized by Vera Lynn in 1939. Henderson and Brown continued to write together for a while for such successful shows as *Hot-Cha!* (1932), *Strike Me Pink* (1933), and especially *Scandals of 1931*, which alone gave them five hit songs, including 'Life Is Just a Bowl of Cherries', popularized by Ethel Merman, and 'This Is the Missus', sung by Rudy Vallee. The show also notched up a recording industry first, when Brunswick Records issued a 12-inch disc containing all the hit songs, sung by Bing Crosby and the Boswell Sisters—perhaps the first ever attempt to bring songs from a show to the public all on one record.

Soon, however, the lure of Hollywood also attracted Lew Brown to the west coast to produce and direct, leaving Ray to find other lyric writers for his music. With Ted Koehler he wrote for *Say When* in 1934, and with Jack Yellen for *George White's Scandals of 1935*, although nothing especially memorable emerged, apart from the song 'Oh You Nasty Man', which put Alice Faye on the map. However, writing with Ted Koehler and Irving Caesar for the 1935 Shirley Temple movie *Curly Top*, he produced another never-to-be-forgotten song, 'Animal Crackers'.

Ray Henderson continued composing throughout the 1940s, including a 1948 collaboration with Lew Brown, 'An Old Sombrero and an Old Spanish Shawl', but during the 1950s he retired to live in Greenwich, Connecticut, where he tried to adapt his musical talents to more serious things, and just before he died was said to be contemplating writing an opera. But whatever successes the three men may each have achieved on their own, if only the songs of the DeSylva, Brown and Henderson partnership survived, they alone would justify a place for the team in the history books.

Some other outstanding DeSylva, Brown and Henderson songs:
'It All Depends on You' (1925), 'I'm on the Crest of a Wave' (1928), 'Together' (1928), 'To Know You Is to Love You' (1928), 'You Wouldn't Fool Me, Would You?' (1929), 'My Lucky Star' (1929), 'I Wonder How I Look When I'm Asleep' (1927), 'Broken-Hearted' (1927).

DIAMOND, Neil, composer, author, singer, guitarist.

Born Brooklyn, New York, 24 January 1941. Neil seems to have been attracted to music from a very early age, and at 10 he was a member of a group of kids called The Memphis Backstreet Boys, probably because the only place they could play was on the back streets of Brooklyn. He was educated at local schools during these early years, but at 13 ran away from home and ended up in Kansas City, where he got together a rather folksy group called The Roadrunners, playing in whatever cafés or coffee bars would have them. After two years of this he returned home to Brooklyn in an attempt to continue his education, which included a stint at New York University. But it did not last, and he took various jobs with music publishers in the hope that one day he would become a professional songwriter.

During this period of the 1950s, New York's Tin Pan Alley was still basically working as it has always done. Publishers contracted likely talent to write songs for a few dollars a week, hoping sooner or later to sell the songs to big recording artists. Young Diamond endured some six years of this, mostly with no success at all, although he did get some of his songs recorded, often as 'B' sides. He finally hit a stroke of luck when two songs became million-sellers for The Monkees—'I'm a Believer', and 'A Little Bit Me, A Little Bit You'. The composer got nothing except his salary.

Two record-producing friends, Jeff Barry and Ellie Greenwich, were ultimately responsible for persuading Neil to try recording his own songs, the first attempt being 'Solitary Man' in 1966. This did well enough to spark off two more later in the same year, 'Cherry, Cherry' and 'I Got the Feelin'', which reached 6th and 16th positions in the US charts respectively. This convinced Neil Diamond that he was never going to make it as a hack writer for Tin Pan Alley, and that his only chance of success was, as he himself has said: '. . . to gear my music to my own point of view. To write what moved me'.

The turning point came in 1969, when his record of his song 'Sweet Caroline' swept to the number 4 spot in the US charts. Ironically, in view of the huge success that Neil was later to have in England, that record achieved nothing in the UK until it was re-released in 1971, when it shot up to No 8, obviously because of his number 1 success in 1970 with 'Cracklin' Rosie'. Neil Diamond may seem to be typical of the modern generation of singer/songwriter/ performers. But in many ways he is not, particularly because his burning wish has always been, and still is, to be a songwriter, and because, as he says, 'I only took to performing because I was desperate to get my songs heard'. He has also said: 'Performing seemed quite natural for me—my father was an amateur performer. Performing ... is the most joyful thing I do. It's also the happiest thing I do. The bigger the audience, the more anticipated, the more excitement. When you're writing, it's a solitary profession, and you wonder about people's reactions'. And again: 'For what other reasons am I going on stage than to please my audience? I have never understood the kind of artist who thinks he has some kind of divine right to play, and the audience has to work to get inside what he's trying to communicate'.

That his main desire is to write songs has also been demonstrated by his attempts to move away from areas involving his own performance, such as his suite 'African Trilogy', and the fact that he wrote the music for the film version of *Jonathan Livingston Seagull*. The film flopped, and the music was not particularly memorable, but, along with such diversions as putting together his own TV specials, these are all pointers to the fact that writing takes preference over performing. Between 1969 and 1973, he followed the success of 'Sweet Caroline' with such major hits as 'Holly Holy' (1969, No 6 in US), 'I Am ... I Said' (1971, No 4 in US and UK), and 'Song Sung Blue' (1972, No 1 in US, No 14 in UK). At that point in his life, he decided to take a complete break from performing of any kind. He married when he was quite young, but it was not a success, and he was divorced. He was re-married to Marcia Murphey, and they soon had two sons, Jesse and Micah. When Jesse was two-and-a-half, Diamond says he suddenly realized: 'I'd been away from family and friends, I'd been on the road for six years, and I felt he needed me more than the audience did. So for four years, I devoted myself to my son Jesse, being home with him doing normal things like waking up in the same city everyday'. During that lay-off, *Jonathan Livingston Seagull* was completed, and so were two albums, especially the gold award winner *Beautiful Noise*. When he did start concert appearances again, in 1976/77, it was with an enormously successful tour of Australia.

By the end of 1978, Neil Diamond had won 20 platinum and/or gold albums, and had over 30 hit singles, almost all of which were of his own compositions (there was an exception in 1970, when he had a hit with the Russell/Scott song, 'He Ain't Heavy, He's My Brother'). In 1981 he had yet another hit with 'Love on the Rocks'.

But perhaps his most ambitious achievement was his 1980

involvement with the re-make of the classic Al Jolson film *The Jazz Singer*. Neil wrote all the music, and starred in the film, his first major acting role. Indeed it is from *The Jazz Singer* album that the single 'Love on the Rocks' was taken. The film was a box office flop and the critics were unkind to it. But musically its success cannot be denied, with the soundtrack reaching No 5 in the album charts.

Neil Diamond is a complex character. He never takes his wife or family on tour, as some stars do, because, as he says, 'involving my family in my business life is not fair to them or me. I need a refuge to retreat to from the world of make-believe, and they need and deserve a life of their own'. To Neil, his private life is private. The fact that in 1978 he underwent a 12-hour operation for the removal of a tumour on his spinal cord, followed by three months in a wheelchair, uncertain if he would ever walk again, received absolutely minimal publicity, and that only because he collapsed on stage. Certainly he is a man of the current generation whose work can truly be said to rank alongside that of the greatest of previous generations.

Some other outstanding Neil Diamond songs:
'You Got to Me' (1967), 'Girl, You'll Be a Woman Soon' (1967), 'I Got the Feelin'' (1966), 'Thank the Lord for the Night Time' (1967), 'Red, Red Wine' (1968), 'Brooklyn Roads' (1968), 'Brother Love's Traveling Salvation Show' (1969), 'Touching You Touching Me' (1971), 'I Am . . . I Said' (1971), 'Done Too Soon' (1968), 'Soolaimon' (1971), 'Stones' (1972), 'Play Me' (1972), 'Walk on Water' (1973), 'You Don't Bring Me Flowers' (1978), 'Mama Don't Know' (1980), 'The Grass Won't Pay No Mind' (1969), 'Crunchy Granola Suite' (1971), 'Glory Road' (1971).

DIETZ, Howard, *see* Schwarz, Arthur.

DONALDSON, Walter, composer, author, pianist, publisher.

Born Brooklyn, New York, 15 February 1893. Died Santa Monica, California, 15 July 1947. Although his mother was a music teacher, he took no interest in it until he taught himself to play piano, simply so that he could write some songs for a school show. On leaving school he spent a short time working for a Wall Street broker, but this was obviously not for him, and he struck out on his own as a songwriter in 1915 with three songs, the first of which was 'Back Home in Tennessee', with lyrics by William Jerome. So effective were those three songs of 1915 that together they sold 8 million copies. During World War I he was in the entertainments division of the US Army, where he met Sergeant Irving Berlin, for whose music company he went to work immediately on discharge. He stayed with the Berlin company for some 10 years, during which time he wrote a string of hits, among them 'How Ya Gonna Keep 'Em Down on the Farm?', and 'My Mammy' (which was not originally written for Al Jolson as is often thought, although it appeared in Jolson's 1918 show *Sinbad*. It was originally performed in vaudeville by comedian Bill Frawley). 'My Mammy' was not published until 1921, by which time it had become totally associated with Jolson. Between 1921 and 1927 Walter Donaldson wrote no fewer than six million-sellers: 'You're a Million Miles From Nowhere When You're One Little Mile from Home', 'My Buddy', 'Carolina in the Morning', 'Yes, Sir, That's My Baby', and 'My Blue Heaven'. 'My Mammy' was the sixth. During his heyday in the 1920s, Donaldson used a number of well known lyricists, including Sam Lewis and Joe Young (for 'My Mammy'), but perhaps his greatest association was with Gus Kahn, who was responsible for the lyrics of four of those six million-sellers. 'My Blue Heaven' had words by George Whiting. Donaldson severed his connection with Berlin's publishing company in 1928 and formed one of his own, Donaldson, Douglas and Gumble. This company produced more hits, many with Gus Kahn, but others with Edgar Leslie, Johnny Mercer, Mitchell Parish, and two never-to-be-forgotten tunes for which Donaldson himself wrote the words as well as the music—'Little White Lies' and 'You're Driving Me Crazy'.

In 1926 he made his first contributions to a Broadway show, *Sweetheart Time*, followed in 1928 by the complete score (lyrics by Gus Kahn) for *Whoopee*, starring Eddie Cantor and Ruth Etting, and featuring a string of hits, including 'Making Whoopee'.

In 1929 Donaldson was in Hollywood, along with so many other top writers. Here he contributed songs to *Glorifying the American Girl* as did Irving Berlin, Rudy Vallee (who along with Eddie Cantor was one of the stars), and Yip Harburg. For an unremarkable film, it had some star writers. Other films for which Donaldson wrote complete scores were *Kid Millions* (1934), with Eddie Cantor again, Ethel

Merman and Ann Sothern (Gus Kahn wrote the lyrics); *Operator 13* (1933), starring Marion Davies, Gary Cooper and The Mills Brothers; and *The Great Ziegfeld* (1936) starring William Powell and Myrna Loy, with lyrics by Harold Adamson. And there were many others, including two pictures starring Jean Harlow. Throughout the war years he stayed in Hollywood writing, and his last picture, *Follow the Boys*, starring Marlene Dietrich, George Raft, Orson Wells, W C Fields, Jeanette MacDonald, Sophie Tucker and the Delta Rhythm Boys, was produced in 1944. It only contained one of his songs, ('Tonight'), many other distinguished composers also contributing to the score. By 1946 ill-health had forced him to retire, and he died the following year at the age of 53. Without doubt he was a true son of Tin Pan Alley, and a major contributor to the art of American popular song.

Gus Kahn, his major collaborator, was born at Coblenz in Germany in 1886, and died in Beverly Hills, California, in 1941. He was one of the great lyric-writers, who never aspired to compose. In addition to his hits with Walter Donaldson, he also wrote many lyrics for such composers as Richard Whiting, Buddy DeSylva, Al Jolson, Vincent Youmans, George Gershwin, Harry Woods, Arthur Johnston, Sigmund Romberg and Harry Warren.

Some other outstanding Walter Donaldson songs:
'That Certain Party' (with Gus Kahn, 1926), 'I Wonder Where My Baby Is Tonight' (with Gus Kahn, 1926), 'Beside a Babbling Brook' (1923), 'Mary—What Are You Waiting For?' (1927), 'Love Me or Leave Me' (with Gus Kahn, 1929), 'My Baby Just Cares for Me' (with Gus Kahn, 1930), 'It's Been So Long' (with Harold Adamson, 1936), 'Mister Meadowlark' (with Johnny Mercer, 1940), 'Sleepy Head' (1934).

DOZIER, Lamont, *see* Holland, Dozier, Holland.

DUBIN, Al, *see* Warren, Harry.

DUKE, Vernon (Vladimir Dukelsky), composer, author, pianist.

Born Parafianovo, Russia, 10 October 1903. Educated Kiev Conservatoire. Fled Russia after the Revolution for London. Has composed for Diaghilev's Ballet Russe, and has written many serious works including six songs from 'A Shropshire Lad'. Wrote for the London production of *Yvonne* (1926), and *The Yellow Mask* (1928), which starred Bobby Howes and Phyllis Dare. In 1929 he went to New York and began writing for Broadway shows, including *Walk a Little Faster* starring Beatrice Lillie, with lyrics by E Y Harburg (1932), *Ziegfeld Follies* (1934, 1936), *Cabin in the Sky*, starring Ethel Waters (1940), *Sadie Thompson* (1944), and others. His chief collaborators were E Y Harburg and Howard Dietz, and with Ira Gershwin he completed the score for *The Goldwyn Follies* after George Gershwin's death. Vernon Duke is a good example of a composer with a prolific output of songs, but who is included here because of a few classics that the world will always remember: 'April in Paris' (1934), 'Autumn in New York' (1932), 'I Can't Get Started With You' (immortalized by trumpeter Bunny Berigan, 1936), and 'Taking a Chance on Love' (from *Cabin in the Sky*, 1940).

DYLAN, Bob (Robert Allen Zimmerman), composer, author, singer, guitarist.

Born Duluth, Minnesota, 24 May 1941. The family soon moved to Hibbing, not too far away. Bob Dylan (the surname he adopted when he became a performer, from his favourite poet, Dylan Thomas), was educated at Hibbing High School. His only other education was a brief enrolment at the University of Minnesota when he was about 19. He was expelled after six months. On no fewer than 10 occasions he ran away from home for short or longish periods, mostly it is suggested, because he seems to have been born with a kind of wanderlust. Whatever the truth of the matter, his excursions brought him his first taste of the kind of music that was to make his name, for he learned his craft from the old travelling blues singers. Somebody gave him an old guitar at the age of 10, which he taught himself to play. He also listened to itinerant folksingers such as Woody Guthrie.

Dylan soon moved to New York where, for a time, he earned a few dollars by playing and singing in the streets, sleeping in subways at night when he could not afford a roof. Occasionally he would land a minor engagement for a week, or a few days, singing and playing in one of the numerous coffee bars of the period. It was during a spell in one of these that he was heard by journalist Robert Shelton of *The New York Times*, who gave him a rave write-up. Within a month he had made his first album for Columbia Records. By 1961 he had given his first concert at the Carnegie Chapter Hall, and by 1962 he was at last able to afford to rent a small apartment, where he started to create songs and poetry in large quantities. On his second Columbia album he included his composition 'Blowin' in the Wind', which was recorded in 1963 by Peter, Paul and Mary, and ultimately achieved sales of almost 2 million. So Bob Dylan, the original voice of protest of the 1960s, broke into the big time in a big way.

Dylan songs of the 1960s expressed protest about everything that the young generation of the period felt moved to protest about, which is why, once he had become established, Dylan drew unto himself a whole world of what might almost be called young disciples. His songs protested about racial problems, civil rights, war (traditional and especially nuclear), the profit motive, the generation gap, and sexual relations. Along the road came such compositions as 'With God on Our Side', 'A Hard Rain's A-Gonna Fall', 'The Ballad of Hollis Brown', 'The Times They Are A-Changin'', 'All I Really Want to Do', and 'It's Alright Ma, I'm Only Bleeding'. Among all these there was 'Mr Tambourine Man', a multimillion hit for The Byrds in 1965. From about that time on The Band, a group Dylan had originally found in Atlantic City, was adopted by him to back him on his recordings. By the 1970s the group had become a major rock group in its own right.

After the mid-1960s, Dylan's style began to change—summed up perhaps in the title of his 1964 album *Another Side of Bob Dylan*. He began to weld the influence of rock music onto what had hitherto been pure folk. His fans were appalled (or professed themselves so), accusing him of selling himself to mammon. He was by that time becoming a very rich man, and had acquired not only a wife (Sarah Lowndes), but also a son and a daughter. At the Newport Folk Festival in 1965, he appeared playing an amplified guitar, thus perhaps unwittingly giving rise to the phrase 'folk rock'. He himself said he no longer wanted to write as the observer—'I want to write from inside me'. He was later to say, 'I got bored with my old songs. I can't sing "With God on Our Side" for 15 years. I couldn't go on and play like that. I was thinking of quitting'.

In 1966 he was involved in a near fatal motorcycle accident, and it was a considerable time before he was able to sing and play and record again. When his new album, *John Wesley Harding*, appeared in 1968, it was noted that he had apparently dropped the amplified guitar, but included in the backing were harmonica, piano, bass and drums, and the recording was made in Nashville. An immediate best-seller, it showed clearly that Dylan had progressed into what the music business dubbed 'country rock'. Between 1965 and 1968, however, Dylan the performing songwriter (as opposed to the songwriter who contributed to the success of other artists) had probably his best time with chart successes. It began with 'Subterranean Homesick Blues' in 1965, continuing in the same year with 'Like a Rolling Stone', 'Rainy Day Women' (1966), 'I Want You' (1966), 'Leopard-Skin Pill-Box Hat' (1966), 'I Threw It All Away' (1967), and 'Tonight I'll Be Staying Here With You' (1969). And the successful *John Wesley Harding* album was soon followed by the even more successful *Nashville Skyline*.

Bob Dylan had always been somewhat of an introvert, and as the years progressed, each one more successful than the last, he became almost a recluse, rarely appearing in public, so that when he did undertake a concert (a notable one was the Madison Square Garden Concert for Bangladesh organized by ex-Beatle George Harrison in 1971), his promoter was guaranteed a sell-out as soon as the concert was announced. During the 1970s he also began to further the interest in movies which he had begun to show in the late 1960s. He appeared in *Don't Look Back* (1967), and something that was originally intended as a TV special, *Eat That Document* (1969). During 1972 and 1973, however, he spent his time on a major movie project, *Pat Garrett and Billy the Kid*, in which he appeared with Kris Kristofferson. In 1974 he undertook a 21-city concert tour, something he had not attempted for years. Whatever his original fans may have thought about his changing music, no sooner were the details announced than they oversubscribed it by mail order 10 times over. It seems the Bob Dylan story is by no means over.

The important Bob Dylan songs have been referred to in the text, so we have not felt it necessary to append a list of further titles.

ELLINGTON, Edward Kennedy ('Duke'), composer, pianist, arranger, conductor.

Born Washington DC, 29 April 1899. Died New York, 24 May 1974. Educated at local schools, then at Wilberforce University where he obtained an Hon MusD, followed by an LHD at Milton College. In his early days he had various jobs playing piano in local bands when, in 1923, a group called The Washingtonians of which he was a member, was offered an engagement at the Hollywood Club in New York. From then on the career of Duke Ellington as a musician and bandleader never looked back.

He began writing songs quite early, and his first tune with lyrics is believed to have been titled 'What Are You Going to Do When the Bed Breaks Down?' but it does not appear to have been published. Duke started recording with The Washingtonians as early as 1925, and by 1926 was already recording his own instrumental compositions with the band, of which 'East St Louis Toodle-oo' (their first signature tune) is a good example. But in many cases Ellington compositions were being played and recorded years before they were published, largely because they were purely instrumental. As a result, such famous compositions from the 1920s as 'Birmingham Breakdown', 'Black and Tan Fantasy', 'The Mooch', and 'Hot and Bothered' are outside the scope of this book. 'The Mooch' subsequently acquired lyrics by publisher Irving Mills, who was quick to spot Ellington's composing talents and sign him up.

Probably Duke's first published song was 'Blues I Love to Sing' (1927), with lyrics by his trumpet player 'Bubber' Miley. And possibly his first song to approach hit status was 'Ring Dem Bells (1930), again with lyrics by Irving Mills, for the film *Check and Double Check*, starring Amos 'n Andy, then big names on American radio. 'Mood Indigo' (1931) was again conceived as an instrumental (Irving Mills later supplying yet more lyrics), and 'Creole Love Call' (1932) was a song without words, because the classic vocal by Adelaide Hall is a melodic wail, in which she makes her voice sound like an instrument in the band. But with 'Best Wishes' (1932), which had words by that great lyricist Ted Koehler, Duke Ellington could really be said to have arrived as a writer of popular songs.

Throughout the 50 years of Duke's career as a bandleader, his abilities as a songwriter, as opposed to those of a composer for his orchestra, always took second place. Nevertheless, his roster of hits is a very creditable one. His bandleading career has been more than adequately chronicled by other writers, but here is a list of his major songwriting achievements. His main lyrical collaborators, in addition to publisher Irving Mills, have been Billy Stryahorn, Mitchell Parish, Henry Nemo, Bob Russell, Paul Francis Webster, Eddie de Lange, and Carl Sigman.

Some outstanding songs by Duke Ellington :
'It Don't Mean a Thing' (1932), 'Sophisticated Lady' (1933), 'Drop Me Off at Harlem' (1933), 'Solitude' (1934), 'In a Sentimental Mood' (1935), 'Caravan' (1937), 'I Let a Song Go Out of My Heart' (1938), 'Do Nothin' Till You Hear from Me' (1943), 'I Didn't Know About You' (1944), 'Don't Get Around Much Anymore' (1942), 'I'm Beginning to See the Light' (1944), 'Just A-Sittin' and A-Rockin'' (1945), 'Just Squeeze Me' (1946).

The following instrumentals deserve a mention :
'Rockin' in Rhythm', 'Saturday Night Function', 'Echoes of Harlem', 'Jack the Bear', 'Harlem Air Shaft', 'Mornin' Glory', 'Cotton Tail', 'Crescendo in Blue', 'Diminuendo in Blue', '"C" Jam Blues', 'Come Sunday', 'Satin Doll'.

Suites :
Black, Brown and Beige, New World a-Comin', Sepia Panorama, A Drum Is a Woman, Suite Thursday, Liberian Suite, Such Sweet Thunder, Far Eastern Suite, Perfume Suite, New Orleans Suite. Duke Ellington also wrote the scores for the shows *Jump for Joy* (1941), and *Beggar's Holiday* (1946), and the background music for the films *Anatomy of a Murder* (1959) and *Paris Blues* (1961).

ELLIS, Vivian, composer, author, pianist.

Born Hampstead, London, 29 October 1904. Vivian Ellis grew up with music. His grandmother was a member of the Royal Academy, friend of Sir Arthur Sullivan and composer of a successful opera called *Carina.* His mother was a brilliant violinist. Music and the theatre were in his blood. While he was still a schoolboy, the great concert pianist Dame Myra Hess was so impressed by his piano playing that she took him as a pupil. He studied at the Royal Academy but in spite of his ability as a pianist he had no ambition to become a concert performer. He wanted to compose his own music and with this in mind took a job in the professional department of a music publisher. Before he was out of his teens he was contributing songs to West End revues such as *The Curate's Egg, The Little Revue, Still Dancing,* and others.

His first big success came in 1929 with the show *Mr Cinders,* which gave Binnie Hale a song always associated with her, 'Spread a Little Happiness', and the duet she sang with Bobby Howes, 'I'm a One Man Girl'.

In 1930 Vivian Ellis began what was to be a long association with the noted impresario Charles B Cochran. He wrote the score for *Cochran's 1930 Revue* (which had 'additional numbers' by Richard Rodgers and Lorenz Hart), and the most popular Ellis hit was 'The Wind in the Willows', sung by Leslie Hutchinson, who became better known as Hutch. It was following the Cochran revue that Vivian Ellis really got into his stride as a first-rate show composer. He wrote the entire score for *Follow a Star,* which had three numbers he created for Sophie Tucker—'I Can Never Think of the Words', 'That's Where the South Begins' and 'If Your Kisses Can't Hold the Man You Love'—as well as 'The First Week-End in June' for Jack Hulbert. For *Little Tommy Tucker* he produced two fair-sized hits with 'Follow the Girl' and 'Let's Be Sentimental'. He celebrated the opening of 1931 with three West End productions in the first month: *Folly to Be Wise,* with the song 'The South is the Place for Me'; *Blue Roses,* which had the charming song 'I Saw the Moon Through the Window'; and 'The Sun in Your Eyes' from the Drury Lane show *The Song of the Drum.* Later in the same year he contributed to the Jack Buchanan show *Stand Up and Sing.*

Maybe it was through over exposure (it was shortly after these successes) that, for no apparent reason, his career began to falter. The incessant demand for his work suddenly stopped. Quite undismayed, Vivian started on what was to become a second career—writing books. The novel he wrote at that time was not exactly sensational, but he continued with others that were much more successful, including two volumes of autobiography and some children's books. His most popular books were his humorous 'How to' series: *How to Be a Man About Town* (which he was), *How to Enjoy Your Operation* (which he had), *How to Bury Yourself in the Country* (which he did), and *How to Make Your Fortune on the Stock Exchange* (which he didn't).

That bad patch Vivian Ellis went through lasted for over two years, and it was Cochran who came to the rescue with an invitation to compose the score for a new revue he was presenting. Not only that, but he was to have A P Herbert as his collaborator, which turned out to be an inspired piece of theatrical match-making on Cochran's part, and one which was to affect the future of all three of them. The revue *Streamline* opened in November 1934. It starred Meg Lemonnier, who sang 'You Turned Your Head', and Florence Desmond, with the song 'Kiss Me Dear'. His score also included a song that became a minor classic. It was sung by Norah Howard and told the story of an elderly nanny whose life had been devoted to 'Other People's Babies'. While *Streamline* was having a successful run at the Palace Theatre, *Jill Darling* opened at the Saville. It was another Ellis hit, and when later he wrote that second volume of autobiography he called it *I'm on a See-Saw*, the hit song from the show. It was sung by a young juvenile called Johnny Mills who later developed into the brilliant film star Sir John Mills. Among the other good tunes from the show were two sung by the glamorous Frances Day, 'Let's Lay Our Heads Together' and 'Dancing With a Ghost'. When Vivian decided in 1936 to write some of his own words as well as music, the first lyric he wrote was a speciality for Frances Day called 'Me and My Dog'.

In 1937 came the opening of *Hide and Seek*, with Cicely Courtneidge and Bobby Howes. For Miss Courtneidge Vivian wrote two songs ideally suited to her talents as a comedienne, 'I'll Follow the Birdie' and 'May-Belle', while Bobby Howes had the good fortune to be given a song which became 'his' song, and he continued singing it for the rest of his life—'She's My Lovely'. In the summer of 1938 Vivian Ellis scored a hat-trick by writing the music and lyrics for three West End shows, *The Fleet's Lit Up*, in which Frances Day had a hit with 'How Do You Do, Mister Right?', *Running Riot*, with Leslie Henson, and *Under Your Hat*, which reunited Cicely Courtneidge with Jack Hulbert and appropriately featured a duet called 'Together Again'. Courtneidge also had a burlesque patriotic song, 'The Empire Depends on You'.

It was during the run of this show that World War II began for Vivian Ellis. He volunteered for the navy, and this stopped him composing for the next five years. A couple of months before the end of the war Lieutenant Commander Ellis was invalided out. But for composer Vivian Ellis it was difficult getting back into the theatre after being out of the public eye for so long. New faces and new names had appeared. It was Cochran who again came to the rescue when he teamed him up once more with A P Herbert, and a great theatrical partnership was back in business. Their first production was *Big Ben*, which opened in 1946 at the Adelphi, a theatre they were to occupy for the next three years with three outstanding British musicals. It was in this show that Cochran spotted Lizbeth Webb, a pretty girl of 19 who made one short appearance singing a reprise of the theme song 'I Want to See the People Happy'. With his innate ability to exploit and develop talent better than most, Cochran quickly decided to commission Ellis and Herbert to write a show especially for her. The result was *Bless the Bride*. A P Herbert's book and lyrics had wit, charm and romance, and Vivian Ellis wrote what was probably his best score to date. The show was a triumph, with Liz Webb singing 'I Was Never Kissed Before' and 'This Is My Lovely Day', while the young Greek singer Georges Guétary stopped the show nightly with 'Ma Belle Marguerite'.

After almost 900 performances *Bless the Bride* was followed in 1949 by *Tough at the Top*, the third and last of the Cochran operettas. Although this had another fine score it didn't have quite the same appeal as the others. With his next efforts Vivian Ellis went solo, writing the words and music for *And So to Bed* (1951), in which the title song became a hit for Keith Michell, and a highly successful children's play *Listen to the Wind* (1954). In the following year Vivian and A P Herbert joined forces once more for a musical version of Herbert's popular novel *The Water Gypsies*, which starred Dora Bryan as Lily, the girl who loathed her name and asked in the song 'Why Did You Call Me Lily?' Among the other good tunes were 'Clip-Clop', 'When I'm Washing Up' and 'This Is Our Secret'.

Vivian Ellis worked untiringly for his fellow composers as deputy president of the Performing Rights Society, and in 1973 was honoured with an Ivor Novello Award for Outstanding Services to British Music.

His most important compositions are referred to in the text, so no further listing is included here.

EVANS, Ray, *see* Livingston, Jay.

EVANS, Tolchard, composer, author, pianist, conductor.

Born Paddington, London, 1901. Died Willesden, London, 12 March 1978, the district where he had lived ever since he was a boy. In 1916 he took his first job as a 15-year-old office boy in the London music publishing house of Lawrence Wright. This was in Denmark Street, London's own Tin Pan Alley, and Tolchard Evans remained a Tin Pan Alley man (that is, a professional songwriter to his fingertips) until the end. In 1919 he had his first song published, 'Candlelight', but it was not a great success, and although he kept on trying, he had to wait until 1926 for his first hit, 'Barcelona', a million-seller.

From then on success followed success. Sometimes, as with 'Barcelona', he would write both music and words. At other times he collaborated with such successful authors as H B Tilsley and Stanley Damerell. He will best be remembered for his 1931 song, 'Lady of Spain' (lyrics by Errell Reaves). It is impossible to estimate how many millions of song copies this has sold since it was born. Nor can one say how many records by various artists it has sold over the years. Certainly Eddie Fisher had a million-selling record with it in 1952, 21 years after its publication. Less successful, although only slightly so, was his 1934 song, 'If'. Like 'Lady of Spain', this suddenly had a rebirth in 1951, when Perry Como made a record of it which was another million-seller.

Most of Tolchard Evans's hits were written during the 1930s, although he had a somewhat surprising re-emergence during the 1950s, inspired perhaps by that million-seller of Perry Como's in 1951. 'Everywhere' won him an Ivor Novello Award in 1955, and 'I'll Find You' (from the film *Seawife* starring Richard Burton) an award in 1957. He received another award for his 1956 song 'My September Love' which was a big hit record for David Whitfield, and his own piano recording of his song 'The Singing Piano' was a big seller in 1959.

The other side of Tolchard Evans's career involved his bandleading activities, which started back in 1925 when he had a band at the Queen's Hotel, Westcliff-on-Sea. From there he moved to the Palace Hotel, Southend, where he remained for most of the 1930s. During the 1940s and 1950s he was heavily featured on BBC radio, in particular with his Tuneful Twenties series, which started in 1949, and another series called John Bull's Band, which started in 1951. In addition he often appeared as a featured performer on TV, notably in such productions as *The Black and White Minstrel Show* and *The Billy Cotton Band Show*.

Although Evans may not have written as many hits as some of his contemporaries, his big hits were usually bigger than theirs, and if you wanted a song written, all you had to do was pick up a telephone, commission 'Tolch', and he would write one for you. During his life he composed over 1,000 songs. He was always willing to write for the top singers, bands, and variety performers of the day, and several of his songs were adopted as signature tunes, including one called 'The Bells of Normandy', which was used in the 1930s by the then commercial radio station, Radio Normandy.

Some other outstanding Tolchard Evans songs:
'A Message From Missouri' (1926), 'The Road to Loch Lomond' (with H B Tilsley, 1926), 'Dreamy Devon' (with Hargreaves and Damerell, 1930), 'Unless' (with Hargreaves and Damerell, 1934), 'Song of the Trees' (with S J Damerell, 1935), 'There's a Lovely Lake in London' (with Damerell and Butler, 1935), 'I Hear Your Voice' (with Ralph Butler, 1942), 'Sailor, Who Are You Dreaming of Tonight?' (with Damerell and Butler, 1944), 'I'll Find You' (with Richard Mullan, 1957).

FAIN, Sammy, composer, singer, pianist.

Born New York, 17 June 1902. The family moved to Sullivan County, where Sammy was educated at the local high school. He was a self-taught pianist, and as a schoolboy he vainly pestered New York publishers by post with his songs. On leaving school he moved back to New York, where he was lucky enough to get a job in Tin Pan Alley as staff pianist to publisher Jack Mills. He also worked the vaudeville circuit as an accompanist, teaming up with Artie Dunn, and working with him on early radio programmes. Thus he had made something of a name for himself as an entertainer before his first song was published. This song appeared in 1925, and with lyrics by Irving Mills and Al Dubin bore the title 'Nobody Knows What a Redheaded Mama Can Do'. Two years later he met lyricist Irving Kahal, and a songwriting team that was to last 17 years and produce many number one hits, was born. The partnership ended only with

Kahal's death in 1942, although Fain wrote some songs with other authors before that date, and many more after it.

It seems that the very first Fain/Kahal song was destined to be a hit. It was the 1927 smash, 'Let a Smile Be Your Umbrella'. In the same year they produced another less well known opus that was, nevertheless, to be of inestimable value to three young men just starting out on their careers—Paul Whiteman's Three Rhythm Boys—Bing Crosby, Harry Barris and Al Rinker. The song was 'I Left My Sugar Standing in the Rain'.

Unlike many of his contemporaries, Sammy Fain contributed songs to movies before Broadway shows, notably 'You Brought a New Kind of Love to Me' for Maurice Chevalier's 1930 epic, *The Big Pond*. His first contribution to Broadway came only a year later, with songs for the revue *Everybody's Welcome*. Other successful films in which he was involved were *Footlight Parade* (1933) with Jimmy Cagney, Joan Blondell, and Ruby Keeler (Dick Powell sang 'By a Waterfall'); *Vogues of 1938* from which his song was 'That Old Feeling'; *I'll Be Seeing You* (1944) with Ginger Rogers and Joseph Cotton, for which he wrote the title song, although he had first used it six years earlier in a revue called *Right This Way*; *Thrill of a Romance* (1945) starring Van Johnson and Esther Williams, and the song 'Please Don't Say No'; and *April Love* (1957) for which again he wrote the title song, sung this time by Pat Boone. There was also *Calamity Jane* with Doris Day and 'Secret Love' (1953); *Love Is a Many-Splendored Thing* (title song, 1955, and an Academy Award winner); *A Certain Smile* (title song, 1958); and several others. Unlike many composers, he seldom wrote complete film scores, but his contributions were prolific, for in addition to those mentioned, between 1930 and 1958 he wrote songs for more than 30 other films. Similarly, he contributed to many Broadway shows, especially *Hellzapoppin* (with the Tobias Brothers, 1938), and *George White's Scandals of 1939*.

Besides collaborating with Irving Kahal, Sammy Fain also wrote with Sammy Cahn, Jack Yellen, Lew Brown, Mitchell Parish, Bob Hilliard, E Y Harburg and Paul Francis Webster. During the year 1949/50, he had the distinction of having two of the three top songs in the hit parade at the same time, 'Dear Hearts and Gentle People' being No 2, and his 1938 hit 'I Can Dream Can't I?', was revived to become No 3.

Irving Kahal, his lyricist, was born in Houtzdale, Pennsylvania, 5 March 1903 and died in New York 7 February 1942. He, too, had been a singer in his early days, with Gus Edwards's Minstrels, but after his meeting with Fain he concentrated on their successful songwriting partnership.

Some other outstanding Sammy Fain songs:
'Was That the Human Thing to Do?' (1931), 'When I Take My Sugar to Tea' (1931), 'Spin a Little Web of Dreams' (1934), 'That Old Feeling' (with Lew Brown, 1937), 'I'll Be Seeing You' (1938), 'The Second Star to the Right' (with Sammy Cahn, 1951), 'Home Is Where the Heart Is' (with Sammy Cahn, 1953).

FIELDS, Dorothy, *see* McHugh, Jimmy.

FLETCHER, Guy, composer, author.

Born St Albans, Herts, 23 April 1944. Educated at Sir Joseph Williamson's School, Rochester, Kent. His first song, called 'Step by Step' was published in 1965, and turned out to be a big hit in Scandinavia, thanks to a record by Wishful Thinking.

Since then he has had many major successes, of which perhaps the most notable have been 'I Can't Tell the Bottom From the Top' (The Hollies, 1969), 'With the Eyes of a Child' (Cliff Richard, 1970), 'Sing a Song of Freedom' (Cliff Richard, 1970), 'By the Devil I Was Tempted' (Blue Mink, 1971), 'Power to All Our Friends' (Cliff Richard, 1973—a Eurovision Song Contest winner), 'Fallen Angel' (Frankie Valli, 1977), 'Save Me' (Clout, 1978), and 'Dedication' (Bay City Rollers, 1977).

He also contributed the song 'Wonderful World' to the movie *Live a Little, Love a Little,* which was sung by Elvis Presley. He has been commissioned to write material for Ray Charles, Tom Jones and other singers, including Elvis Presley (for whom he wrote 'Just Pretend' and 'The Fair's Moving In' in addition to 'Wonderful World'). All of these were composed in collaboration with his writing partner Doug Flett. They won an Ivor Novello Award in 1973/4 for their song 'Power to All Our Friends'.

Doug Flett was born in Sydney, Australia, 13 October 1935, and his family emigrated to England when he was quite small. He was educated at Hull Grammar School. He has partnered Guy Fletcher from their earliest days.

FLETT, Doug, *see* Fletcher, Guy.

FREED, Arthur, *see* Brown, Nacio Herb.

GAY, Noel (Richard Moxon Armitage), composer, author, pianist, organist, arranger.

Born Wakefield, Yorkshire, 15 July 1898. Died London, 3 March 1954. Not many of the songwriters in this book come from wealthy or cultured backgrounds. Some do—in America Cole Porter is a prime example. In the UK an equally good example would be Noel Gay. His father was sufficiently well off to provide for his son an education that, after starting at a local school, took him straight on to the Royal College of Music, and subsequently to Christ's College, Cambridge. He ended up with MA, and MUSBac degrees, as well as FRCO and ARCM.

When he was a small boy, his parents recognized that perhaps they had a musical prodigy on their hands. At the age of 14 he frequently deputized for the regular organist at Wakefield Cathedral. During his musical studies in London he also became organist at St Anne's, Soho and sub-organist at the Chapel Royal. He was just 17. But it was at Cambridge that he first showed not just a talent for, but also the inclination to write and perform in, the popular music idiom. Studying at Cambridge at the same time was the late Lord Louis Mountbatten, who was running a university dance band. Noel Gay wrote songs and did arrangements for them, and thus found himself introduced to the world of musical comedy which, in those years in England, was such a prolific provider of the popular tunes of the day.

Through various contacts he met André Charlot, the major revue impresario of the day, who asked the budding songwriter to do a score for *The Charlot Show of 1926*, which first brought Jessie Matthews to public notice, and which also featured Anton Dolin. Nothing memorable remains of Noel Gay's contribution, although one song, 'Journey's End', was published, but it made enough impression for him to be asked to write for another show, *Clowns in Clover*, in 1927, starring Jack Hulbert and Cicely Courtneidge. This produced a number of good songs, of which the two best remembered, 'Ladies Are Running Wild' and 'On Wings of Love', were not, as it happens, featured by the two stars. It was about that time that he elected to call himself Noel Gay for his popular compositions, doubtless to leave a door open to return to serious music as Richard Armitage if he needed it. He had to wait until 1930 for a really big hit, the song 'All the King's Horses', which Cicely Courtneidge made into an instant success when she sang it in the show *Folly to Be Wise*.

The next year he followed this with another. The show was called *Hold My Hand*, the lyrics for Noel's music were by Desmond Carter, and the stars were Stanley Lupino, Sonnie Hale, and Jessie Matthews, who alone took the title song into the best sellers. There had been an earlier near hit called 'Tondeleyo', in 1928, for the film *White Cargo*, which had the honour of being the first song to be synchronized in a British talking picture.

During the 1930s Noel Gay contributed to, or wrote complete scores for such well known productions as *She Couldn't Say No* (1932), *That's a Pretty Thing* (1933), *Jack O' Diamonds* (1935), *Me and My Girl* (probably his biggest ever, starring Lupino Lane, and featuring 'The Lambeth Walk', 1937), *Wild Oats* (1938); and *The Little Dog Laughed* (starring Bud Flanagan, with the song 'Run Rabbit Run', 1939). In the 1940s he continued to prosper with such productions as *Present Arms* (1940), *Susie* (1942), *The Love Racket* (1943), and *Meet Me Victoria* (1944). Many of the hit songs that started life in these shows are listed below. There were films, too, such as *Me and Marlborough* (1935), in which Cicely Courtneidge sang 'There's Something About a Soldier'; *Okay for Sound* (1937), and the song 'The Fleet's in Port Again'; *Father Knew Best* (1937), in which George Formby introduced 'Leaning on a Lamppost'; and *The Camels Are Coming* (1934), in which Jack Hulbert introduced 'Who's Been Polishing the Sun?'. In addition to his writing, playing and conducting, Noel Gay also started his own publishing company in 1938, and quickly turned this into a success as well. In 1939 he produced the score for the West End show *Lights Up*, starring Evelyn Laye, and featuring such hits as 'You've Done Something to My Heart', and 'Let the People Sing'.

After the mid-1940s, Noel Gay suffered increasingly from deafness. He had a hearing aid, which he hated, and frequently refused to use when it suited him, or when the company was boring. And because of this he wrote less and less after 'My Thanks to You', which Vera Lynn popularized in 1950. After his death, the company did publish one last song, 'Love Me Now'.

Noel Gay has been described by several people who knew him well as 'short, pink, and cherubic, a chubby-faced man who beamed over his spectacles'. His son Richard also said, in an interview with author Eddie Rogers for his book *Tin Pan Alley* that 'he was often subject to flashes of impatience, anger or perverseness'. This is surprising, perhaps, in someone who was basically a gentle and unassuming man.

Some other outstanding Noel Gay songs:
'I Don't Want to Go to Bed' (from *Sleepless Nights*, 1932), 'The Sun Has Got His Hat On' (popularized by Jack Hulbert in 1932, and revived as a hit by Jonathan King in 1971), 'I Took My Harp to a Party' (popularized by Gracie Fields in 1933), 'La-di-da-di-da' (from *That's a Pretty Thing*, 1933), 'Let's Have a Tiddley at the Milk Bar' (1936), 'All for a Shilling a Day' (from *Me and Marlborough*, 1935), 'Love Makes the World Go Round' (from *These Foolish Things*, 1938), 'Only a Glass of Champagne' (from *Lights Up*, 1939), 'All Over the Place' (from *Sailors Three*, 1940), 'Hey Little Hen' (1941), 'Happy Days Happy Months' (from *The Love Racket*, 1943), 'I'll Always Love You' (popularized by Lupino Lane in *Sweetheart Mine*, 1946), 'When Alice Blue Gown Met Little Boy Blue' (1946), 'I Was Much Better Off in the Army' (1946), 'Let's All Be Good Elizabethans' (1952), 'You Smile at Everyone but Me' (1953).

GERSHWIN, George (Jacob Gershvin), composer, pianist, arranger.

Born Brooklyn, New York, 26 September 1898. Died Beverly Hills, California, 11 July 1937. Educated at various public schools in New York, and until the age of six showed no interest in music. This was not surprising because there was no tradition of music in his family. His elder brother Ira was inclined to be the serious one, and George was mostly concerned with neighbourhood street games. A school chum, Maxie Rosenzweig (later Max Rosen, famous violinist), already something of a prodigy, assured young George that he had no musical talent whatsoever. But when he was 12 the Gershwin family acquired an upright piano, and the boy started to teach himself to play, and to finger original melodies.

By 14 he was taking piano lessons, and within a year he had a job as staff pianist at the Remick Music Company. Later he worked as accompanist for such artists as Nora Bayes, of 'Shine on Harvest Moon' fame. Soon he was hired by Max Dreyfus of Harms Music, on the unusual basis that for $35 per week all he had to do was to write songs and show them to Dreyfus, who had the right to publish them if he wished. With Gershwin's talent bursting at the seams, the arrangement was profitable for both of them, and George felt that he had repaid himself for taking Irving Berlin's earlier advice not to work for him as his arranger. In David Ewen's *Great Men of American Popular Song* he quotes Berlin as saying to Gershwin, 'The job is yours at $100 a week if you want it. But I hope you don't take it. You are much too talented'.

Gershwin's first published song was 'When You Want 'Em, You Can't Get 'Em, When You've Got 'Em, You Don't Want 'Em', in 1916, which Sophie Tucker added to her repertoire. His first for Harms Music was 'Some Wonderful Sort of Someone', two years later. It was not a hit, but Dreyfus still had faith, and got Gershwin the job of writing the music for a revue, *Half Past Eight*. It opened and closed out of town. It was not until the publication of 'Swanee' (lyrics by Irving Caesar) in 1919, which was taken by Al Jolson and included in the show *Sinbad* that the first solid-gold Gershwin hit had arrived. Within a year it had sold more than 2 million records and more than 1 million copies of sheet music. In spite of all that, however, if did not qualify for a golden disc because the records were made by a number of different artists. Nevertheless, no other single Gershwin song ever achieved the commercial success of that first hit.

The next big step was when he was asked to write songs for *George White's Scandals of 1920*, which he continued to do for subsequent *Scandals* through 1924. These marked the continuation of his collaboration with brother Ira as lyricist, who had used the pseudonym Arthur Francis, because Ira did not want to ride to success on his brother's back. The two best known tunes from this period were 'I'll Build a Stairway to Paradise' and 'Somebody Loves Me'. After Ira had emerged from his self-imposed secrecy, the two brothers wrote the music for the show *Lady, Be Good* in 1924, which starred Fred Astaire and his sister Adèle, and produced not only the title song, so beloved of generations of jazz musicians, but also a beautiful ballad, 'The Man I Love'. In spite of the success of the George and Ira team, it is worth noting that George had already been writing with such distinguished names as Irving Caesar and Buddy DeSylva, although with the exception of *Swanee* it is the songs written with Ira that have really made the Gershwin reputation.

That George Gershwin was destined to become one of the great composers for stage musicals is demonstrated by the fact that he continued to write them until *Porgy and Bess* was completed, two years before his death. During the 11 or 12 years in question, among the successful shows were *Tip-Toes* (1925), starring Jeanette MacDonald, which produced 'Looking for a Boy' and 'That Certain Feeling'; *Oh Kay* (1926), with Gertrude Lawrence, and the song 'Someone to Watch over Me'; *Funny Face* (1927), with Fred and Adèle Astaire and the song ''S Wonderful'; *Rosalie* (1928), written in conjunction with Sigmund Romberg, the best known Gershwin contribution being 'How Long Has This Been Going On?'; *Show Girl* (1929), with Jimmy Durante and Ruby Keeler, and the song 'Liza', another beloved of jazz musicians; *Strike Up the Band* (1930), which in addition to the title song produced 'I've Got a Crush on You'; *Girl Crazy* (1930), in which both Ethel Merman and Ginger Rogers made their Broadway debuts, and from which came 'Bidin' My Time', 'Embraceable You', and another one for the jazzers, 'I Got Rhythm'; and *Of Thee I Sing* (1931), which produced 'Love Is Sweeping the Country'. There were some less successful shows during 1933 and 1934 and, of course, the never-to-be-forgotten operetta *Porgy and Bess* in 1935.

While all this was going on, George Gershwin had, like all the other big names of his time, been busily engaged in writing for Hollywood movies as well. Some of these works were film adaptations of his successful Broadway shows such as *Girl Crazy*, but others were purely films, such as *A Damsel in Distress* (1937) for Fred Astaire, with such songs as 'A Foggy Day' and 'Nice Work if You Can Get It'. In the same year, his last, he wrote *Shall We Dance*, the Fred Astaire/Ginger Rogers movie in which almost every song was memorable, particularly 'They Can't Take That Away From Me'. Also in 1937, he wrote for *The Goldwyn Follies*, although the movie did not appear until 1938. It contained his last hits, 'Love Walked In', and 'Love Is Here to Stay'. In 1945 Warner Bros produced a film called *Rhapsody in Blue*, based on Gershwin's life, full of his hit songs; and in 1947 20th Century-Fox produced *The Shocking Miss Pilgrim*, starring Betty Grable and Dick Haymes, using a number of hitherto unpublished Gershwin tunes.

I have already said that a number of George Gershwin's tunes became jazz favourites, and were also much loved by the great singing stars who made their names with the Big Bands. George had been influenced by jazz and its performers from his early childhood—indeed for a time the family even lived in Harlem, the birthplace of New York jazz. But all through his life he had, as a major ambition, the desire to become the first American composer of popular music to bring to the medium the quality and acclaim that for centuries had been reserved for classical composers. He felt he had achieved this in 1924 when he was commissioned by Paul Whiteman to write 'Rhapsody in Blue', which was first performed at New York's Aeolian Hall. Critics of the day say it drew an ovation from the audience, although by no means all of them gave it praise, one describing it as '. . . trite and feeble and conventional'. By the same token, generations of jazz musicians who rate Gershwin tunes highly as vehicles for their art, have continuously knocked it with such phrases as 'you can't dress up jazz in those sort of fancy clothes'. Nevertheless, it has become a standard part of the light music concert repertoire, as has the work which followed it in 1925, 'Concerto in F'. Out of three more instrumental compositions, the best known is 'An American in Paris' (1928).

George Gershwin died from a tumour on the brain. For weeks prior to his death he had been in extreme pain, but was believed to be suffering from a nervous breakdown. Ultimately he was sent to the Cedars of Lebanon Hospital for exploratory surgery. There the tumour was discovered and an operation performed, but it was unsuccessful. Had he survived, he would almost certainly have been disabled, blind, or both. Mercifully he died the following morning. David Ewen, in *Great Men of American Popular Song* provides a fitting epitaph: 'Gershwin may have died leaving many a masterwork unwritten, but not before he had achieved his destiny'.

Ira Gershwin was born in New York on 6 December 1896, and at the time of writing is still living in Beverly Hills, California. Words and writing seem to have appealed to him from his schooldays, when he wrote sketches and verse for a college magazine. But on leaving school he had to earn a living doing whatever jobs came his way, and he wrote only in his spare time (in 1918 he sold a sketch for $1). His early pseudonym, Arthur Francis, was made up of the names of the youngest Gershwin brother Arthur, and sister Frances, and it appears on a Gershwin song copy as early as 1920. But his biggest break as a lyricist came the following year, when he wrote his first Broadway show, *Two Little Girls in Blue* to Vincent Youmans' music. By 1924, for a show called *Be Yourself* which lasted a bare 93 performances, he felt able to assume his true identity as Ira Gershwin. From there on, his collaboration with brother George has already been chronicled.

After George's death, Ira found it difficult to adjust to writing with other composers. That he did so successfully is in itself a testimony to the man. To write with Jerome Kern ('Long Ago and Far Away'), Harold Arlen ('The Man That Got Away', a huge hit for Judy Garland), and others such as Harry Warren and Kurt Weill (*Lady in the Dark*), says all that needs to be said about his talent. He has retained throughout his life that dry, wry, sense of humour often heard in his lyrics, and which is typified by the following incident. Arthur Freed, himself a good lyricist, but perhaps better known as a film producer, told Ira that he was having a little problem with Jerome Kern, while he was working on the film of Kern's life. Kern it seems, did not want his name to be used for the story, but wanted Freed to think up a fictitious one. 'A good idea', commented Ira. 'You can call Kern "J. Fred Coots"'.

Some other outstanding George Gershwin songs:
'Fascinating Rhythm' (1924), 'Sweet and Low-Down' (1925), 'Do, Do, Do' (1926), 'Clap Yo' Hands' (1926), 'My One and Only' (1927), 'But Not for Me' (1930), 'Summertime', 'I Got Plenty o' Nuttin'', 'It Ain't Necessarily So', 'Bess, You Is My Woman' (from *Porgy and Bess*, 1935), 'Let's Call the Whole Thing Off', 'I've Got Beginner's Luck', 'They All Laughed', and 'Shall We Dance?' (from *Shall We Dance?*, 1937).

GERSHWIN, Ira, *see* Gershwin, George.

GOFFIN, Gerry, *see* King, Carole.

GORDON, Mack, *see* Revel, Harry.

GREENAWAY, Roger, composer, author, publisher, producer.

Born Southmead, near Bristol, 23 August 1938. Educated Soundwell Junior and Kingswood Grammar Schools, Bristol. On leaving, he worked for a printer and paper manufacturer, and then completed his National Service in The Royal Berkshire Regiment, 1957–1959. In 1960 he joined a Bristol group called The Kestrels, where he also met the man who was to become his songwriting partner. This was **COOK, Roger,** composer, author, publisher, producer. Born Bristol, 19 August 1941. Educated Fishponds Junior and Speedwell Secondary Modern Schools, Bristol. Before he, too, joined The Kestrels, he did semi-pro work locally with a group called The Sapphires, as well as various odd jobs to earn money.

After a spell with The Kestrels, the two Rogers decided to start on their own as a singing/songwriting duo, David and Jonathan, in which they were ably aided and abetted by Beatles producer George Martin. While David and Jonathan had a good deal of success (their biggest hit was 'Lovers of the World Unite' in 1966), it soon became evident that it was the songwriting capabilities of the pair that were going to take them along the road to the big time, rather than their efforts as performers.

Their first published songs were a group of three that all came out in 1965—'Everything in the Garden', recorded by Petula Clark, Jimmy Justice and Arthur Prysock; 'This Golden Ring', for The Fortunes; and, biggest of all, 'You've Got Your Troubles', which was recorded by The Fortunes, Jack and Mari Blanchard, and surprisingly, Neil Diamond, its total sales topping 4 million. Dating as it does from the relatively early days of their career, that last figure is a very significant one because, out of the many hundreds of Greenaway/Cook songs to date, when looking for their major successes, those that have sold less than half a million hardly seem to rate.

Apart from their writing talents, Greenaway and Cook have made it a point over the years to perform from time to time as part of groups with which they have been associated. For instance, Roger Greenaway has sung with White Plains, The Pipkins, and Brotherhood of Man. Roger Cook has appeared with Blue Mink, as well as solo under his stage name of Roger James Cook. Artists who have ridden to success on the back of Greenaway/Cook songs have been Whistling Jack Smith (with over 3 million copies of 'I Was Kaiser Bill's Batman', 1967, No 5 UK and No 20 US); Gary Lewis and The

Playboys (850,000 with 'Green Grass', which reached No 4 in the US charts); Gene Pitney (380,000 of 'Something's Gotten Hold of My Heart', 1967, No 5 in the UK charts); White Plains (1½ million of 'My Baby Loves Lovin'', 1970, No 9 UK and No 13 US, and 500,000 of 'I've Got You on My Mind', 1970, No 17 UK); Blue Mink (450,000 of 'Melting Pot' and 300,000 of 'Banner Man', 1971, No 3 UK); Cilla Black (550,000 of 'Something Tells Me', 1971, No 6 UK); The Hollies (1,800,000 of 'Long Cool Woman in a Black Dress'); The Drifters (450,000 of 'Kissin' in the Back Row of the Movies'); The New Seekers (world-wide sales of over 5 million of 'I'd Like to Teach the World to Sing' 1971, No 1 UK and No 7 US, which started out in life as a TV commercial jingle); Tom Jones (1,300,000 of 'Say You'll Stay Until Tomorrow'); Crystal Gayle (1 million plus of 'It's Like We Never Said Goodbye'); The Fortunes (1½ million of 'Here Comes That Rainy Day Feeling'); and Andy Williams (385,000 of 'Home Lovin' Man' 1970, No 7 UK).

In the case of some of the songs listed above, other collaborators have been involved. For instance, Roger Greenaway has had four big hits with Barry Mason, six with Geoff Stephens, and eight with Tony Macaulay, Roger Cook not being involved in all of them. Cook on the other hand has also had big hits with other writers, notably 'Talking in Your Sleep' by Crystal Gayle (1980, co-written with Bobby Woods), and '7-6-5-4-3-2-1' by Gary Toms Empire (1980, both words and music by Cook, which was in the US charts for six months). It is clear that the two Rogers are far from being one-hit wonders, and that they will continue for a long time to turn out chart-topping songs. Roger Greenaway is married, with three children—two boys and a girl, and continues to live in London. Roger Cook is also married, with three children, and for the last few years has lived in Nashville, Tennessee.

Some other outstanding Greenaway/Cook songs:
'Sunny Honey Girl' (1970), 'Doctor's Orders' (1973), 'The Way It Used to Be' (lyrics only, 1968), 'Softly Whispering I Love You' (1967), 'Hello Summertime' (1974), 'It Oughta Sell a Million' (1974), 'Freedom Come Freedom Go' (1971), 'Sugar and Spice' (1971), 'Good Times Better Times' (1970), 'Jeans On' (1976).

HAMLISCH, Marvin (Frederick), composer, pianist.

Born New York, 2 June 1944. Marvin Hamlisch began his musical career very early in life. At the age of five he was playing on the piano songs he'd heard on the radio; at six he began taking piano lessons; and at seven he became the youngest student ever enrolled at the Juilliard School of Music after an audition in which he played 'Goodnight Irene' in seven different keys. His original ambition was to be a concert pianist, but he soon gave up this idea and turned to composition and songwriting.

It was while he was working at a summer camp that he first had his songs performed. One of them was 'Travelin' Man', which his good friend Liza Minnelli later included in her first album. She also sang it with her mother, Judy Garland, at the London Palladium in 1964. In the following year he had his first hit song, 'Sunshine, Lollipops and Roses', recorded by Lesley Gore. It was in the charts for 11 weeks. By now Marvin had begun moving in show business circles, and it was through Liza Minnelli that he started working on Broadway as a rehearsal pianist for shows such as *Funny Girl* and *Fade Out—Fade In.*

While he was playing piano at a party given by movie producer Sam Spiegel he heard that Spiegel was searching for a musical theme for his next production, *The Swimmer* (1968). Three days later Hamlisch presented him with the theme music he had worked up. Spiegel immediately hired him and Marvin moved to Hollywood. This led to assignments for other films, including two Woody Allen comedies, *Take the Money and Run* (1969) and *Bananas* (1971), also the Jack Lemmon films *The April Fools* (1969) and *Save the Tiger* (1972). In 1971 he had his first nod of recognition when his song from the Walter Matthau film *Kotch*, called 'Life Is What You Make It', with lyrics by Johnny Mercer, was nominated for an Academy Award. This was just an appetizer. On 2 April 1974 he gathered an armful of Oscars by winning an unprecedented three Academy Awards. With lyric writers Alan and Marilyn Bergman he won Best Original Song as well as Best Score for the Barbra Streisand/Robert Redford film *The Way We Were*, and another for his adaptation of Scott Joplin's ragtime music for *The Sting.*

In 1975 his first Broadway show, *A Chorus Line*, opened to rave reviews and became a long-running and established success. Marvin's score included the hit songs 'One', 'I Felt Nothing' and 'What I Did for Love', the last of which has been recorded by such singers as

Johnny Mathis, Tony Bennett, Shirley Bassey, Jack Jones and Andy Williams. The year after *A Chorus Line* opened, Marvin Hamlisch wrote the music for a highly regarded musical TV version of John Osborne's play *The Entertainer*. He composed eight songs for the programme, the best of which was 'The Only Way to Go'. For the two-character film *Same Time Next Year* (1978), he again worked with Alan and Marilyn Bergman on the song duet, 'The Last Time I Felt Like This', which resulted in another Oscar nomination.

It was around that time that he began a highly successful collaboration with lyric-writer Carole Bayer Sager. Together they wrote the theme song for the 1977 James Bond film *The Spy Who Loved Me*, sung by Carly Simon and called 'Nobody Does It Better'. It has become a Hamlisch standard. The couple continued with a series of hit film songs. 'Better Than Ever' for the film *Starting Over* (1979), 'Through the Eyes of Love', the theme from *Ice Castles* (1979), 'If You Remember Me', from the sound track of *The Champ* (1979), as well as an independent number, 'Two Boys'. This culminated in Marvin's most recent musical *They're Playing Our Song* (1979), a big success on Broadway and in London. With a book by Neil Simon, it's the story of a love affair between a successful New York songwriter and his scatterbrain lyric-writer. The Hamlisch score included the hit songs 'Fallin'', 'If He Really Knew Me', 'I Still Believe in Love' and 'When You're in My Arms'. Although Marvin's most recent score was for the Robert Redford film *Ordinary People* (1980), the signs are that he has become somewhat disenchanted with Hollywood. He is currently working on a new Broadway musical, and we can confidently expect more entries in the Marvin Hamlisch songbook.

Marvin Hamlisch's best known songs are referred to in the text, so no further list is necessary.

HAMMERSTEIN 2nd, Oscar, *see* Kern, Jerome *and* Rodgers, Richard.

HANDY, William Christopher, composer, cornetist, bandmaster, publisher.

Born Florence, Alabama, 16 November 1873. Died New York, 29 March 1958. Will Handy finds his place here because he has been dubbed 'Father of the Blues' by musical journalists throughout the world, most of whom should know better. Even his autobiography was called *Father of the Blues* (1942). Handy did not invent the blues any more than Irving Berlin invented ragtime. What he did, however, was to put on paper many traditional blues tunes that he heard and remembered during his colourful career (he was born only eight years after the abolition of slavery in the US). He himself knew as a young man what it was to suffer from cold, hunger and homesickness, and he never forgot the 'sorrow songs' he heard in his travels to and from Chicago, St Louis, Memphis, Mobile and generally up and down the Mississippi. He heard them sung by unhappy girls in bawdy houses, by gamblers, by stevedores, and by chain gangs.

The blues as a musical form differs from other popular formats in that it has only 12 bars. It also has what are described as 'blue notes', an effect created by inserting a minor 7th into an ordinary major chord. Of all Handy's famous blues tunes, the most famous is 'St Louis Blues', and this must also be the one that carries most of his original inspiration in it. It has three separate sections, quite unlike most blues, one of which is performed in a sort of tango rhythm. According to Handy, this rhythm was brought by the Moors to Spain, thence by slaves to Cuba, and ended up as the tango after modifications in the Argentine.

Handy's first blues, 'Memphis Blues', was published at his own expense in 1912. Originally he had written it as a campaign song for the then political boss of Memphis, Edward H Crump, calling it simply 'Mister Crump'. He later sold his rights for $50 cash. The experience led him to form his own publishing house and hang on to his copyrights. This eventually made him a rich man until the Depression hit the music business. 'St Louis Blues' must surely be one of the most recorded and played pieces of all time. Performances (apart from the legion by jazz musicians) have included one by The Royal Band of Ethiopia for the Emperor Haile Selassie; by Scottish pipers for King Edward VIII; and by Glenn Miller with his famous 'St Louis Blues March', which got him in such bad odour with his military bosses in World War II. It was also used as the title of a film biography. So let us forgive Handy's understandable ego, and the misguided publicists for dubbing him 'Father of the Blues', and let us say that it is impossible to think of the blues today without thinking of him.

Some other outstanding W C Handy songs :
'In the Cotton Fields of Dixie' (lyrics by Herbert Pace, 1907), 'Jogo
Blues' (1913), 'Yellow Blues' (1914), 'Hesitating Blues' (1915), 'Joe
Turner Blues' (1915), 'Ole Miss' (1916), 'Atlanta Blues' (better known
as 'Make Me a Pallet on the Floor', lyrics by Dave Elman, 1916),
'Beale Street Blues' (1916), 'Aunt Hagar's Blues' (also titled 'Aunt
Hagar's Children's Blues', lyrics by J T Brymn, 1926), 'Loveless Love'
(better known as 'Careless Love', 1921), 'The John Henry Blues'
(1922), 'The Harlem Blues' (1923), 'Basement Blues' (1924), 'Chantez-
les Bas' (1931), 'Way Down Where the Blues Began' (1932), 'East of
St Louis Blues' (1937).

HARBACH, Otto, *see* Kern, Jerome.

HARBURG, E Y (Yip), *see* Arlen, Harold.

HATCH, Tony, composer, author, pianist, arranger, publisher.

Born Pinner, Middlesex, June 1939. **TRENT, Jacqueline (Jackie),**
author, singer, actress. Born Newcastle-under-Lyme, September
1940. Tony was educated at the London Choir School, where he
obtained his first musical training. In 1951 he toured Austria and
Germany with the school choir, and followed this by becoming head
chorister at All Soul's Church, Langham Place, London, for two
years.

When he left school, he took a job as a tea boy in the offices of a
London music publisher, which in turn led him into some extra
work as a producer's assistant at Rank Records. He then served for
three years in the Coldstream Guards, and it was there that further
steps in his musical education took place. Although not a member of
their band, he was fortunate to find himself associated with the
musicians, and learned about arranging—many of his scores
ultimately finding their way into the band's library.

In 1960 he returned to civilian life, taking whatever work he
could get, and it was then that he had his first song published, 'Look

for a Star'. Later that same year he followed this with his first hit, 'Messing About on the River'. In spite of this, financial rewards were modest, and in order to achieve more stability he took a job as a record-producer for Pye Records. There he assisted at sessions with Emile Ford and Lonnie Donegan, and also with Petula Clark, for whom he wrote the big hit 'Downtown' in 1964. This reached number one in many parts of the world, selling over 3 million records in all.

In 1964 he also met singer Jackie Trent, and produced her first record for Pye. This was the beginning of a lasting personal relationship, as well as a song-writing partnership, and the following year they wrote together the song 'Where Are You Now?', which Jackie recorded, and which shot to number one in the charts. This then was the start of the Hatch/Trent team, which continues to this day. In 1966 and 1967 there were more hits, such as 'I Know a Place', 'Call Me', 'My Love', 'I Couldn't Live Without Your Love', 'Don't Sleep in the Subway', and 'Who Am I?', with recordings by such artists as Petula Clark and Adam Faith.

In 1967 Tony and Jackie married, and almost immediately celebrated professionally with a recording of their own song 'The Two of Us', which achieved considerable success. They also wrote 'Colour My World' and 'The Other Man's Grass', both big hits for Petula Clark. In 1968 their song 'Joanna' was pushed into the charts by singer Scott Walker, while Tony also branched out very successfully into themes and jingles for television and radio. Jackie meanwhile produced a daughter, Michelle, and turned her attention to TV acting.

From then on, the performing side of their joint careers rather took over from songwriting, although not completely. Between 1969 and 1973 they appeared together in a Max Bygraves show at the London Palladium, made three tours of Australia, and appeared frequently on TV and radio. In 1970 Jackie played the title role in London in the musical *Nell*, for which Tony orchestrated the music and directed. All this seems to have given them a taste for the musical theatre and in 1973 they wrote the musical *The Card*, which starred Jim Dale and Millicent Martin. In 1975 they wrote a second musical in collaboration with David Wood, *Rock Nativity*.

Tony and Jackie continue to write, sing, make radio and TV appearances, and undertake concert tours. They currently live in Ireland.

Jackie Trent was educated at Broadmeadow School, Chesterton, and developed a taste for the theatre at the age of nine, when she began appearing in school pantomimes and other productions. She started singing with local bands at 13, and by 17 had become a professional. This led to tours of Germany, Turkey, Italy and Greece. She also appeared successfully in cabaret in London, and in summer shows with Lonnie Donegan. She made records for the Oriole label in 1962, until she first auditioned for Tony Hatch at Pye Records in 1963.

The most important Hatch/Trent songs have been referred to in the text, so there is no need for an additional list.

HENDERSON, Ray, *see* DeSylva, Brown and Henderson.

HERBERT, Victor, composer, conductor, cellist.

Born Dublin, 1 February 1859. Died New York, 26 May 1924. His father died when he was only three, and he was taken to live at Sevenoaks in England, with his maternal grandfather. He received piano lessons from his mother, who then moved to Stuttgart after marrying a German doctor, and young Victor's musical education was continued there. But his interest in music was overwhelming, and at 15 he left school to study the cello, later being appointed first cellist to the Stuttgart Royal Orchestra. In 1886 he married Theresa Förster, leading soprano of the Stuttgart Opera, and in the same year they went to New York, where his wife was due to appear in a season at the Metropolitan. The best that Victor could do for himself at that time was to take a job playing his cello with the opera house orchestra.

A year later, however, he was giving solo performances with the New York Symphony Orchestra, and was busy forming an orchestra of his own. He pursued his musical career with distinction, being appointed musical director of the National 22nd Regiment Band in 1893, and principal conductor of the Pittsburgh Symphony Orchestra from 1898 to 1904.

But that was the age of the operetta. In his book *Great Men of American Popular Music* David Ewen reports 'During the single season 1894–95, fourteen companies were touring the United States with foreign operettas'. Although Victor Herbert had already entered the realms of composition, contributing to the serious repertoires of the various orchestras with which he was associated, he became more and more attracted to the musical theatre. After failing to get his first operetta *La Vivandière* (1893) performed, he still declared to his wife 'I *must* write for the theatre'. In 1894 his *Prince Ananias* was first performed in Boston, and the critics were kind to it.

From then on it was as a composer of operetta and light music that he really became known. By the time of his death in 1924, he had completed the scores for 49 productions. Details of these are outside the scope of this book, but the songs from so many of them have entered the repertoire of popular music that a summary of the most important are given below. Although he spent most of his life in America (he became an American citizen in 1902), he never absorbed any of the influences of American popular music (ragtime, syncopation, the blues, etc.), remaining to the end steeped in the traditions of European operetta and musical comedy. David Ewen says 'He died thinking he was a has-been'. His importance, however, in the context of this book, lies not in the success or failure of his productions as shows, but in the never-ending succession of up-dated treatments that his most famous melodies continue to receive more than 50 years after his death.

Outstanding Victor Herbert songs:
'Gypsy Love Song' (*The Fortune Teller*, 1898), 'Toyland' (*Babes in Toyland*, 1903), 'Absinthe Frappé' (*It Happened in Nordland*, 1904), 'Kiss Me Again' (*Mlle Modiste*, 1905), 'I Want What I Want When I Want It' (*Mlle Modiste*, 1905), 'Everyday Is Ladies' Day With Me' (*The Red Mill*, 1906), 'Because You're You' (*The Red Mill*, 1906), 'When You're Pretty and the World Is Fair' (*The Red Mill*, 1906), 'Moonbeams' (*The Red Mill*, 1906), 'In Old New York' (1906), 'Rose of the World', (*Algeria*, 1908), 'Tramp! Tramp! Tramp!' (*Naughty Marietta*, 1910), 'I'm Falling in Love With Someone' (*Naughty Marietta*, 1910), 'Ah! Sweet Mystery of Life' (*Naughty Marietta*, 1910), 'Sweethearts' (*Sweethearts*, 1913), 'When You're Away' (*The Only Girl*, 1914), 'Thine Alone' (*Eileen*, 1917), 'A Kiss in the Dark' (*Orange Blossoms*, 1922), 'Indian Summer' (*An American Idyll*, 1919).

HERMAN, Jerry, composer, author.

Born New York, 10 July 1932. Educated University of Miami (BA Drama). Started out as a TV scriptwriter. His first published song was 'Your Good Morning' (1958). He finds a place here for his contribution to the musical theatre, which began with off-Broadway productions such as *I Feel Wonderful* (1954), *Parade* (which he also directed, 1960), and *Nightcap* (revue). He also gained much experience in his early years by writing special material for such performers as Tallulah Bankhead, Jane Froman, and Hermione Gingold (who used one of his songs in her revue *A to Z*). In 1961 he had two Broadway shows, *Milk and Honey* and *Madame Aphrodite* which, although they had good scores, did not contain any hit songs.

But all that changed in 1964 when Jerry Herman wrote the score for the show *Hello, Dolly!*, starring Carol Channing. This was made into an equally successful film starring Barbra Streisand in 1969, and of course Louis Armstrong's recording of the title song became a million-seller (Louis's first, at the age of 64). *Mame* followed in 1966, starring Angela Lansbury. This was almost as big a hit as *Hello, Dolly!*, with the title song being once again the best known item from the score.

Other Jerry Herman shows have been *Dear World* (1969), and *Mack and Mabel* (1974), based on the story of silent-movie producer Mack Sennett and his star Mabel Normand.

Some other outstanding Jerry Herman songs :
'The Next Time I Love' (1960, *Parade*), 'The Girls Who Sit and Wait' (1961, *Madame Aphrodite*), 'Milk and Honey' (1961, *Milk and Honey*), 'Let's Not Waste a Moment' (1961, *Milk and Honey*), 'Hello, Dolly!' (1964, *Hello, Dolly!*), 'Elegance' (1964, *Hello, Dolly!*), 'Goodbye Dearie' (1964, *Hello, Dolly!*), 'Mame' (1966, *Mame*), 'When Mabel Comes in the Room' (1974, *Mack and Mabel*).

HOFFMAN, Al, composer, author.

Born Minsk, Russia, 25 September 1902. Died New York, 21 July 1960. His family emigrated to America when he was six years old, and settled in Seattle, Washington. Noticing that his son seemed to have an ear for music, his father bought him a harmonium, and that was the start of his musical training. He also sang in local choirs as a boy soprano, and took an early interest in acting, which at first seemed as though it might become his career. Ironically this role fell to his brother David, who was trying to become a musician, so their futures became reversed.

He was educated at Franklyn High School, Seattle, where he formed a college band and became its drummer, an activity that he carried on professionally with local bands after graduating. He soon became a local bandleader and tried his hand at songwriting, but with no success, so he left home for New York in 1928, determined to break into Tin Pan Alley. This was a lot harder than he had imagined, but fortunately he had taken his drum kit with him, and survived on various gigs and one-night stands until he had his first successful song, 'Heartaches', published in 1931, with lyrics by John Klenner. Although this was successful, it did not become a smash hit until 16 years later. In 1947, a disc jockey on a radio station in Charlotte, North Carolina, found the old Ted Weems recording and made it into a million-seller both for composer and bandleader.

In 1934, Gaumont British Pictures invited Hoffman to London to write for their musical films, and he remained in England until 1937, writing successfully for both stage and screen. For the latter he composed 'Everything Stops for Tea', from the 1935 Jack Buchanan movie *Come Out of the Pantry*; 'Everything's in Rhythm With My Heart', in the same year, for the Jessie Matthews film *First a Girl*; 'My First Thrill' for the 1936 picture *She Shall Have Music*, featuring Jack Hylton's Band; and in 1937 'Gangway', the title song of another Jessie Matthews film. For the British stage he contributed 'I'm in a Dancing Mood' and 'This'll Make You Whistle' (the title song) as part of his score for the 1936 Jack Buchanan/Elsie Randolph show of that name; and 'A Little Co-operation From You', one of the songs from the 1937 show *Going Greek*, starring Leslie Henson, Fred Emney and Richard Hearne among others (Alan Jay Lerner was one of the three lyric-writers).

Although Al Hoffman's first big hit was 'Heartaches', his first published song had appeared in 1929, and during the next five years he had minor successes with other compositions through recordings by such artists as Kate Smith and Bing Crosby. But for him 1934 was a particularly fruitful year with 'I Saw Stars', and 'Little Man You've Had a Busy Day'.

After his return to America in 1937, he seldom had less than two hit songs per year in the American charts. He went to Hollywood in 1948 to write the score for the Walt Disney film *Cinderella* (1950), from which 'Bibbidi-Bobbidi-Boo' was the big hit. He continued as a writer of hits through the 1950s, with such standards as 'If I Knew

You Were Comin' I'd 've Baked a Cake', 'Papa Loves Mambo', 'Allegheny Moon', 'Hot Diggity' and others that were brought to the charts by such artists as Bob Hope and Bing Crosby, Perry Como, and Patti Page.

His chief collaborators and lyricists over the years have been Al Goodhart, Maurice Siegler, Jerry Livingston, Mack David and Bob Merrill.

Some other outstanding Al Hoffman songs:
'Why Don't You Practise What You Preach?' (1934), 'I'm in a Dancing Mood' (1936), 'There Isn't Any Limit to My Love' (1937), 'She Shall Have Music Wherever She Goes' (1936), 'Story of a Starry Night' (1942), 'Mairzy Doats and Doazy Doats' (1944), 'Gilly Gilly Ossenfeffer Katzenelenbogen by the Sea' (1954).

HOLLAND, DOZIER, HOLLAND, composers, authors, producers.

Brian Holland, born Detroit, Michigan, 15 February 1941; **Lamont Dozier,** born Detroit, Michigan, 16 June 1941; **Eddie Holland,** born Detroit, Michigan, 30 October 1939. This songwriting team achieved its greatest fame in the 1960s when it was signed up by the producer Berry Gordy, soon after he started the Tamla-Motown Record Company in 1961. Of the three, Lamont Dozier is the most innovative, and has been the driving force behind their success. Eddie Holland has confined himself mostly to lyrics, and could perhaps be best described as the quiet member of the team. Brian Holland collaborated with Dozier on the music. Lamont Dozier was the first to join the Tamla circus. He had headed a local group playing in the Detroit area in the late 1950s, but it never amounted to anything. His wife, however, was working for Berry Gordy's wife in a small record company called Anna Records. Although the little company was never successful, and ultimately went broke, the introduction had been made, and was taken up when Tamla began operations. In those early days Lamont had two moderately successful songs of his own, before joining the Hollands. He wrote 'Locking Up My Heart' for The Marvelettes, and 'Contract on Love' for Stevie Wonder.

As a team, Holland, Dozier, Holland's first hit was 'Come and Get these Memories', for Martha and The Vandellas, who were then Motown's latest acquisition. At that time Lamont was still working with other writers, and one of his biggest hits was the early 1960s song, recorded by The Marvelettes, 'Please Mr Postman', in which the Hollands played no part. It was revived as a hit all over again in the early 1970s for The Carpenters, and has now become a standard. But it was with the launching of Diana Ross and The Supremes that the team of songwriters really began to make the big time. Between 1964 and 1969 (up to the time Diana Ross left the group) they wrote no fewer than 14 major hits for them, including seven that reached the American No 1 spot. All this earned numerous gold discs for the group and produced sales between 1964 and 1975 of over 100 million singles and albums.

Curiously, no single record achieved a million sales on its own in the Billboard RIAA Certified Million-Sellers chart, not even their biggest hits such as 'Baby Love' (1964) or 'Stop! In the Name of Love' (1965).

In addition to their work for The Supremes, the team also wrote several big hits for The Four Tops, including a US No 1 in 1965 with 'I Can't Help Myself' (which never even entered the UK charts), and a joint US/UK No 1 in 1966, 'Reach Out, I'll Be There'.

By about 1966, Lamont Dozier began to feel that he was not getting his just reward from the team's agreement with Motown, and indicated his wish to set up his own publishing company. But the Hollands persuaded him that they should all stick together and set up their own record company instead. Their contract with Tamla-Motown was a very tight one, and Berry Gordy was not going to let his top writing team go without a fight. This led to a singularly unpleasant and lengthy legal case, with each side suing for millions of dollars. It was not resolved until 1969, at which time Lamont Dozier and the Hollands set up their own company, Invictus Records. For a while they were still legally tied as writers to Motown, so anything they composed for the new company had to be recorded under pseudonyms. Two early hits on Invictus, Freda Payne's 'Band of Gold' and Chairman of the Board's 'Give Me Just a Little More Time' bore no Holland, Dozier, Holland composer credits.

By 1972, Lamont Dozier was becoming dissatisfied again, this time because Invictus did not seem to be progressing fast enough, and also because he felt a need to develop his talents on his own. A second protracted lawsuit resulted, this time brought by the Hollands, to restrain him. It was not finally resolved until 1973/4 when he made his first appearance on the ABC label, with an album on which he sang. Once again, for legal reasons, none of the songs bore his name. From then on his career developed along the lines of the singer/songwriter/producer. In 1975, in an interview with Jess Levitt of *Cashbox* he said of his days at Motown, 'We milked it dry, and then I wanted to do my own thing. I try to take my tunes into the life experience. It's hard for another person to interpret your message. I think the feeling is more penetrating when the writer does it'. He has since released a number of albums under his own name, although no worldwide hit songs have resulted. He has also continued to do more live performances. By the late 1970s, it seems he had become somewhat disillusioned by the disco craze, and in another interview late in 1978 (this time for *Melody Maker*) he said, 'Where does music fit in? I don't think anybody's writing true songs, or trying to be daring anymore'.

The Holland brothers, meanwhile, faded from the scene. Perhaps they were never quite as dedicated to the music business as Lamont Dozier. As far back as 1969, in an interview with Ritchie Yorke for *New Musical Express*, Eddie Holland said that he never found writing lyrics easy. 'It always took me a long time. I've often spent 10 or 12 hours a day, day after day, getting a song right'. Even at the height of the Motown success, the Hollands had other interests, including a racehorse. Together with Lamont Dozier they had always been involved in record production as well, and it is in this area that their main interests lie today.

Some other outstanding songs by Holland, Dozier, Holland:
'Where Did Our Love Go?' (1964, No 3 UK, No 1 US), 'I Hear a Symphony' (1965), 'Back in My Arms Again' (1965), 'Come See About Me' (1965), 'You Keep Me Hanging On' (1966, No 6 UK, No 1 US), 'You Can't Hurry Love' (1965, No 3 UK, No 1 US), 'The Happening' (1967, No 6 UK, No 1 US), 'Reflections' (1967, No 5 UK, No 2 US), 'In and Out of Love' (1967, No 13 UK, No 9 US), 'Love Is Here and Now You're Gone' (1967, No 17 UK, No 1 US), 'Forever Came Today' (1968). All the foregoing were with Diana Ross and The Supremes. 'I Can't Help Myself' (1965, No 1 US, The Four Tops), 'Same Old Song' (1966, The Four Tops), 'Bernadette' (1969, No 8 UK, No 4 US, The Four Tops), 'This Old Heart of Mine' (1966, The Isley Brothers).

JOHN, Elton (Reginald Dwight), composer, pianist, singer, producer.

Born Pinner, Middlesex, 25 March 1947. Educated at local schools, he was given piano lessons at an early age. Subsequently he was sent to the Royal Academy of Music but he admits that he never took his classical studies very seriously. Music had always been part of his home environment, however, because both his mother and father used to buy records by the popular artists of the 1950s, and it was on this diet that young Elton grew up. He says that the first records to make a real impact on him were by Bill Haley, and subsequently Little Richard and Jerry Lee Lewis. From then on it was the rock 'n' roll style of piano playing that absorbed him till he eventually joined a small local group at the age of about 14. They played on Saturday and Sundays nights in any pub or club where they could get an engagement. On leaving school he took a job as teaboy-cum-packer in a music publisher's office, while continuing to earn extra money with the group in the evenings and at weekends.

Following an appearance at a talent contest, the group were advised to turn professional. As a result, they travelled up and down the country accompanying a variety of visiting American singers. Elton's biggest break came in 1966 when blues singer Long John Baldry asked him to join a new band he was forming called Bluesology. But it was still a touring job with more one-night stands, and Elton was already finding the life monotonous and depressing. He managed an audition for Liberty Records, at which he played some of his own compositions. But at that time these had no words, so when asked to sing he performed five Jim Reeves songs and got turned down as a performer. Ray Williams of Liberty, however, did put him in touch with Bernie Taupin, the man who was to become his partner in all his most successful songs. At first their contact was only by telephone and through the post, Taupin sending batches of lyrics to John, who would then compose music for them. The first time they met was when Elton was recording some demonstration tapes in a studio owned by music publisher Dick James. James signed them up as writers on a contract that gave them a weekly advance against royalties of £10, and Elton quit the Bluesology group to become a professional songwriter. It was then that he changed his name from Reg Dwight to Elton John—Elton from Elton Dean (Bluesology's sax player) and John from Long John Baldry.

Bernie Taupin was born at Sleaford, Lincolnshire, on 22 May

1950. Even at school he showed an interest in writing poetry, and at 16 he left to work as an apprentice printer for a local newspaper. This was not at all what he had had in mind when he tried for the job—he had ambitions to be a journalist—so it was not surprising that before long he was fired. There followed long spells out of work, interspersed with a variety of odd jobs. These included many visits to London to try and sell his ideas for pop music lyrics, something he had taken up when he realized that nobody was going to make a living writing poetry. On one of these visits he, too, had been to see Liberty Records, and it was then that Ray Williams advised him to send some lyrics to Elton John.

It seems to good to be true, but Taupin assured author Paul Gambaccini in conversation for the book *Elton John and Bernie Taupin*, that the story of posting his first lyrics to Elton is correct. He threw the package in the waste paper basket in a fit of despair, and it was his mother who fished it out and told him to post it anyway, which he finally did. Following their signing by Dick James, they spent a year writing what they thought their publisher wanted—ballads suitable for singers such as Engelbert Humperdinck. Few of these were published, and finally they were told it was all terrible. Why didn't they try writing what they thought they could do best? The result was their first minor hit, recorded by Elton John, the song 'Lady Samantha'. It was written in late 1968 and the record appeared in 1969. Their first published song had been called 'I've Been Loving You', which was also Elton John's first record, early in 1968, but it did not exactly shake the world. The first major John/Taupin hit was 'Your Song', written for the album *Elton John* in 1970. As a single, the record reached No 7 in the UK charts, and made No 1 in the US, while the album itself rapidly climbed to No 4 in the US album charts, and to No 11 in the UK. The album also won Elton his first gold record in 1971.

While perhaps not typical of the singer/songwriter genre which began to take over the popular music scene in the 1960s, dominated it in the 1970s, and continued into the 1980s, Elton John nevertheless, is certainly an example of the species. All his hits have been his own compositions (with lyrics by Bernie Taupin, which is what makes him atypical), and he has only once recorded another composer's song. This was in 1974, when his record of Lennon and McCartney's 'Lucy in the Sky With Diamonds; reached No 1 in the US charts. On the other hand many artists have recorded Elton John compositions, including perhaps surprisingly, Andy Williams. Yet only once have he and Bernie written a song specially for another artist, and that was 'Don't, You're Breaking My Heart' for Kiki Dee (1976). In the event, Elton sang it with her on the record, which was a big hit. Since 1973 he has had his own record company called Rocket.

As Elton John was both pianist and singer, inevitably he had a head start over other embryo stars when it came to live concert appearances. From the beginning his act was always polished, if too extreme and gimmicky for some tastes. His initial American tour in 1970 started with a sell-out performance at the Troubadour Club in Los Angeles, and most Elton John concerts have been sell-outs ever since. He has also made many TV appearances, both in his own spectaculars and as a guest on other people's shows. His extremes of dress and stage antics are really updated versions of tricks from the heyday of rock 'n' roll artists such as Little Richard and Jerry Lee Lewis, and they should not detract from his very real talent as a composer.

Some outstanding Elton John/Bernie Taupin songs:
'Friends' (1971), 'Levon' (1971), 'Tiny Dance' (1972), 'Rocket Man' (No 6 US, 1972), 'Crocodile Rock' (No 1 US, No 2 UK, 1972), 'Daniel' (No 2 US, 1973), 'Goodbye Yellow Brick Road' (No 2 US, No 6 UK, 1973), 'Candle in the Wind' (No 11 UK, 1974), 'Bennie and the Jets' (No 1 US, 1974), 'Don't Let the Sun Go Down' (No 1 US, 1974), 'Philadelphia Freedom' (No 1 US, No 12 UK, 1975), 'Island Girl' (No 1 US, 1975).

JOHNSTON, Arthur James, composer, conductor, pianist, arranger.

Born New York, 10 January 1898. Died Corona del Mar, California, 1 May 1954. Learned piano at an early age, and went to work for Fred Fisher's publishing company as a staff pianist at the age of 16. Learned the rudiments of arranging, and soon met Irving Berlin, who hired him to transcribe and arrange his songs (Berlin could only play piano in one key, and could neither read nor write music). From there Johnston went on to become musical director for Berlin's early *Music Box Revues.* His own first hit song was 'Mandy Make Up Your Mind', written with George Meyer, Roy Turk and Grant Clarke in 1925 for the great Florence Mills in the show *Dixie to Broadway.* In 1929 he went to Hollywood with Berlin, orchestrating for him the scores of the films *Puttin' on the Ritz*, *Mammy* and *Reaching for the Moon*, together with the background music for Charlie Chaplin's *City Lights*.

His own next hit song was 'Just One More Chance', written and published in 1932 with lyrics by Sam Coslow for the movie *College Coach*, starring Dick Powell, Ann Dvorak and Pat O'Brien. By this time Berlin, along with many other writers, had returned to New York in the aftermath of the Depression, but Johnston stayed in Hollywood. He was thus able to continue writing for such films as *College Humour* with Bing Crosby (1933), and contributing the song 'Cocktails for Two' to the film *Murder at the Vanities* (1934), which turned Carl Brisson into a film star, and which also featured Duke Ellington's orchestra. In 1933 he also wrote the songs for *Too Much Harmony* (another picture with Bing Crosby) and *Hello Everybody* starring Kate Smith, who made a big hit of his 'Moon Song'.

In all these films he had continued working with Sam Coslow, but *Murder at the Vanities* introduced him to Johnny Burke, another contributor to the picture, and between them these two wrote all the songs for the huge 1936 hit film *Pennies From Heaven*, with Bing Crosby and Louis Armstrong. In the Bing Crosby/Martha Raye 1937 film *Double or Nothing* the songs were by Johnston and Coslow as well as Johnston and Burke. In 1935 he wrote for another Dick Powell/Ann Dvorak film, *Thanks a Million* (Gus Kahn was the lyricist this time). He visited Britain in 1937 to write the music for the 1938 British picture *Sailing Along*, which starred Jessie Matthews, Roland Young and Jack Whiting. The big song was 'My River', dedicated to the Thames.

He served in the US Army in World War II, writing an army show. *Hut-Two-Three-Four*, and returned to writing for movies in 1947 in *Song of the South*. His last two songs were 'Live and Love Tonight', and 'If I Only Had a Match'.

Sam Coslow, who had such a successful collaboration with Arthur Johnston, was born in New York, 27 December 1902. In addition to his work as author and composer, he also co-founded the publishing firm of Spiers & Coslow, and later became a producer and film writer. As well as collaborating with Johnston, Sam Coslow was responsible for the lyrics of many more hit songs with composers Sammy Fain, Ralph Rainger, Sigmund Romberg, Jimmy Van Heusen, Richard Whiting and others. For two songs in particular, he wrote both words and music: 'You'll Have to Swing It (Mr Paganini)', immortalized by Ella Fitzgerald, and 'I'm in Love With the Honourable So-and-So'.

Some other outstanding Arthur Johnston songs:
'The Day You Came Along' (with Sam Coslow, 1933), 'Learn to Croon' (with Sam Coslow, 1933), 'Moonstruck' (with Sam Coslow, 1933), 'Thanks' (with Sam Coslow, 1933), 'My Old Flame, (with Sam Coslow, 1934), 'Thanks a Million' (with Gus Kahn, 1935), 'One Two, Button Your Shoe' (with Johnny Burke, 1936), 'Down the Old Ox Road' (with Sam Coslow, 1933), 'Let's Call a Heart a Heart' (with Johnny Burke, 1936), 'The Moon Got in My Eyes' (with Johnny Burke, 1937), 'All You Want to Do Is Dance' (with Johnny Burke, 1937), 'It's the Natural Thing to Do' (with Johnny Burke, 1937).

KAHAL, Irving, *see* Fain, Sammy.

KAHN, Gus, *see* Donaldson, Walter.

KENNEDY, Jimmy, *see* Carr, Michael.

KERN, Jerome, composer.

Born New York, 27 January 1885. Died New York, 11 November 1945. Educated at public school, then at Thirteenth Avenue School and Newark High School after the family moved to Newark, New Jersey, in 1897. He learned to play the piano at a very early age, taught by his mother. Later he entered the New York College of Music where his talents could be developed further, and where, in addition to serious work, he wrote songs for college shows. From there he went to London, where he took a modest job with impresario Charles Frohman writing musical inserts for various productions, the most notable being a song called 'Mr Chamberlain'. The significance of this was that the lyric was written by P G Wodehouse, and it started a collaboration which was to last on and off for a number of years. Kern returned to the States in 1904, but this song was to achieve some success for him two years later when it was sung in the London production of *The Beauty of Bath* by the then top-ranking actor Seymour Hicks, the man who had introduced Kern to Wodehouse.

Back in New York, Jerome went to work plugging songs for the publishing house of Shapiro–Remick. At the same time he contributed four songs to the imported English show *Mr Wix of Wickham*, which brought him to the notice of Max Dreyfus, boss of Harms Music. He signed him up both to write and plug songs for his company—an association that lasted until Kern's death. Between 1905 and 1912, Broadway called for almost 100 Kern songs to interpolate into other people's musicals—quite a common practice at the time. But 1912 was a red letter year for the composer because it heralded his first complete Broadway score, the music for *The Red Petticoat*.

Two years previously, on another visit to England, he married Eva Leale. In 1945, when his life story was being filmed under the title *Wait Till the Clouds Roll By*, the film company publicity department described it as '... the mammoth musical of Jerome Kern's dramatic life story'. The composer himself commented, 'Why, I've only had one wife, but the studio feels that I need more than one woman in my past, so they've stuck in as many as they liked'. As Jack Burton in his *Blue Book of Tin Pan Alley* says, '... there was nothing dramatic about the life of Jerome Kern, a small, bespectacled, mild-mannered man, who might have been mistaken for a college professor'.

The music for *The Red Petticoat* produced no gigantic hit for its composer. For his first hit he had to wait until 1914, when he wrote a song that was interpolated into another imported British show, *The Girl From Utah*. The title of the song was 'They Didn't Believe Me' (lyrics by Herbert Reynolds), and that was when the magic of Jerome Kern's music really began. It's worth going back a little to look at what this man did for the world of popular music. In 1910 critic Alan Dale had written: 'Who is this Jerome Kern, whose music towers in an Eiffel way above the average primitive hurdy-gurdy accompaniment of the present day musical comedy?'.

In his book *Great Men of American Popular Music*, David Ewen says, 'Structurally, Jerome Kern's songs—both the early and the later ones—were not far different from the formulas accepted both on Broadway and in Tin Pan Alley during Kern's lifetime. He adhered to the 16-measure verse and the 32-measure chorus. The sentiments of a Kern song are not far different from those of other song hits of those days. And yet there is a difference between Kern and all those who had preceeded him, or who were his contemporaries before 1920, that sets him completely apart from the song business, putting him in a class by himself. 'They Didn't Believe Me' . . . is all the more remarkable when we come to realize how new and revolutionary this song was for its times. A climax is achieved with a magical (and totally unexpected) change of key; a new 4-measure thought is suddenly interpolated into the recapitulation section of the chorus . . . the rhythm is changed from consecutive quarter and half notes to triplets without warning. All of this provided continual interest to an exquisite melody, and it continues to catch and hold the ear to this day when well sung'.

It is clear, therefore, that with the advent of Jerome Kern we also are dealing with a man who was one of the major influences on American popular music of this century. George Gershwin was to write: 'I paid him the tribute of frank imitation, and many things I wrote at this period sounded as though Kern had written them himself'. A 14-year-old Richard Rodgers was so bemused by the music Kern wrote for the 1915 production *Very Good Eddie*, that he spent his pocket money returning to see the show a dozen times. He later said, 'The influence of the hero on such a hero-worshipper is not easy to calculate. A large part of one winter most of my allowance was spent for a seat in the balcony listening to *Love o' Mike*. This was one of Kern's less successful shows, which ran for only 192 performances.

Between 1912 and 1939 Kern wrote either complete scores or contributed the major part of the music for no fewer than 37 Broadway shows, including *Oh, Boy!*, ('Till the Clouds Roll By', 1917), *Sally* ('Look for the Silver Lining', 1920), *Sunny* ('Who?', 1925), *Show Boat* ('Ol' Man River', 1927), *The Cat and the Fiddle* ('She Didn't Say "Yes"', 1931), *Music in the Air* ('I've Told Every Little Star', 1932), *Roberta* ('Smoke Gets in Your Eyes', 1933), *Joy of Living* ('You Couldn't Be Cuter', 1938), and *Very Warm for May* ('All the Things You Are', 1939). In addition, between 1902 and 1930 he had too many songs to mention interpolated into other people's shows.

Like most of the other writers of his time, he had a spell in Hollywood, commencing in 1934. Many of his successes there were, naturally, movies of his Broadway hits, but not all. There was the 1936 Fred Astaire/Ginger Rogers film *Swing Time*, with 'A Fine Romance', 'The Way You Look Tonight' and 'Pick Yourself Up'. In 1937 there was an Irene Dunne/Randolph Scott picture, *High Wide and Handsome*, with 'The Folks Who Live on the Hill'; in 1941 there was *Lady, Be Good*, starring Eleanor Powell and the song 'The Last Time I Saw Paris' (although this song had originally been written with no show or film in mind, a year earlier, when it was first performed by Kate Smith on a radio show). In 1942 Fred Astaire was there again, this time with Rita Hayworth, in the film *You Were Never Lovelier*, and the song 'Dearly Beloved'; and in 1944 there was the Rita Hayworth/Gene Kelly spectacular *Cover Girl*, and the song 'Long Ago and Far Away'.

His last departure from Beverly Hills to New York was in 1945. He was scheduled to co-produce a revival on Broadway of *Show Boat*, and to write the score for a new musical based on the character of Annie Oakley, which turned out in the end to be written by Irving Berlin as *Annie Get Your Gun*. Jerome Kern collapsed in a New York street with a cerebral haemorrhage on 5 November 1945. He was rushed to hospital but died on 11 November with only his lyricist, Oscar Hammerstein 2nd, at his side. Ironically, Irving Berlin, who called that same day to visit the sick man, became the first visitor to learn that Kern was dead. At his funeral Oscar Hammerstein 2nd read the eulogy. In it he said: 'Let us thank whatever God we believe in that we shared some part of the good, bright life Jerry led on this earth'. The *New York Herald Tribune* said simply: 'Genius is surely not too extravagant a word for him. He left us rare treasures'.

Some further details about the man must be added. One concerned *Show Boat*, for which Oscar Hammerstein 2nd wrote both the book and the lyrics. In adapting Edna Ferber's serious novel for this production, something which Kern found particularly appealing, he and Hammerstein must have been among the first, if not indeed the very first, to transform a serious book into a smash hit musical. They certainly preceded the famous Lerner/Loewe classic conversion of Shaw's *Pygmalion* into *My Fair Lady* by almost exactly 30 years. As a man, Jerome Kern had many hobbies and many moods. He collected valuable paintings, books, stamps, and silver among other things (a sale of some of his paintings in 1929 brought him $2 million). Once, when both his cars were in use and no taxi was available, he bought a new car rather than miss a Giants baseball game. To quote David Ewen again: 'On the one hand he was extravagant with his money; on the other hand, particularly in business dealings, he was parsimonious as a fishwife. He was a big man in a great many things, but he was also excessively petty in blowing up a small incident out of all proportion. Yet he enjoyed both perpetrating puns, and telling funny stories (which he did exceedingly well), in short, to laugh and be laughed at'.

Did Oscar Hammerstein 2nd prophetically sum up his character when he wrote in 1939 the lyrics for Jerry Kern's immortal song 'All the Things You Are'?

Kern's other main lyrical collaborators included Dorothy Fields, Johnny Mercer and Yip Harburg. But undoubtedly the longest associations were with P G Wodehouse, Oscar Hammerstein 2nd and Otto Harbach. The Wodehouse alliance was formed in 1904. It comes as a surprise to many people to realize that the novelist who created the immortal characters of Jeeves and Bertie Wooster also wrote a great many good lyrics. He was born in Guildford in 1881, and after that initial co-operation over 'Mr Chamberlain', he did not work with Kern again until 1917, when he wrote the lyrics for the show *Oh, Boy!*. So successful was it that in 1918 there was a follow-up called *Oh, Lady! Lady!*, which was even more successful, and for which a song, 'Bill' was written but dropped before the first night. The song found its rightful place when many years later it became part of the score of *Show Boat*. During the 1930s Wodehouse was mainly concerned with his novels, although he was part author of the book for the 1934 Cole Porter show *Anything Goes*. For most of this period he made his home at Le Touquet in France, where he was interned by the Nazis in World War II. He was released on condition that he broadcast to the English-speaking peoples on German radio, a condition to which he agreed, and for which the British only very belatedly forgave him. After a number of years the stigma began to wear off, Wodehouse himself always maintaining that the broadcasts were done tongue-in-cheek. After the war he lived in America, becoming an American citizen in 1955.

Kern's collaboration with both Otto Harbach and Oscar Hammerstein 2nd stemmed from the fact that they all worked together on the 1925 musical *Sunny*. Hammerstein's contributions to the art of lyric-writing are truly great (see Rogers, Richard). Harbach, whose parents emigrated from Denmark, was born in Salt Lake City in 1873. Originally destined to pursue a career in teaching English and public speaking, he fell in love with Broadway and the musical while on a visit to New York in 1901. This changed his life, and he decided to put his knowledge of the language to use as a lyricist. He had many hard times, working with young composers whose shows flopped, and earning his living meanwhile as an advertising copywriter. In 1907 he had songs in a successful show, although all but one of its hits ('Cuddle Up a Little Closer, Lovey Mine') had been written by another lyricist.

It was not until 1910, when he wrote *Madame Sherry*, with composer Karl Hoschna, that he could really be said to have arrived. Hoschna died the following year, but Harbach was soon lucky enough to become associated with Rudolf Friml. The result was the enormously successful operetta. *The Firefly*, a success which they topped in 1924 with *Rose-Marie*. Before the meeting with Kern, Harbach had already started writing lyrics with the young Oscar Hammerstein 2nd, one of their most successful ventures being in 1923 with *Wildflower* (music by Herbert Stothart and a youthful Vincent Youmans). This was followed by an even more successful collaboration with Sigmund Romberg in 1926 for *The Desert Song*. After his first show with Kern (*Sunny*), Otto Harbach also worked with him on *Criss-Cross* (1926), *Lucky* (libretto only, 1927), *The Cat and the Fiddle* (1931), and *Roberta* (1933). Otto Harbach wrote with many other distinguished composers after that, including George Gershwin. He died in New York, 24 January 1963.

Some other outstanding Jerome Kern songs :
'Ka-lu-a', 'Good Morning, Dearie' (1921), 'Raggedy Ann', 'Stepping Stones' (1923), 'Why Was I Born?', 'Sweet Adeline' (1929), 'Why Do I Love You?', 'Only Make Believe', 'Can't Help Lovin' That Man' (all from *Show Boat*, 1927), 'Lovely to Look At', 'I Won't Dance' (*Roberta* film, 1935), 'Can I Forget You?' (1937), 'You Couldn't Be Cuter' (1938), 'The Last Time I Saw Paris' (1941), 'Dearly Beloved', 'I'm Old-Fashioned' and 'You Were Never Lovelier' (all from *You Were Never Lovelier*, film, 1942), 'Long Ago and Far Away' (*Cover Girl*, film, 1944).

KING, Carole (Carole Klein), composer, author, singer, pianist.

Born Brooklyn, New York, 9 February 1942. Educated at local schools and Queens College, New York. There was no special musical influence in her home, other than that to be born in Brooklyn in the 1940s meant that you grew up in the dying days of the big bands, and on into the era of the ballad singers of the early 1950s, before rock 'n'roll. So it was that later, while still at college, it was the Bill Haley/Elvis Presley/Fats Domino early rock music that made the biggest appeal to young Carole, and before she left she had already begun to try her hand at writing songs loosely in that idiom. It was at college, too, that she first met the man who for more than 10 years was to be her husband and lyricist, Gerry Goffin.

They had written their first hit before they were 20, 'Will You Still Love Me Tomorrow?', which got to No 3 in the UK and to No 1 in the US via the 1961 recording by The Shirelles. They had had a song published earlier, 'Natural Woman' (1960), but they had to wait until 1967 before anything happened to it. In that year it was recorded very successfully by Aretha Franklin. Carole herself had tried recording some of the early songs she and Gerry had written, but they were not successful. She had her first hit as a singer in 1962 with 'It Might As Well Rain Until September', which made No 3 in the UK and No 22 in the US. It was covered by a girl called Little Eva, whose recording in the same year reached No 2 in the UK and No 1 in the US. The irony is that Little Eva had been discovered by the Goffins. She used to work for them in their New York apartment as a baby-sitter, and it was they who arranged for her to make her record. The song remains one of the best of the Carole King/Gerry Goffin songs to this day.

Gerry Goffin was born in Queens, New York, 11 February 1939, so he was only just out of his teens when the early King/Goffin hits were being written, and the first job they had on leaving college was as professional writers for the Al Nevins/Don Kirshner publishing company, Aldon Music. This occupied part of the Brill building in New York, in which were other publishing houses, so that it became to the 1950s and 1960s what the old Tin Pan Alley had been to the 1930s and 1940s. There were writers everywhere, housed in little cubicles with pianos, hopefully churning out hit after hit for what was referred to as the 'hit factory'.

Before the partnership with Goffin, Carole had written one song of which she was both composer and author. At the end of 1959, Neil Sedaka and Howie Greenfield wrote Neil's big hit 'Oh, Carol', which they said was dedicated to Carole King, who had known Sedaka from his college days. Carole in return wrote 'Oh Neil', but it was never a hit.

Carole King and Gerry Goffin must have been among the last of the teams of truly professional songwriters whose work succeeded through the 1960s and into the 1970s, because it was in the 1960s that the trend of the singer-songwriter first started, a trend which was ultimately to take over the business of popular songwriting almost completely. Carole and Gerry were 'pros' as so many generations of songwriters before them had been. They were in the business of writing songs for anybody who would sing them, and they must have been among the last of a fast dying breed. In 1961 Carole partnered Howie Greenfield with a hit and also with her own recording in 1974 of the song 'Jazzman', which she took to No 2 in the US charts.

During the 1970s, having firmly established herself as a recording artist as well as a distinguished songwriter, Carole began more and more to explore the world of albums, and the consequent touring and concerts that followed. The first album, *Carole King—Writer*, was good but not notable, but the second, *Tapestry*, in 1971, was a huge success, and resulted in an equally successful tour with a bill that included singer James Taylor. By 1973 the album had won more than one gold record, and a Grammy Award. Small wonder, therefore, that the following album *Music* won a gold almost as soon as it was on sale, as did *Fantasy* in 1973. Later successful Carole King albums were *Carole King—Simple Things* (1977), and *Carole King—Welcome Home* (1978).

What kind of person is Carole King? 'Her particular gift has always been to write music in which the rhythm and melody are inseparable. In a typical Carole King song the music is always gently carrying the words along, and there's little of the heavy rhythm of the traditional ballad or rock 'n'roll song'. (From *The Story of Pop* edited by Jeremy Pascall). As a teenager herself when she first started writing, it is obvious that she had just the right feel for a song to capture the young audience which was just beginning to take over the music market. Later, when she began writing both words and music, as well as recording and performing her own material, Jon Landau wrote in *Rolling Stone*: 'Carole King is thoroughly involved with her music; she reaches out towards us and gives everything she has'. Again, Jeremy Pascall in *The Story of Pop* says: '... post-teenagers who had come through the roller-coaster of adolescent feelings, faithfully recorded in songs like those Carole King *used* to write, this audience was ready for songs about friendship as well as love, about the intermediate relationships as well as the black and white'. Jon Landau, in *Rolling Stone* again: 'Carole's voice has often been criticised for being too thin. That may be, but ... it is marvellously expressive from first to last'. Robert Hilburn, reviewing a concert in the *Los Angeles Times* in 1971 said: 'She was the same warm, gentle Carole King who made her debut last year at The Troubadour with James

Taylor, and she gave what was, musically, the most significant concert I've been to this summer at the Greek, (theatre) because it reflected most accurately the current mood of contemporary pop music. Miss King came out in a simple red dress, sat down at the piano, looked a little shyly at the full Greek Theater house, and merely said "Hello". It set the mood for the evening'.

Carole King songs have been recorded by almost everybody, from the early days of Gene Pitney and Tony Orlando, through groups such as The Animals, The Byrds and The Rockin' Berries, to Rod Stewart, Johnny Mathis and Andy Williams. In the lyrics she wrote for her song 'You've Got a Friend', Carole King may unwittingly have summed up herself: 'When you're down and troubled/And you need some loving care/And nothing, nothing is going right/Close your eyes and think of me/And soon I will be there/To brighten even your darkest night'.*

Some other oustanding Carole King songs :
'Don't Bring Me Down' (1966), 'Don't Say Nothin' Bad 'Bout My Baby' (1963), 'Every Breath I Take' (1961), 'Goin' Back' (1966), 'Halfway to Paradise' (1961), 'Hung on You' (1965), 'I'd Never Find Another You' (1964), 'Oh, No, Not My Baby' (No 2 in the US in 1964 for Maxine Brown, No 11 in the UK for Manfred Mann in 1965, No 6 in the UK for Rod Stewart in 1973), 'One Fine Day' (1963), 'Show Me Girl' (1964), 'So Far Away' (1971), 'Up on the Roof' (1962), 'Victim of Circumstance' (1963), 'Wasn't Born to Follow' (1968), 'At the Club' (1965), 'Don't Ever Change' (1962), 'Let's Turkey Trot' (1963), 'Sharing You' (1962), 'Sweet Seasons' (1972), 'God Only Knows' (1977).

*© 1971 Screen Gem–EMI Music Inc. (USA). Reproduced by permission of Screen Gems–EMI Music Ltd.

LANE, Burton, composer, author.

Born New York, 2 February 1912. Educated New York High School of Commerce, and Dwight Academy. Started piano lessons at 11, and although showing considerable promise, was made to finish his studies before considering music as a profession. But at 14 he auditioned for impresario J J Shubert, and found himself with a commission to write music for Shubert's *Greenwich Village Follies*.

Unfortunately, because the star fell ill, it never opened. Lane, by then 15, became staff pianist and writer at the Remick publishing company, with whom he remained for 20 years. Perhaps his experience with *Greenwich Village Follies* put him off, because his first published songs did not appear until 1931, when he contributed with other writers to a revue called *Three's a Crowd* in 1930, and to a show called *Earl Carroll's Vanities of 1931*. His first hit did not come until 1933, a song called 'Tony's Wife', with lyrics by Harold Adamson.

Burton Lane is best known for his score for the 1947 Broadway musical, *Finian's Rainbow* (book and lyrics by Fred Saidy and Yip Harburg), which gave us such songs as 'How Are Things in Glocca Morra?', 'When I'm Not Near the Girl I Love', 'Old Devil Moon', and 'If This Isn't Love'. Prior to that he had written for a show called *Laffing Room Only* (1944), which produced the song 'Feudin' and Fightin'', although this did not become a hit until three years later. In 1965 he wrote the title song for the show *On a Clear Day You Can See Forever*, which won him a Grammy Award.

He also contributed songs to movies, notably 'Everything I Have Is Yours' for the 1933 Joan Crawford/Clark Gable musical (in which Fred Astaire made his film debut) *Dancing Lady*; 'The Lady's In Love With You' from the 1939 Bob Hope/Shirley Ross picture *Some Like It Hot*; 'How About You?' for the 1941 Judy Garland/Mickey Rooney film *Babes on Broadway*; and the whole score for the 1951 Fred Astaire/Jane Powell film *Royal Wedding* (re-titled *Wedding Bells* in the UK).

Among his most famous collaborators have been Ralph Freed, Ted Koehler, Al Dubin, Yip Harburg, Alan Jay Lerner, Frank Loesser and Ira Gershwin.

Some other outstanding Burton Lane songs:
'Howd'ja Like to Love Me?' (1938), 'Says My Heart' (1938), 'How Could You Believe Me?' (1951), 'I Hear Music' (1956).

LEE, Bert, *see* Weston, R P (Bob).

LEGRAND, Michel, composer, pianist, conductor.

Born Paris, February 1932. The son of Raymond Legrand, who himself was a well known composer, pianist and conductor. Michel

Legrand entered the Conservatoire Nationale de Musique at the age of 12, where he was a pupil of Nadia Boulanger. With his family background, his musical interests tended to lean more towards the popular than the classical, and he was soon playing jazz in night clubs, writing songs, and orchestrating for French radio. For a time he was also accompanist to such popular singers as Juliette Greco, Lili Jean Marie and the great Maurice Chevalier.

In 1958 he made an album. *I Love Paris*, an arrangement of 16 popular French tunes, which sold well over a million copies and helped establish him as a success. By then he had already become interested in composing film music and worked with many of the top French film directors. Two of these films, in particular helped, him gain an international reputation. *Les Parapluies de Cherbourg* (*The Umbrellas of Cherbourg*), which was really a film-opera because it has no dialogue in it. It included three songs which, with English lyrics by Norman Gimbel, became popular—'I Will Wait for You', 'If It Takes Forever', and 'Watch What Happens'. The other film was *Les Demoiselles de Rochefort* (*The Young Girls of Rochefort*), which produced the song, with English words by Alan and Marilyn Bergman, 'You Must Believe in Spring'. Several years before this, when he was just out of his teens, he had written his very first song–a little thing in waltz time, which a young French singer, Reneé Le Bas, recorded. It was a complete flop and for seven years it was forgotten. Then jazz singer Blossom Dearie took it to America and played it for Johnny Mercer. Johnny loved the melody, wrote an English lyric with the title 'Once Upon a Summertime', and it immediately became a hit with records by Andy Williams, Barbra Streisand and Tony Bennett.

For about six years Michel continued working in Paris and wrote the music to over 50 films until, with this experience behind him, he decided to have a crack at Hollywood. After a couple of mediocre films, he had the opportunity to write the music for *The Thomas Crown Affair*, which starred Steve McQueen and Faye Dunaway. It was in this film that he scored a popular success with 'The Windmills of Your Mind', which won an Academy Award as Best Song of 1968. It was sung in the film by Noel Harrison. This was no doubt a turning point in Legrand's Hollywood experience. He was fortunate enough to arrive at a time when the ranks of the veteran songwriters and film composers were diminishing. He was in at the beginning of a new era, and talented enough to combine the roles of songwriter and composer of original music for the screen. Legrand is one of the most distinguished names in contemporary music.

Some other outstanding Michel Legrand songs:
Several of them have lyrics by Alan and Marilyn Bergman: 'One at a
Time' (from the film *La Piscine*); 'What Are You Doing the Rest of
Your Life?' (from the film *The Happy Ending*, an Oscar nomination
in 1969'; 'Sweet Gingerbread Man' and 'Nobody Knows' (from the
film *The Magic Garden of Stanley Sweetheart*); 'Pieces of Dreams' (from
the film of the same title); 'The Summer Knows' (from *The Summer
of '42*, the Oscar-winning score of 1972); 'There'll Be a Time' (from
the film *Ode to Billy Joe*); 'Happy' (the song version of the love theme
from the dramatic score Michel Legrand wrote for the film biography
of Billie Holliday, (*Lady Sings the Blues*); 'Wonder Where I'll Be
Tomorrow' (the song version of the theme from the film *Sheila Levine
Is Dead and Living in New York*); 'One Day' (from *The Plastic Dome of
Norma Jean*); 'The Years of My Youth' (with words by the British
lyricist Hal Shaper, from the original French song 'Comme Elle Est
Longue a Mourir Ma Jeunesse', and sung by Jack Jones); 'I Will Say
Goodbye'; 'Blue, Green, Gray and Gone'; 'The Saddest Thing of All'
(an adaptation of the original French song 'Toi et Moi C'est Rien
C'est Tout', which, with English words by Carl Sigman, was
introduced by Frank Sinatra.

LEIBER, Jerry (Jerome), composer, author, producer.

Born Baltimore, Maryland, 25 April 1933. **STOLLER, Mike,**
composer, author, producer, born New York, 13 March 1933. Jerry
Leiber's parents emigrated to America from Poland, where his father
had been a teacher of Hebrew. He died when Jerry was five, so his
son hardly knew him. To make ends meet, his mother opened a candy
and grocery store, right on the edge of Baltimore's black area, and in
between getting some kind of education at local schools, Jerry Leiber
helped his mother in the shop from his earliest days, humping
potatoes or delivering goods, mainly to the homes of black customers.
So musically he grew up in an aura of rhythm and blues, churned out
daily on the local R & B radio station, which seemed to be the one
his mother's customers always listened to.

An early ambition was to be a drummer and a tap dancer. When
he was nine he was given piano lessons, but he never got far because
the piano was in his uncle's house, and uncle didn't care for the
youngster's attempts at boogie-woogie. But life took on a new

meaning for him in 1945 when mother sold up and moved with her son to Los Angeles, to an apartment that was not far from the RKO–Paramount studios. This opened a new world for Jerry Leiber. Drumming and tap-dancing were out, and acting was in. He went to school, and studied music and drama, and took a job as a general dogsbody at the Circle Theater. But by the time he was 16 music had taken over again. He worked in a record store, making his first attempts at writing lyrics, since he could write no music. And it was a school friend who eventually introduced him to a struggling piano player called Mike Stoller, and so another great songwriting partnership was born.

Mike Stoller's family background was quite different from that of Jerry's. Born in the Long Island district of New York, his father was a engineer and draughtsman, while his mother had been a model and dancer before her marriage. It was, you could say, a pretty conventional middle class American family. Mike's mother liked going to Broadway shows and would often take her son. There was also an aunt who was a qualified pianist, and who gave the youngster piano lessons. But this did not last. He was only seven when he first heard boogie-woogie, and after struggling to play it (to his teacher's disgust) managed, by the time he was 11, to have lessons from the daddy of them all, James P Johnson. But by the time he was 14 he had lost interest again, and was hanging around the bepop clubs on 52nd Street, trying to catch the great jazzmen of the day such as Thelonius Monk, Charlie Parker and Dizzy Gillespie.

In 1949 the family moved to Los Angeles. Young Mike took up the study of music again, more seriously this time, even learning the rudiments of composition and arranging. This did not stop him playing in local bands to earn a few dollars and when he got the chance, jamming with any jazz musicians who happened to be around. Then came the meeting with Jerry Leiber. Mike tried to put him off. To the classical/jazz musician, songs were junk, full of 'Moon and June'. But when Jerry produced a few sketchy lyrics obviously written in the blues idiom, his attitude changed. To quote Robert Palmer in *Baby That Was Rock 'n'Roll*, 'Mike said "I didn't know you were talking about the blues". He began flipping through the exercise book, playing chords here, boogie-woogie figures there. "Yeah" he said finally. "Okay, let's write some songs"'.

So, at 17 years old, the two boys, so different in background, education and personality, started on the long haul to fame as songwriters. The year was 1950. In 1952 they produced their first successful song, 'Kansas City', a regional hit by Little Willie Longjohn, which was later accepted as a blues standard and performed by many well known artists. A year later they wrote their first hit, 'Hound Dog', for Willie Mae 'Big Mama' Thornton. They didn't know at the time that it *was* to be their first big hit. They only found out three years later, in 1956, when an unknown singer called Elvis Presley recorded it at the Sun Studio in Memphis and took it to No 2 in both the US and the UK charts.

At first the partnership depended very much on Jerry Leiber for writing the words and Mike Stoller for the music. To a large extent it remained this way as their careers progressed, although the two functions overlapped at certain points. As individuals, they were total opposites. Jerry, a ball of energy and restlessness, spewed out ideas incessantly. Mike, a laid-back, relaxed character, had the typical approach of the cool jazzman. Of their composing sessions, Leiber says, 'Often we would just sit down with nothing to go on. He'd start playing, and I'd start shouting'. Stoller says, 'There was some kind of a balance in our metabolisms. Jerry's energy motivated me. I could be sprawling on a couch, and he would suddenly shout out some words to me and I'd respond' (from *Baby That Was Rock 'n' Roll*).

The other important factor in their early success was their total involvement with the blues and black music. This stemmed from Jerry Leiber's background, but he had no difficulty in involving Mike Stoller because of the latter's devotion to jazz. 'We found ourselves writing for black artists', Leiber says, 'because these were the voices and rhythms we loved. By the fall of 1950, when both Mike and I were in City College, we had black girlfriends, and were into a black life style' (from *Baby That Was Rock 'n' Roll*).

Their first published song was 'That's What the Good Book Says', on a 1951 recording by a group called The Robins. It came about through a chance meeting in the record shop where Jerry Leiber worked with a man from a local independent record company, Modern Records. The man's name was Lester Sill, who many years later was to become head of EMI Screen Gems Publishing in America. True to form, the orthodox channels of music publishing did not want to know about two white kids who wanted to write black music.

Another first came for Leiber and Stoller when they became, quite by chance, the first independent record producers in the history of rock. It was on the Willie Mae Thornton session of 'Hound Dog'. The producer was drummer Johnny Otis of The Johnny Otis Road

Show. The session was going so badly that he left the control room to play drums, leaving Leiber and Stoller in charge of production. By 1953, together with Lester Sill, they started their own company, Spark Records, and it was not long before the new company had its first Leiber/Stoller hit, 'Riot in Cell Block No 9', recorded by The Robins. In 1956, after approaches from Atlantic Records, they decided to set themselves up as independent producers, their first deal to be with Atlantic. Success was not slow to come once the group, The Coasters, had been formed, and they had a No 5 in the US charts in 1957 with 'Searchin''. Six years later the British group, The Hollies, revived the song and took it to No 12 in the UK charts. And other and bigger Coasters hits were to follow. 'Yakety Yak' (1958, No 1 in the US), 'Along Came Jones' (1959), and 'Charley Brown' (1959). Throughout the late 1950s and early 1960s Leiber and Stoller songs and Leiber and Stoller-produced records were seldom out of the international top ten. Their biggest hit song of all was the 1960 'Spanish Harlem' (1960), which Ben E King originally took to No 10 in the US charts, but which has since been recorded by more than 130 artists, ranging from Long John Baldry and Andy Williams to the James Last Orchestra and Sonny and Cher. In 1971 Aretha Franklin's record went to No 14 in the UK and No 2 in the US.

All this leaves out 'The Presley Connection'. Following the success of Presley's version of 'Hound Dog', the Presley management constantly called for more songs by Leiber and Stoller. This led to the title songs from the Presley films *Loving You* in 1957, *King Creole* in 1959 and *Jailhouse Rock* (1957). The writers were very impressed with Elvis. They liked working with him for his perfectionism and professionalism. But they were less than pleased with the restrictions automatically imposed on any writers by the processes involved in film-making. The disciplines of having to write a particular type of song to fit a particularly type of scene and to last exactly so many minutes and seconds were not for these young freewheelers. But they did it, and did it successfully.

This same period also saw them involved in both writing for and producing records with The Drifters. There was 'There Goes My Baby' (1959), which they wrote, and 'Save the Last Dance for Me' (1960). This was written by Doc Pomus and Mort Schuman, and is an early example of producers Leiber and Stoller being quite happy to record other people's songs. Throughout the 1960s and the 1970s, Leiber and Stoller began to devote more and more of their time to record production and less and less to songwriting. In 1964 they had another go at running a record label. This was called Red Bird Records, but it really did seem as if the business side of running a company was not for them, and they sold out their interest in 1966. Curiously, 1966 was the year when they wrote one of the greatest of all their songs (some even say there was an unconscious element of autobiography in it), although it was never one of their biggest hits. The title was 'Is That All There Is?', and there is no doubt that Peggy Lee's 1969 recording of it has passed into the archives of all-time great performances of all-time great songs. The lyrical content approaches the genius of a Lorenz Hart or a Cole Porter of a previous generation.

If having one's songs recorded by the widest possible range of artists is a sign of greatness, then Leiber and Stoller are up there with the big names. Apart from the obvious pop stars the groups of the 1950s and 1960s already referred to, their songs have also been performed by Edith Piaf and Vaughn Monroe (they each recorded 'Motorcycle Boots'); by Werner Muller, Ronnie Aldrich and Frank Chacksfield, among the orchestra leaders; and by Perry Como, Johnny Mathis and Cliff Richard among the standard singers. In 1975 they produced Peggy Lee's album *Mirrors*, for which they wrote all but two of the songs. And in 1976 they produced an album by Elkie Brooks, which, in addition to old Leiber/Stoller hits, also contained three new songs.

Some other outstanding Leiber/Stoller songs:
'Bossa Nova Baby' (1959), 'Down Home Girl' (1965), 'Framed' (1954), 'I Who Have Nothing' (Jerry Leiber wrote the English lyrics for this continental composition by Mogol and Donida, 1963), 'I'm a Hog for You' (1959), 'I'm a Woman' (a hit for Peggy Lee, 1963), 'Little Egypt' (1961), 'Love Me' (1954), 'My Claire de Lune' (1961), 'On Broadway' (1963), 'Poison Ivy' (1959), 'Ruby Baby' (1956), 'Saved' (1961), 'Searchin'' (1957), 'Treat Me Nice' (1957), 'Trouble' (1958), 'Young Blood' (a hit for The Coasters, 1957), 'Professor Hauptmann's Performing Dogs' (1968), 'On the Road Again' (1974), 'The Case of Mary Jane' (1975), 'Pearl's a Singer' (1974), 'Night Bird' (1977).

LENNON, John Winston, composer, author, singer, guitarist, bandleader. Born Liverpool, England, 9 October 1940. Murdered outside his New York apartment 8 December 1980.

McCARTNEY, James Paul, composer, author, singer, guitarist, producer, bandleader. Born Liverpool, England, 18 June 1942.

As two of the 'fab four'–The Beatles–it is difficult at least prior to their break-up, to separate the careers of Lennon and McCartney, songwriters, from the story of that historic group. But the Beatles story has been more than adequately set out by others, and as this book ia about songwriters, we must concentrate on that side of Lennon and McCartney.

John's father, Fred Lennon, worked on the transatlantic liners that sailed between Liverpool and New York, and other ports on America's eastern seaboard. Thus he often brought home from his travels records of American popular music that were unobtainable in England. He taught John's mother, Julia, to play the banjo, and although mother and father separated when John was quite young, some of the music he heard must have remained with him through the years that followed, while he was being brought up by his aunt Mimi. He went to Quarry Bank School in a Liverpool suburb, and hated it, spending a lot of time fighting. He enjoyed reading, and quite early on began writing stories of his own. Things picked up for him a bit when his mother Julia, who he still saw a lot, gave him £10 to buy an old guitar which he taught himself to play, not very well, and with other school friends formed a skiffle group called The Quarrymen. After leaving school he also had a spell at Liverpool College of Art, but as with the rest of his education, this was unsuccessful. He was not allowed to concentrate on cartoons, a medium for which he showed some talent. All in all, the picture of the tough, rebellious Liverpool school kid from the broken home is inescapable, and with the advent on the teenage music scene of Bill Haley, Lonnie Donegan, and then Elvis Presley, the seeds were sown almost inevitably for the development of John Lennon, rock musician and composer.

Paul McCartney's early years were completely different. By the social standards of the day, the McCartneys were definitely a rung or two up the social ladder from the Lennons. Paul was educated at local schools and then at Liverpool Institute, one of the best schools in town. His behaviour was the complete antithesis of Lennon's. Paul was always studious, hardworking and diplomatic. He would be more likely to talk himself out of trouble than to bash his opponent over the head. During the 1920s his father, Jim McCartney, played trumpet in a ragtime band that became known as Jim Mac's Band. There was always a piano in the McCartney home, and again there was always the popular music of the day around on which the young Paul could, and did, cut his teeth.

When he was 14, two significant things happened. His mother Mary died suddenly of cancer. Apart from the family trauma, this left serious financial problems, because his mother, who was a nurse, by 1954 was earning more than her husband. The second thing was that Paul developed an obsession to own a guitar, and finally managed to buy one for £15. As with John Lennon, the influences were skiffle, Bill Haley and Elvis Presley. By then he had discovered that he could do impressions of some of his favourites—Little Richard was his best. Then one day in 1956 Paul's school friend, Ivan Vaughan, who was also a friend of John Lennon's, took Paul to a local fête to hear John and The Quarrymen play. This led to Paul's joining The Quarrymen, and to his first stumbling attempts to write songs with John. Beatlewise, the rest is history.

In September 1962, the first published Lennon/McCartney song was also The Beatles' first recording for producer George Martin, of EMI's Parlophone label. It was 'Love Me Do' and it made it to No 17 in the UK charts. This was enough to convince George Martin that he had discovered a group with hit potential, although he was not too keen on their songwriting ability. For their second session he attempted to persuade them to record a song called 'How Do You Do It?', by another then unknown composer, Mitch Murray. The Beatles, with all the arrogance that was to become characteristic of them, refused. George Martin gave the song to another new group, Gerry and The Pacemakers', who took it to No 1 in the UK charts, and to No 9 in the US. But later in the year perhaps the Beatles had the last laugh when George Martin accepted a Lennon/McCartney composition for their second recording session, 'Please Please Me'. This not only put the group and the writers on the map by going to No 2 in the UK and later to No 4 in the US, it also brought to the fore a young and virtually unknown music publisher called Dick James because it was his struggling young company that had the good fortune to obtain the rights.

It is interesting to recall that there is in existence a single copy of a private recording of an unpublished song by McCartney and George Harrison called 'In Spite of All the Danger'. This was made in a small studio in Liverpool in 1958, not long after Harrison joined The Quarrymen, and before they became the Beatles. In 1981, Sotheby's said that at auction the owner of the recording could expect to get a five-figure sum for it if he decided to sell. That owner is Duff Lowe, now a successful stockbroker, but then the pianist with the group.

With the career of The Beatles well and truly launched by 'Please Please Me', the successful songwriting partnership of Lennon and McCartney also never looked back, and a list of their biggest successes is given below. It is frequently difficult, if not impossible, to decide precisely who wrote how much music, and who supplied how many words. Or indeed, even who supplied an initial idea, and who developed it. Throughout the official reign of the Beatles (1962–71), almost every composition was credited jointly. But John and Paul had begun to go their separate ways immediately following their respective marriages. John Lennon married Yoko Ono on 20 March 1969, following his divorce from his first wife Cynthia Pavell by whom he had a son, Julian. Yoko had been born in Japan in 1933, and had two children from a previous marriage. Paul McCartney married Linda Eastman on 12 March 1969. Linda had also been married previously. *McCartney*, Paul's first solo album, was released in 1970, while John Lennon and Yoko Ono had an album they made together issued two years before that, in 1968. From then on their compositions differed as much as did their lives.

Prior to The Beatles's break-up, it is possible to make an educated guess at which of the pair might have been the driving force behind some of the songs. After the initial joint work on the early rock 'n'roll songs, (up to 1964–65), it soon became clear that a song such as 'All You Need Is Love' (1967) was probably mostly Lennon, while there was little doubt that the beautiful straight ballads 'Michelle' (1966) and 'Yesterday' (1965) were almost pure McCartney. Similarly, from 1967, 'Strawberry Fields' was almost certainly by Lennon, and 'Penny Lane' by McCartney. But this does not mean that even in the mid-1960s they had stopped working in close collaboration, and 'Eleanor Rigby', from 1966, was very much a joint effort. It is likely, however, that as McCartney was the balladeer, the McCartney-inspired songs will be the ones to become standards—indeed, 'Michelle' and 'Yesterday' already are.

Two songs which never became hits also fall into that category: 'The Long and Winding Road' and 'Fool on the Hill', the latter perhaps being one of the most moving and beautiful popular songs of the last 20 years. Paul, in addition to his known abilities, has also written the soundtrack music for the movie *The Family Way* (1966), and the theme song for the film *Live and Let Die* (1973, which was nominated for an Academy Award). Both he and John have appeared in the various Beatles films featuring the group's music.

It is also often overlooked that the pair have written numerous songs which they have not recorded themselves, but which have been hits for other artists. For instance, 'Bad to Me' reached No 1 in the UK charts when recorded by Billy J Kramer; 'Goodbye' (not to be confused with 'Hello, Goodbye') got to No 2 in the UK and No 3 in the US via the Mary Hopkin record; Peter and Gordon took 'World Without Love' to No 1 in both UK and the US charts in 1964; in 1968 Cilla Black reached No 8 in the UK with 'Step Inside Love', and in the same year Marmalade took 'Ob-la-di-ob-la-da' to No 1 in the UK. This does not include the hits that Lennon and McCartney songs have made for other artists *after* being recorded by the Beatles, the most notable, perhaps, being Elton John's No 1 in the US charts in 1974 with his revived version of 'Lucy in the Sky With Diamonds'.

What of the two composers in their individual roles after the break-up of the partnership? There can be no doubt that as a composer of popular songs, John Lennon has fared considerably less well than Paul McCartney. The early days of his association with Yoko Ono and The Plastic Ono Band produced a minor hit in 1969 with 'Cold Turkey', and they had a No 2 in the UK in the same year with 'Give Peace a Chance'. In 1971 they reached No 7 in the UK and No 11 in the US with 'Power to the People'. In 1971 John and Yoko went to live in New York, but for most of that year and almost the whole of 1972 they produced little musically. All their efforts were concentrated on fighting a US Government deportation order, because four years earlier they had been convicted in England of possessing marijuana. Once that was settled, in 1975, they began spasmodically devoting time to writing and recording again, with Yoko not only performing on sessions but also contributing to songs with John, and writing others of her own.

But the output was strictly limited, and few individual hit songs of lasting worth emerged. The album *Imagine* had won them a gold disc in 1971, and *Some Time in New York City* got into the US charts in 1972. 'Happy Christmas, War Is Over' reached No 4 in the UK in the same year. 'Mind Games' was both an album and a single in 1973, and then nothing until the fabulously successful *Double Fantasy* album, which came out shortly before John's death in 1980.

In 1975, Yoko gave birth to a son, Sean. John described himself at the time as 'Higher than the Empire State building'. When questioned later about his lack of composing and recording activity, he appeared at peace with life, and would only say, 'I'm busy raising a family and baking bread'. He also began to take an interest, almost for the first time, in his money, investing in everything from apartment blocks to herds of cattle. However, a recent American magazine article (1981) claimed this was just an excuse, and that he had an increasing mental musical block between 1975 and 1979, when he was virtually unable to produce any work at all. The article alleged that he would disappear for days at a time, eventually having to be retrieved by Yoko from some sleazy club. Paul McCartney tried to help, but was snubbed by Lennon with the words: 'If you want to see me, make an appointment'.

Perhaps, unknowingly, John Lennon wrote his own epitaph, not long before he died. In an interview to promote the *Double Fantasy* album, he said, 'It's for the people who grew up with me. I'm saying ... did you get through it all?' In that same interview he clearly felt that he, at any rate, had got through it all, and that he was proud and grateful. He also said, 'If Yoko died, I wouldn't know how to survive'.

After the Beatles' break-up, and Paul McCartney's marriage to Linda Eastman, his life took a completely different turn from John Lennon's. At the beginning of that period the McCartneys lived in a large house in London's Hampstead, but it was not long before they moved to a farm near the Mull of Kintyre, in Scotland. This inevitably gave rise to stories that Paul had withdrawn from the world. Nothing could have been further from the truth. Before they moved from London, his first album, *McCartney*, hit the No 1 spot in the US album charts, and No 2 in the UK. The second, *Ram*, by Paul and Linda, reached No 2 in the US, and No 1 in the UK. Neither produced any memorable songs, although one track, issued as a single, 'Uncle Albert—Admiral Halsey' earned a gold disc in the States.

In 1971 Paul decided he must form a band of his own. Wings was the result, and among its members was Linda, who played electric piano and melotron, and sang with the group, as well as developing into a co-writer of songs with her husband. The first Wings album, *Wings Wild Life* reached No 10 in the US charts and No 8 in the UK by 1972, and it contained seven McCartney songs, although again there were no particularly memorable ones. There were also several singles released in 1972, with only moderate success, the exception being 'My Love', which reached No 1 in the US. A good deal of time was spent during that year working on a TV special, *James Paul McCartney*, for America's ABC Network. It was subsequently also shown in the UK.

In 1973 the album *Red Rose Speedway* did well both at home and abroad, with a gold record also coming for the theme from the James Bond film *Live and Let Die*.

In the same year their next album, *Band on the Run*, reached No 1 in the US, as well as in the UK, but again, as with previous releases, there were not really any memorable songs. The same could be said of *Venus and Mars*, which achieved similar success in both countries. In 1975, 'Listen to What the Man Said' hit No 6 in the UK charts, while the following year both 'Silly Love Songs' (which was an album as well as a single), and 'Let Them In' reached No 2. In 1977, Paul surprisingly released a track from his old *McCartney* album, 'Maybe I'm Amazed', but it did not achieve very much recognition. Later in 1977, he had his biggest hit ever with Wings, 'Mull of Kintyre', which reached the No 1 spot in both the US and UK charts. He spent most of 1978 working on the TV film, *Wings Over America*, which also produced a successful single, 'With a Little Luck', while in 1980 Paul's song 'Girl Friend' became a hit record for Michael Jackson.

There can be no more Lennon. But there can be much more to come from McCartney. As an epilogue to The Beatles period, it is fitting to record that they won six Ivor Novello Awards: 'She Loves You' (1963), 'Can't Buy Me Love' (1964), 'We Can Work It Out' (1965), 'Yesterday' (1965), 'Michelle' (1966) and 'Yellow Submarine' (1966).

Some other outstanding Lennon/McCartney songs:
'All My Loving' (1963), 'Bad to Me' (1963), 'Can't Buy Me Love' (1964), 'Day Tripper' (1965), 'Do You Want to Know a Secret' (1963), 'From Me to You' (1963), 'Get Back' (1969), 'Glass Onion' (1968), 'Goodbye' (1960), 'A Hard Day's Night' (1964), 'Hello, Goodbye' (1967), 'Help' (1965), 'Hey Jude' (1968), 'I Am the Walrus' (1967), 'I Feel Fine' (1964), 'I'll Keep You Satisfied' (1963), 'I Wanna Be Your Man' (1963), 'I Want to Hold Your Hand' (1963), 'Lady Madonna' (1968), 'Love Me Do' (1962), 'Maxwell's Silver Hammer' (1969), 'The Night Before' (1964), 'Nobody I Know' (1964), 'Norwegian Wood' (1965), 'Nowhere Man' (1966), 'Paperback Writer' (1966), 'Revolution' (1968), 'Sergeant Pepper's Lonely Hearts

Club Band' (1967), 'She Loves You' (1963), 'She's Leaving Home' (1966), 'Things We Said Today' (1964), 'Ticket to Ride' (1965), 'We Can Work It Out' (1965), 'When I'm 64' (1967), 'With a Little Help From My Friends' (1967), 'World Without Love' (1964), 'Yellow Submarine' (1966), 'You Can't Do That' (1964), 'Your Mother Should Know' (1967).

LERNER, Alan Jay, *see* Loewe, Frederick.

LESLIE, Edgar, *see* Burke, Joe; Nicholls, Horatio.

LIGHTFOOT, Gordon, composer, author, guitarist, pianist, singer.

Born Orillia, Ontario, Canada, 17 November 1938. He finds his place here because although as a singer/songwriter he grew out of the folk boom of the 1960s, and although his compositions maintain the folk tradition, he has acquired a cult following among a wide variety of artists who have recorded his songs. His output has been small, and in terms of sales figures his hits have been few. But there must be many hundreds of recordings of his best songs. His work is very musical, probably because he studied orchestration after leaving school, first earning a living arranging for vocal groups and writing commercial jingles.

He has never lost the folk influences that marked his early career, although from time to time his songs have veered through country-folk to folk-rock, and have included straight ballads. His earliest song success was in the mid-60s, when Canadian folk artists Ian and Sylvia recorded his 'Early Morning Rain', backed with 'For Lovin' Me'. Not long after that he had a hit on his own in Canada with 'Remember Me', which he followed up during the rest of the decade with 'Spin Spin', 'Go Go Round', 'The Way I Feel', and 'Black Day in July'. After these initial single successes Gordon Lightfoot became almost exclusively an album artist, and remains so to this day.

Subsequent album hits on his own have been *Sundown* (1974), and *Daylight and Katy*, but the mark of his ability is the number of widely differing artists who have recorded his material. These include George Hamilton IV, Lynn Anderson, Anne Murray, Val Doonican, Bob Dylan, Elvis Presley, Peter, Paul and Mary, Judy Collins, Johnny Cash, Lou Rawls, Andy Williams, Barbra Streisand, Ray Conniff,

Glen Campbell, Johnny Mathis, Jack Jones, Roger Whittaker, Liza Minnelli, Buddy Greco and many many more.

His best known and most recorded song is 'If You Could Read My Mind' (also the title track from another of his own hit albums), but other much recorded titles are: 'Cotton Jenny', 'The Last Time I Saw Her Face', 'Miguel', 'Talking in Your Sleep', '10 Degrees and Getting Colder' and 'Summer Side of Life'.

LIVINGSTON, Jay Harold, composer, author, pianist, publisher.

Born McDonald, Philadelphia, 28 March 1915. Started out as a pianist, after organizing a dance band at college. Turned his hand to writing vocal arrangements for radio work, and such things as special material for Olsen and Johnson. He cannot be taken in isolation from his writing and publishing partner, Ray Evans.

EVANS, Ray, composer, author, publisher.

Born Salamanca, New York, 4 February 1915. Ray Evans also started out as a musician but soon teamed up as a songwriter with Jay Livingston.

From 1945 to 1955 they were both in Hollywood under contract to Paramount, and although they wrote complete scores for several musical films, no great hits resulted. They fared better with their single contributions to films, and had hits with 'A Square in the Social Circle' from the 1945 Betty Hutton/Barry Fitzgerald movie *The Stork Club*; the title song for *Golden Earrings*, with Lana Turner and Van Heflin in 1947; 'Buttons and Bows' from the 1948 Bob Hope/Jane Russell film *The Paleface*; 'Silver Bells' from the 1951 Bob Hope/Marilyn Maxwell movie *The Lemon Drop Kid*; 'Home Cookin'' from the 1950 Bob Hope/Lucille Ball film *Fancy Pants*; 'Mona Lisa' from the 1950 film *Captain Carey, U.S.A.*, which later became a huge hit for Nat King Cole; 'Tammy' from the 1957 picture *Tammy and the Bachelor*, starring Debbie Reynolds; and undoubtedly their biggest movie hit of all, 'Que Será Será', for Doris Day in the 1956 picture *The Man Who Knew Too Much*.

The song that started it all was 'To Each His Own' (1946), and it is worth noting that they soon turned their attention very successfully to TV, writing numerous title themes including 'Bonanza' and 'Mr Lucky'. In the 1960s they wrote for two Broadway musicals which, although successful, did not produce any hits. They have also been prolific winners of Oscars, winning more than anyone else for their movie song contributions up to 1960. Ray Evans and Jay Livingston are a genuine songwriting team, and it is impossible to distinguish between them as co-composer and co-author. This is even true when they have been writing with such distinguished names as Victor Young and Henry Mancini. They have also contributed much special material to the repertoires of artists such as Betty Hutton, Cyd Charisse, Mitzi Gaynor, and others. Their best known songs have already been referred to in the text, so we have not included a list of their lesser known works.

LIVINGSTON, Jerry (born Levinson), composer, author, pianist, conductor.

Born Denver, Colorado, 25 March 1909. Educated at the University of Arizona, where he led his own band and started writing music. Made a precarious living playing piano in various local bands after leaving college, but kept trying to break into Tin Pan Alley with his songs. Finally had success in selling his song 'Darkness on the Delta' to a publisher. Mildred Bailey liked the song, recorded it, and gave Livingston his first hit.

His main collaborators in the early days were Marty Symes and Al Neiberg. Later he worked with Mack David, Paul Francis Webster, Mitchell Parish and Bob Merrill, among others. He contributed some fairly unremarkable songs to the 1934 Broadway musical *Bright Lights of 1934*, and after writing many hit songs during the 1930s and 1940s, went to Hollywood in 1949. There he co-wrote the score for Walt Disney's *Cinderella* with Al Hoffman (hit song 'Bibbidi-Bobbidi-Boo'), and several other films, before turning his attention to TV. Prominent in this field were *The Shirley Temple Storybook, Jack and the Beanstalk, Lawman, 77 Sunset Strip, Bugs Bunny, Cheyenne, The Roaring Twenties,* and *Bozo the Clown*. He has also written the music for a religious play called *Hail Mary*.

Some other Jerry Livingston songs:
'Under a Blanket of Blue' (1933), 'I've Got an Invitation to a Dance' (1933), 'Just a Kid Named Joe' (1939), 'Story of a Starry Night'

(1942), 'Mairzy Doats' (1944), 'It's the Talk of the Town' (1933), 'Chi-Baba Chi-Baba' (1947), 'Blue and Sentimental' (1938), 'The 12th of Never' (1964).

LOESSER, Frank, composer, author, publisher, producer.

Born New York, 29 June 1910. Educated Townsend Harris Hall, and the College of the City of New York. Died New York, 28 March 1969. His father, who had emigrated from Germany, was a piano teacher. From the earliest age he showed an interest in music, but to his father's disgust it was always popular music, and although obliged by his family and his teachers to work hard during his school years, he was never really interested. This same disinterest manifested itself in the variety of dead-end jobs he succeeded in obtaining after leaving college. It was clear that his only real concern was songwriting, although through all those early years, in his attempts to get his material published it was always lyrics he submitted to publishers, never music.

Finally the house of Leo Feist hired him for $40 per week to write lyrics for one of their composer's melodies, but at the end of a year they fired him because not one of the songs was ever published. Soon afterwards Feist was nevertheless the first to publish a song with a Loesser lyric, 'In Love With the Memory of You' (1931). But in spite of music by William Schuman, later to become one of America's distinguished serious composers, nothing happened. Failure after failure followed during the next three years. The only song that had any success at all was 'I Wish I Were Twins', in 1934. With music by Eddie de Lange, it was featured by the great artist Valaida in one of Lew Leslie's *Blackbirds* series of revues. During those years Frank Loesser earned a meagre living from playing piano and singing in a New York night club. It was there he met and married Lynn Garland, a popular radio singer of the day.

They were married in Hollywood in 1936, where Loesser had gone to write songs for Universal Pictures. He had equally little success with them, and transferred to Paramount, where at last he had his first hit with 'Moon of Manakoora' (music by Alfred Newman), which was featured by Dorothy Lamour in the 1937 film *The Hurricane*. From then on, although still only as a lyric writer, he had hits with such songs as 'Small Fry' and 'Two Sleepy People' (music for both by Hoagy Carmichael), 'The Boys in the Back Room' (music by Frederick Hollander, made into a hit by Marlene Dietrich), 'I Don't Want to Walk Without You Baby' (music by Jule Styne), and many others with such composers as Jimmy McHugh, Victor Young, Manning Sherwin and Arthur Schwarz.

It was not until the advent of World War II, and the disaster of Pearl Harbor in particular, that Frank Loesser, top-class lyricist, blossomed into Frank Loesser, top-class composer as well. The song that did it was 'Praise the Lord and Pass the Ammunition', in 1942. It seems that Loesser's method of demonstrating his lyrics had been, for a long time, to write what he called a 'dummy' tune for them, which would immediately be discarded when the lyrics were handed over to a professional composer. With 'Praise the Lord and Pass the Ammunition', the dummy tune itself was accepted, and from then on there was no turning back for the man who was once called by Billy Rose 'the greatest natural songwriter since Irving Berlin'. The Kay Kayser record of 'Praise the Lord', became a million-seller. Throughout the war years Loesser continued to write war songs, dedicated variously to the WAC, the Army Air Force, and the infantry, but because these songs were all specifically dedicated to the US forces, it is hardly surprising that they were virtually unknown outside America and American war bases. This applied to perhaps the most famous of them all, 'Roger Young', which was recorded by many artists, including Nelson Eddy and Burl Ives.

The end of the war saw Loesser back in Hollywood, where he had success with the song 'Tallahassee', featured in the 1947 film *Variety Girl*, and in particular with the song 'Baby, It's Cold Outside', featured in the 1949 Red Skelton film *Neptune's Daughter*. This song was originally written for Frank's own amusement, to be performed at Hollywood parties, yet it was his only song to win him an Oscar. It was made internationally famous on record by numerous artists, but the Ella Fitzgerald/Louis Jordan version was perhaps the definitive one.

In 1948 Frank Loesser at last achieved a Broadway success with his score for the musical *Where's Charley?*, an adaptation of the English comedy classic *Charley's Aunt*, dating from 1892. Ray Bolger starred in the New York production, which ran for 792 performances, yet it contained only two memorable songs, 'Once in Love With Amy', and 'My Darling, My Darling'. Coinciding with this success, however, Frank had a simultaneous hit with a straight Tin Pan Alley contribution, 'On a Slow Boat to China', another song helped on its way by a Kay Kayser recording.

But 1950 was the year when the composer had his real blockbuster. This was the adaptation for Broadway of a series of stories by Damon Runyon for which Loesser wrote both music and lyrics. It was, of course, *Guys and Dolls*, starring Vivian Blane, Robert Alda, Sam Levine, Isabel Bigley and Pat Rooney. Not only did it run for more than 1,000 performances, but the 1955 film starring Frank Sinatra, Marlon Brando and Jean Simmons heaped yet more success on the composer. *Guys and Dolls* contained no fewer than five major hits in its score, and full details are listed below.

After the Broadway production, Loesser undertook a new Hollywood assignment—to write the score for the 1952 Danny Kaye picture *Hans Christian Andersen*, another enormously successful movie, also littered with hit songs. This was not the first time Danny Kaye had used Loesser songs to his own advantage. He did very well in 1947 with the comedy number 'Bloop Bleep'. The next Loesser stage musical was *The Most Happy Fella* (1956), an adaptation of Sidney Howard's play *They Knew What They Wanted*. Frank recalls not liking the idea of converting this Pulitzer Prizewinner into a show. 'I thought it was a tragedy about a lot of sad people having a terrible time of things. It was about as musical as a land mine', is how David Ewen quotes him in *Great Men of American Popular Song*. But after much deliberation and reading and re-reading the play, he said, 'Take out all the political talk, the labor talk, the religious talk. Get rid of all that stuff, and you've got a good love story'. The result opened in 1956, ran for two years on Broadway, produced such hits as 'Standing on the Corner' and 'Big D', and gained a new wife for the composer. She was Jo Sullivan, one of the stars of the show, and they were married in 1959.

Another Loesser musical, *Greenwillow*, was staged in 1960. Widely acclaimed by critics, it was perhaps too serious for the public, and it did not have a hit song in it, a combination which doomed it to failure. Such was not the case with *How to Succeed in Business Without Really Trying*, the next Loesser show, which opened in New York in 1961. Among the cast were Robert Morse and Rudy Vallee. It ran for over 1,400 performances, and its biggest hit was the song 'Brotherhood of Man'. It also won the Pulitzer Prize for Drama, an unusual event for a stage musical. In addition to everything else, Loesser had by then been running for some time his own publishing company, Frank Music. He was a man who could never sit still, could never be idle. A holiday for him, he once said, was three days in Las Vegas. He insisted on becoming totally involved in everything he did, but a 16-hour working day, during which he might get through four packets of cigarettes, finally proved too much. He died of cancer in New York at the age of 59.

The work of Frank Loesser's early lyric-writing days will be found under such composers as Burton Lane, Hoagy Carmichael, Jimmy McHugh, Jule Styne and Arthur Schwartz.

Some other outstanding Frank Loesser songs :
'Spring Will Be a Little Late This Year' (*Christmas Holiday*, 1944); 'A Bushel and a Peck', 'If I Were a Bell', 'I've Never Been in Love Before', 'Take Back Your Mink', 'Luck Be a Lady', 'Sit Down, You're Rockin' the Boat' (all from *Guys and Dolls*, 1950); 'The Inch Worm', 'The King's New Clothes', 'Thumbelina', 'The Ugly Duckling', 'Wonderful Copenhagen', 'No Two People' (all from *Hans Christian Andersen*, 1952); 'Poppa, Don't Preach to Me', 'The Sewing Machine' (both from *The Perils of Pauline*, 1947); 'Warm All Over', 'Joey, Joey, Joey', 'The Most Happy Fella' (all from *The Most Happy Fella*, 1956).

LOEWE, Frederick, composer, pianist.

Born Berlin, 10 June 1904. Emigrated to America 1924. His parents were Austrian, and he originally set out to become a concert pianist. It seems incredible that we shall have so little to relate about the composer who, with lyricist and author Alan Jay Lerner, wrote what is perhaps still in many ways the most successful musical of all time, *My Fair Lady* (2,717 performances on Broadway alone), which was only bettered in the 1960s by *Fiddler on the Roof* and *Hello, Dolly!*. Yet as a composer of popular songs Loewe's career only really began with his first meeting with Lerner in Lamb's Club in New York in 1942. Prior to that, all the way through from 1924, he'd had a hard time making ends meet. In addition to taking whatever work he could get as a pianist, he also filled in as busboy, riding instructor, cowpuncher and mailman. Apart from two attempts to present himself as a concert pianist in New York Town Hall (1924), and Carnegie Hall (1942) both of which failed dismally, most of his pianistic work was picked up in silent movie houses, night clubs, and beer halls.

He began composing as young as 15. Before leaving Germany, his song 'Katrina' was selling well in Europe. But of numerous songs written in America between 1931 and 1945, none is notable, and only a few, such as 'Love Tip-Toed Through My Heart' (1934), and 'A Waltz Was Born in Vienna' (1936), are even remembered. The chance meeting with Lerner in 1942 resulted in a show that opened and closed in Detroit only, that same year. But it did lead to a Broadway flop, *What's Up?* (63 performances), in 1943, and a rather better show, *The Day Before Spring* (165 performances), in 1945. Finally, the struggling pair made the big time in 1947 with the delightful show *Brigadoon*, set in the Scottish Highlands, and which gave us such memorable songs as 'Almost Like Being in Love'. In 1954 it was made into a highly successful film with Cyd Charisse and Gene Kelly, and in the early 1960s it came to life yet again as one of America's best TV spectaculars.

In 1951 the team came up with another hit show *Paint Your Wagon*, which included such songs as 'I Talk to the Trees' and 'Wand'rin' Star' (later a huge and unlikely hit for Lee Marvin in the 1969 movie version). And then, in 1956, that all-time great, *My Fair Lady*. Much has been written about this production, and its music and lyrics are now so universally known and acclaimed that there is no need to detail them here, except perhaps to record that when it was made into a film in 1964, it won no less than eight Academy Awards, including 'best picture of the year'. The Lerner and Loewe film *Gigi* preceeded the making of *My Fair Lady*, and was released in 1958, while the stage version of *My Fair Lady* was still running on Broadway. *Gigi*, with its unforgettable music and its talented, not to say inspired, casting, which included Leslie Caron, Louis Jordan, Maurice Chevalier and Hermione Gingold, proved that the success of *My Fair Lady* was far from being a one-off. Again the songs are too well known to need recalling here.

There was to be one more Lerner/Loewe Broadway production, and that was *Camelot*, in 1960. The cast was star-studded enough, with Julie Andrews, Robert Coote, Richard Burton and Robert Goulet. But for a variety of reasons, the magic was lacking. There were several possible reasons for this. Loewe suffered a heart attack in 1958; during rehearsals director Moss Hart, who had also directed *Gigi* and *My Fair Lady* suffered likewise; and Alan Jay Lerner was taken to hospital with ulcers. Be that as it may, it gave us the last of the great Lerner/Loewe tunes, 'If Ever I Would Leave You', and it marked the end of a great songwriting partnership.

Alan Jay Lerner, in birth, upbringing and personality could not

have been more different from Frederick Loewe. He was born of
wealthy parents in New York, 31 August 1918. He was educated at
Bedales School in England, Choate School in Connecticut, and
Harvard University from 1936 to 1940 (during which time he also
spent two years at Juilliard School of Music). He wrote songs and
sketches for college shows, as well as some which were professionally
performed in small revues. Efforts to persuade him to enter the
successful family dress business totally failed, and he spent the next
few years writing radio scripts, and working in an advertising agency.
Again, it was that chance meeting with Frederick Loewe in Lamb's
Club in 1942 that led to the beginning of what had really always
been his ambition, to write for the stage. After the break-up of his
partnership with Loewe, Alan Jay Lerner continued to write songs.
Perhaps his best known efforts being with Burton Lane in 1965, ('On
a Clear Day You Can See Forever'), and subsequently with André
Previn for the show *Coco* (1969).

Some other outstanding Frederick Loewe/Alan Jay Lerner songs:
'Almost Like Being in Love' (from *Brigadoon*, 1947); 'I Talk to the
Trees', 'They Call the Wind Maria', 'Wand'rin' Star' (all from *Paint
Your Wagon*, 1951); 'Wouldn't It Be Loverly?', 'With a Little Bit of
Luck', 'The Rain in Spain', 'I Could Have Danced All Night', 'On
the Street Where You Live', 'Show Me', 'Get Me to the Church on
Time', 'I've Grown Accustomed to Her Face' (all from *My Fair Lady*,
1956); 'How to Handle a Woman', 'If Ever I Would Leave You'
(both from *Camelot*, 1960); 'The Night They Invented Champagne',
'Gigi', 'Thank Heaven for Little Girls', 'I'm Glad I'm Not Young
Anymore', 'I Remember It Well' (all from *Gigi* film, 1958).

McCARTNEY, Paul, *see* Lennon, John.

MACAULAY, Tony (Anthony Instone), composer, author, pianist,
arranger, producer.

Born Fulham, London, 21 April 1944. Educated at King's College
School, Wimbledon. On leaving school he was trained in civil
engineering, but was not pleased to find himself eventually working

for a sewage disposal company. He had always had an interest in music, having grown up during the skiffle rage of the 1950s. Amateur groups abounded and he had on many occasions attempted to write songs. He made the usual round of Tin Pan Alley, trying to find a publisher who might be interested. The nearest he got was the offer of a job as a song-plugger for David Platz of Essex Music. Young Tony jumped at it—at least it had something to do with music, and the money was more than he was getting in the sewage business.

It was at that time that he changed his name. His second cousin was Anna Instone, head of the BBC's Gramophone Department, and in charge of all radio record programmes, and it didn't seem right to have the boss's cousin plugging records to her producers and disc jockeys. The name Macaulay was chosen at random out of the telephone directory and it has stood him in good stead since 1964. It was one year later that Essex Music published the embryo composer's first song, 'I Only Have Myself to Blame'. History does not relate what happened to it, and he had to wait until 1966 for his first hit to be published. This was 'Baby Now That I've Found You', and that did not hit the charts until the 1967 recording by The Foundations, which made No 1 in the UK and No 11 in the US. The Tony Macaulay roll of hits had its first entry.

Between 1967 and 1974 Tony Macaulay, either on his own or with his collaborators had no fewer than 11 hits which reached at least the No 5 spot, and several that reached No 1 in both the UK and the US. They included 'Build Me Up Buttercup' (The Foundations, 1968), 'Love Grows Where My Rosemary Goes' (Edison Lighthouse, 1970), 'You Won't Find Another Fool Like Me' (The New Seekers, 1973), 'Let the Heartaches Begin' (Long John Baldry, 1967), 'Sorry Suzanne' (The Hollies, 1969), and 'That Same Old Feeling' (Pickettywitch, 1970).

Yet for two years, between 1971 and 1973, Tony hardly wrote a song. During that period he was involved in a lengthy legal battle with publishers Schroeder Music, over a 10-year contract he had signed as a young composer. The battle could have bankrupted him, in spite of the royalties from all his hits, for it went right up to the House of Lords, and there was no legal precedent, except for a case in 1916 between master and servant. The argument revolved round the legality or otherwise of a contract that offered no work, but prevented the composer from working for anyone else. Macaulay won his case but the strain was enormous, and it took him some time to get back to writing hits again.

In 1974 he came right back on form with a hit for The Drifters, 'Kissin' in the Back Row of the Movies', which he followed in 1975 with 'Love's Games', and in 1976 with 'You're More Than a Number in My Little Red Book', a UK No 1. In 1977 he had a series of hits with David Soul, which included 'Don't Give Up on Us', a US/UK No 1, and 'Let's Have a Quiet Night In'. In 1977 he was voted Songwriter of the Year, beating Stevie Wonder to the honour.

It is hardly surprising that with this kind of success behind him, he should turn to record production, as well as writing for stage and screen. These things became a challenge that Tony simply had to take up. He started with two special productions for the Theatre Workshop at The Theatre Royal, Stratford. The two shows were *Is Your Doctor Really Necessary?* and *Gentlemen Prefer Anything.* They were followed by co-operation with Ian le Frenais and Dick Clement on a musical based on the lives of Stan Laurel and Oliver Hardy to be called *Stan and Babe,* which awaits production at the time of writing. So do the projects on which he was working into 1981. These are a film called *Percy's Progress,* as yet uncast, and a musical, *The Cellar,* which it was hoped would feature Dame Flora Robson and Beryl Reid. And throughout the 1970s he produced almost as many hit records of other people's songs as those of his own.

Tony Macaulay has worked with various lyric-writing partners, but probably the most distinguished is Geoff Stephens. Geoff was born at Southgate, London, on 1 October 1934. He was educated at Collyers Grammar School Horsham, and Southend High School. When he left school at the end of the 1940s, he tried his hand at various jobs to earn a living, but found that he had a great interest in writing, especially lyrics, and in the early 1950s formed a company called The Four Arts Society, which specialized in the presentation of original revues. Thus began his first association with the music business. His first published song was called 'Problem Girl', in 1962. He had his first hit in 1964 when a group called The Applejacks recorded 'Tell Me When', for which Les Reed had written the music. A year later he had his second hit, 'The Crying Game', for which he wrote both words and music, and which went to No 5 in the UK charts via Dave Berry's recording. One of his biggest hits appeared in 1966—'Winchester Cathedral'—another song for which he wrote both words and music. Recorded by an outfit called The New Vaudeville Band, it went to No 4 in the UK and to No 1 in the US. There have been over 3,000 cover versions of this, ranging from

Dizzy Gillespie to Frank Sinatra. Geoff Stephens had made it to the big time.

Other songs for The New Vaudeville Band followed, but it was in 1967 that a return to collaboration with Les Reed produced the song which has become a standard, 'There's a Kind of Hush'. His association with Tony Macaulay began in 1969, with a song called 'The Lights of Cincinnati', followed later the same year by 'Sorry Suzanne' for The Hollies. The association continued on and off through the 1970s, and included such hits as The New Seekers' success, 'You Won't Find Another Fool Like Me', and several with David Soul.

Geoff has had many other successful collaborators, including more hits with Les Reed ('Daughter of Darkness'), Mitch Murray and Peter Callander ('Hello Sam, Goodbye Samantha'), Roger Greenaway ('Doctor's Orders'), and another with Roger as recently as 1980, Crystal Gayle's hit 'It's Like We Never Said Goodbye'.

Another lyricist who has had many hits with Tony Macaulay is John MacLeod. Originally a member of the top vocal group The Maple Leaf Four, his collaboration with Tony resulted in many of the mid-1960s hits already mentioned by such artists as Long John Baldry, The Foundations, The Paper Dolls, Herman's Hermits and Pickettywitch.

Barry Mason has also contributed to the Macaulay songbook over the years, notably the huge Edison Lighthouse hit from 1970, 'Love Grows Where My Rosemary Goes', No 1 in the UK and No 3 in the US.

Some other outstanding Tony Macaulay songs:
'Smile a Little Smile' (1969), 'Something Here in My Heart' (1968), 'Baby Make It Soon' (1969), 'I Can Take or Leave Your Loving' (Herman's Hermits, No 10 in the UK, No 20 in the US, 1968), 'Back on My Feet Again' (1968), 'Sad Old Kinda Movie' (1970), 'Baby Take Me in Your Arms' (1968), 'Sweet Inspiration' (1970), 'Pony Express' (1970), 'I Didn't Get to Sleep at All' (1973), 'Home Lovin' Man' (Andy Williams, No 10 UK, 1970), 'Comes That Rainy Day Feeling' (1971), 'Letter to Lucille' (Tom Jones, 1973), 'I Get a Little Sentimental Over You' (New Seekers, 1974), 'Play Me Like You Play Your Guitar' (Duane Eddy, No 10 UK, 1975), 'Goin' in with My Eyes Open' (David Soul, No 2 UK, 1977), 'Can't We Just Sit down and Talk It Over' (Donna Summer, No 1 Album Charts US, 1978), 'It Sure Brings Out the Love in Your Eyes' (1978).

McHUGH, Jimmy, composer, pianist, publisher.

Born Boston, Mass, 10 July 1894. Died Beverly Hills, California, 23 May 1969. Educated St John's Preparatory School and Holy Cross College (Hon Mus D). Unlike so many of the Tin Pan Alley greats, Jimmy McHugh received professional piano and music tuition, initially from his mother, so that his first job was that of a rehearsal pianist at the Boston Opera House. But before long the idea of popular music claimed him and he took a job as a song-plugger with the Boston office of Irving Berlin Music (he was one of 22 such pluggers), his job being to demonstrate Berlin songs to artists in local theatres. For this he earned $8 per week, with bicycle thrown in. He sson decided that this was not for him, and in 1921 went to New York. There, after one or two unsuccesful efforts, he had a hit song in 1924, 'When My Sugar Walks Down the Street', with lyrics by Irving Mills and Gene Austin, a song that soon became a favourite with jazz musicians. In 1926 he had another in that category, 'I Can't Believe That You're in Love With Me', with lyrics by Clarence Gaskill. Prior to that he had also written some songs with lyrics by Al Dubin, but they didn't amount to much.

By that time he had begun writing the music for the sensational *Cotton Club Revues*, something which he did for seven years. He also became professional manager of Mills Music, Irving Mill's publishing company. His really big break came when he was asked to write all the music for Lew Leslie's show *Blackbirds of 1928*. This was his first successful collaboration with lyricist Dorothy Fields, the start of another of one of the most famous partnerships in songwriting. The show starred Adelaide Hall and Bill Robinson, and contained numerous songs that were destined to become standards, the most famous of all being 'I Can't Give You Anything but Love'. Legend has it that it was the last song to be written for the show, and was inspired by the writers overhearing a conversation between two impoverished lovers gazing into the jewellery windows of Tiffany's store in New York. They heard the man say, 'Gee honey, I'd like to get you a sparkler like that right now, but I can't give you nothin' but love'.

The partnership with Dorothy Fields continued almost to the end of the 1930s, although it was not an exclusive one. Together they wrote for more Broadway shows, including *Hello, Daddy* (1928), and *The International Revue* (1930). This included in the cast Gertrude Lawrence and Harry Richman, and produced two more record-breaking hits, 'On the Sunny Side of the Street', and 'Exactly Like You'. With Al Dubin he wrote for *Down Argentine Way* (1939), which featured Carmen Miranda and the song 'South American Way'; and with Al Dubin and Howard Dietz for *Keep Off the Grass* (1940), which starred Jimmy Durante, and included Ray Bolger, Larry Adler and Jane Froman; while in 1948 there was *As the Girls Go*, with lyrics by Harold Adamson, who became McHugh's next regular partner after Dorothy Fields.

But like so many other writers of his time, it was in Hollywood in the 1930s that he had perhaps his greatest successes, many of them with Dorothy Fields. Out of some 50 or 60 musical films (by no means all with Dorothy), among the best known were: *The Cuban Love Song* (title song, 1930); *Dancing Lady* (1933), with Fred Astaire, Joan Crawford and Clark Gable; *Dinner at Eight* (1933), with an all-star cast including John and Lionel Barrymore, Jean Harlow and Billie Burke, and which produced the song 'Don't Blame Me'; *Have a Heart* (1934), with the song 'Lost in a Fog'; *Every Night at Eight* (1935), starring George Raft, Alice Faye and Frances Langford, which produced the song 'I'm in the Mood for Love'; *Hooray for Love* (1935), with Ann Sothern and Bill Robinson; and *Roberta*, the classic 1935 Fred Astaire/Ginger Rogers film for which McHugh collaborated with Jerome Kern. All those were written with Dorothy Fields.

In addition there were such pictures as *King of Burlesque* (1935), with lyricist Ted Koehler (Fats Waller, who was in the film, had a hit with 'I'm Shootin' High'); *You're a Sweetheart* (1937), lyrics by Harold Adamson, and starring Alice Faye and George Murphy; *Higher and Higher* (1944), lyrics by Harold Adamson, and featuring Frank Sinatra, Jack Haley, and the song 'I Couldn't Sleep a Wink Last Night'; *Happy Go Lucky* (1943), with Mary Martin and Dick Powell, and the song 'Murder, He Says', sung by Betty Hutton, this time with lyrics by Frank Loesser; *Follow the Boys* (1944), with George Raft and Vera Zorina, and lyrics once again by Dorothy Fields, which produced the classic 'I Feel a Song Coming On'; *The Princess and the Pirate* (1944), with Bob Hope; *Four Jills and a Jeep* (1944), with Martha Raye, Alice Faye, Betty Grable, Carole Landis, Dick Haymes and Jimmy Dorsey's Orchestra; *Doll Face* (1946), with Perry Como and Carmen Miranda; *Calendar Girl* (1947), which produced the song 'Have I Told You Lately That I Love You?'; *A Date With Judy* (1948), with Wallace Beery, Jane Powell, Elizabeth Taylor and Carmen Miranda, and the song 'It's a Most Unusual Day'. All the foregoing were in collaboration with Harold Adamson. Jimmy

McHugh was still writing songs up to 1959, when he produced 'Let's Have an Old-Fashioned Christmas'. A bachelor all his life, he was awarded a Presidential Certificate of Merit during World War II; he founded the Jimmy McHugh Polio Foundation; and his own publishing company.

In view of his long associations with both Dorothy Fields and Harold Adamson, it might be appropriate to say a few words about them.

Dorothy was born 15 July 1905 at Allenhurst, New Jersey. Her father, Lew Fields, was a well known comedian. In Max Wilk's book, *They're Playing Our Song*, she recalls numerous stories of her association with Jimmy McHugh, including how their song 'I Can't Give You Anything but Love' was described by a reviewer as 'sickly and puerile'. She says, 'It sold over 3,000,000 copies!' After her first collaboration with Jerome Kern over the song 'Lovely to Look At', she wrote with him for numerous other pictures, including the Astaire/Rogers film *Swing Time*. Max Wilk says, '. . . a sharp-tongued man, possessed of sharp opinions, Kern obviously enjoyed working with Miss Fields. And the feeling remained mutual. The two wrote songs for another film, *Joy of Living*, and were originally slated to do the score of *Annie Get Your Gun*. Kern's death ended a joyful collaboration'.

In 1939 she found herself writing with Arthur Schwartz for the Broadway musical *Stars in Your Eyes*, and she worked with him later on *By the Beautiful Sea* (1954), and *A Tree Grows in Brooklyn* (1951). In addition to her lyrics, Dorothy Fields also developed into one of the foremost writers of books for musicals, many in collaboration with her brother Herbert, including the Cole Porter musical *Something for the Boys*. When she was writing books, Max Wilk asked her if she ever found it difficult to retire as a lyricist and bequeath that spot to Cole Porter. 'Oh honey, let me tell you, it's great', she said fervently. In 1946 she found herself in exactly the same position again, when Irving Berlin was signed to write the songs for *Annie Get Your Gun* and she was contracted to do the book. But just to show that she could still write lyrics as well as ever, she found a brand new composer with whom to collaborate in 1965. This was Cy Coleman, and together they wrote the score of *Sweet Charity* (1966), perhaps one of the last Broadway shows to have the distinction of including a song that was not only a hit with theatre audiences, but also with radio and TV audiences: 'Big Spender'. Dorothy Fields died in New York on 28 March 1974.

Harold Adamson, McHugh's other main collaborator, was born in Greenville, New Jersey, 10 December 1906. In addition to the references already made to his work with Jimmy McHugh, the other main composers with whom he has had successful partnerships included Hoagy Carmichael ('My Resistance Is Low'), Walter Donaldson ('It's Been So Long'), Vincent Youmans ('Time on My Hands'), Burton Lane ('Everything I Have Is Yours'), and Victor Young ('Around the World').

Some other outstanding songs by Jimmy McHugh:
'Diga Diga Doo' (1928), 'I Must Have That Man' (1928), 'Doin' the New Lowdown' (1928), 'Where Are You?' (1937), 'You Say the Nicest Things' (1948), 'Can't Get Out of This Mood' (1942), 'I Get the Neck of the Chicken' (1942), 'A Lovely Way to Spend an Evening' (1944), 'Let's Get Lost' (1943), 'Spreading Rhythm Around' (1936), 'There's Something in the Air' (1936), 'Coming in on a Wing and a Prayer' (1943).

McLEAN, Don, composer, author, singer, guitarist.

Born New Rochelle, New York, 2 October 1945. Don McLean's output as a songwriter is small but he merits a place in this book because five of his songs have been huge hits, and each one had had about it something quite special. As a teenager, he was a great Buddy Holly fan, but at the age of 18 decided rock-'n'-roll was not for him, and spent quite a few years as a follower of folk heroes such as Josh White and Brownie McGhee. The Beatles brought him back to rock as a performer (he still had not written a song that he cares to talk about), and he spent the decade singing and playing wherever he could earn money, in folk clubs or with rock bands.

Gradually he found himself involved with writing poetry, and editing a book about a voyage he and a group of folk-singing environmentalists had undertaken, called *Songs and Sketches of the First Clearwater Crew.* The success of this led to TV appearances, and to having 25 of his songs accepted for a film called *Other Voices.* In 1970 he was signed to record by United Artists, and with only his second release he hit a major jackpot, 'American Pie', in 1972. The song immediately went to No 2 in the UK and No 1 in the US, and by now has become a standard recorded by hundreds of other artists.

Later the same year he had another triumph with his song 'Vincent' (about the painter Van Gogh), and his album *Tapestry*, originally his first release for United Artists in 1970, found its way into the album charts again.

In 1973 he had another hit, 'And I Love You So'. It was a song he had written in 1970, and it completely revitalized the recording career of Perry Como. This was followed by his own recording of 'Wonderful Baby', a hit in the US but a song that never entered the UK charts, although it, too, has become a standard and has been recorded by many artists, including Fred Astaire.

Although he continues to write, the performing side of Don McLean has come more and more to the fore, and he has had successes with other composers' material, such as Buddy Holly's 'Every Day' and the Roy Orbison song 'Crying' (1980).

A young middle-of-the-road composer and singer, despite his background, Don McLean has resigned himself to the fact that his audience is never going to consist simply of young people. His material is equally pleasing to the Frank Sinatra and Roberta Flack fans. In a 1980 interview with Colin Irwin for *Melody Maker* he said, 'I'm more interested in melodies. But then I've always offended the purists. I was always trying to combine Woody Guthrie with Sinatra—that was my goal. Singer-songwriters are going to become as scarce as hen's teeth pretty soon. It's become a real old-fashioned thing. What's coming is whether you're gonna be able to sing or not'. In some of his songs he has totally rejected the pop star syndrome, and has not hesitated to take digs at himself. The overwhelming success of 'American Pie' undoubtedly shook him to the core. When not performing he prefers to live quietly in the country in up-state New York. As he said in one of his own lyrics, 'I could not be a part of your cocktail generation'.

Some other outstanding Don McLean songs:
'Castles in the Air' (1970), 'Magdalene Lane' (1970), 'Respectable' (1970), 'Everybody Loves Me Baby' (1972), 'Winterwood' (1972), 'Dreidl' (1973), 'The Pride Parade' (1973), 'If We Try' (1974), 'Oh My, What a Shame' (1974).

MACLEOD, John, *see* Macaulay, Tony.

MANCINI, Henry, composer, conductor, arranger, pianist.

Born Cleveland, Ohio, 16 April 1924. Educated Carnegie Technical Music School, and the Juilliard School of Music. His father and mother had emigrated to the USA from the Italian province of Abruzzi, and soon settled in Aliquippa, Pennsylvania, where young Mancini started learning the flute, an instrument favoured by his father. This was followed by piano lessons at the age of 12. In Juilliard he also studied arranging, but was drafted into the air force in 1943, serving overseas until 1945. On discharge, he was lucky enough to secure his first professional job as pianist/arranger with what was then called The Glenn Miller Orchestra led by Tex Beneke. It was during his years with this band that he met and married his wife Ginny, who sang with the band as Ginny O'Connor, and who had formerly been a member of Mel Tormé's group, The Meltones.

Henry Mancini grew up before the war in the great era of the big bands, and was at first devoted to the music of Artie Shaw, until he heard the original Glenn Miller band, following which, he confessed: 'I became a Miller nut'. Nothing could have suited him better, therefore, than the job after the war with Tex Beneke. He left the band in 1948, and had a hard time trying to break into the freelance world of arrangers and pianists, doing odd jobs as deputy for absent pianists, and a few arrangements for night club singers and small combos. Suddenly, in 1952, his luck changed, when he landed a two-week contract to write music for Universal-International in Hollywood.

To say his luck had changed is really an understatement, since his first assignment was to score the music for *The Glenn Miller Story* (which won him his first Academy Award nomination). This was quickly followed by *The Benny Goodman Story*, and Orson Welles' *Touch of Evil*. Altogether he stayed six years at Universal–International, contributing to over 100 films. Soon after leaving in 1958, Mancini had his first taste of writing for TV, and at the same time his first acceptance as a composer, with his theme music for the series *Peter Gunn*. But this assignment was much more than just writing a theme tune. Mancini stayed with the series throughout its run, providing as he says, between 10 and 15 minutes of music for every show, and Blake Edwards the producer, was unstinting in his praise for Mancini's work as a major contributory factor to the success of the show. The RCA album of music from the series won two Grammies

(Best Album of the Year and Best Arrangement of the Year), and the recording by the Ray Anthony Orchestra won a gold disc.

Another Edwards/Mancini collaboration *Mr Lucky*, followed. It was not a TV success, but in spite of that, recordings of the music won two Grammies, and Henry's own recording with orchestra became a best-seller.

In 1960 he returned to Hollywood, and in 1961 had another turning point in his career with the music for the movie *Breakfast at Tiffany's*, which also produced his first real song hit, 'Moon River' (lyrics by Johnny Mercer). He won two Academy Awards. Audrey Hepburn starred in the film and Andy Williams' record of 'Moon River' earned two gold discs. In 1962 he had an instrumental hit with 'Baby Elephant Walk' from the film *Hatari*, and later the same year came his next major song hit, again with lyrics by Johnny Mercer, 'Days of Wine and Roses', the title song of the film starring Jack Lemmon and Lee Remick. Once more an Andy Williams record earned a gold disc. By now it seemed as though every picture that had a Henry Mancini score must not only have at least one hit, but also earn a stack of awards. Into this category fell 'Charade' (theme song, 1963, lyrics by Johnny Mercer), 'Dear Heart' (theme song, 1964, lyrics by Jay Livingston and Ray Evans), 'The Pink Panther' (background music, 1964), and 'The Sweetheart Tree' (from *The Great Race*, 1965), as well as the score of *Sunflower* (1971).

During the 1970s and early 1980s Henry Mancini has continued to write prolifically for films—almost 30 up to 1980. Nor did he neglect TV, making many guest appearances conducting an orchestra, as well as contributing themes and other music for many successful series. He also undertook many concerts worldwide, conducting his orchestra, often with singers such as Andy Williams appearing on the same bill. Country music singer Charley Pride took a Mancini song, 'All His Children' to number one spot in the record charts in 1974, and the services of this composer, arranger, conductor and pianist continued to be in demand.

His daughter Monica has become an accomplished singer with various highly paid backing groups for records, films and TV; a second daughter, Felice, wrote the lyrics for what must surely be the first father/daughter collaboration—the song 'Sometimes', recorded by The Carpenters on a million-selling album, as well as by Johnny Mathis, and Peggy Lee. His son Chris is into the group scene as composer, author, and keyboard specialist. Chris and Monica have also appeared together in TV shows.

Hank Mancini is a quiet, modest man, spending all his off-duty time either with his family or pursuing his hobbies of photography, ski-ing, and swimming. He is also keen to put something back into the business that has taken him to the top of the tree. Thus he has endowed a chair at the University of California for screen composition, as well as other scholarships and fellowships, including one at Juilliard in New York. Altogether he must have spent well over $2 million in this way.

The most outstanding of Henry Mancini's songs have been referred to in the text, but others include 'Bachelor in Paradise' (1961), 'Theme From Romeo and Juliet' (1969), 'Whistling Away' (from *Darling Lili* 1970), 'It's Easy to Say' (from *10*, 1979).

MANN, Barry, composer, author, pianist, singer.

Born Brooklyn, New York, 9 February 1942. **WEILL, Cynthia,** author, composer, singer, dancer. Born New York, 18 October 1937. They married in 1961. Barry, after education at local schools, and receiving classical piano tuition, suddenly discovered that he could play the popular songs of the day by ear, and so began his first attempts at composing on his own. He was 12. After leaving school, he was training to be an architect, and continuing with his music strictly as a hobby. He soon had songs accepted by such artists as Steve Lawrence ('Footsteps'). At the same time he started making demo discs of his work, singing the songs himself, and it was this that led to a contract with the Al Nevins/Don Kirshner publishing organization. His first success for them came in 1961 with a song called 'Who Put the Bomp in the Bomp Ba Bomp Ba?', his own recording going to No 7 in the US charts. Later in the year a recording by The Viscounts went to No 15 in the UK. The lyrics were by Gerry Goffin, who later teamed up with Carole King.

Cynthia Weill was educated at high school in New York, followed by the Sarah Lawrence College, until she graduated at 18. She had always been fascinated by show business, and throughout her college days she also studied acting, dancing and singing. On leaving school she was talented enough to get a job as a dancer and showgirl at New York's Copacabana. This was later followed by acting parts in TV, and more singing and dancing in night clubs, as she progressed from the line to solo spots. Then she found that she needed special material, and couldn't afford to pay a songwriter to write for her, so decided to do it herself, with considerable success. Before long she began to concentrate on writing rather than performing.

Cynthia was once quoted as saying: 'I suddenly knew what I wanted to do. Performing no longer seemed important. Writing was my scene. It felt natural'. Having taken the decision, she did not find it all that easy to get 'in' professionally, and admits she was drifting until she, too, was lucky enough to get an introduction to Al Nevins and Don Kirshner, As a result, she ended up in the Brill building, or the 'song factory' as it was frequently called at that time, because the publishers had so many contract writers working there. Barry Mann once said, years later: 'It was insane. Cynthia and I would be in this tiny cubicle, about the size of a closet, with just a piano and a chair. No window or anything. We'd go in every morning and we'd write songs all day. In the next room Carole (King) and Gerry (Goffin) would be doing the same thing. Sometimes when we all got to banging on our pianos you couldn't tell who was playing what'.

Before Cynthia was really aware of Barry in the Brill building, she was working with several other writers, including singer Teddy Randazzo, Carole King, and Gerry Goffin. She first met Barry when he came to sell a song to Randazzo, and found Cynthia there working with him on another song. The year was 1961, and it marked their partnership in both music and marriage. Twenty years later they were still going strong.

The singer ended up with the Mann song as the 'A' side and the Randazzo/Weill song as the 'B' side of his record.

Their first big hit was 'Bless You' by Tony Orlando (1961, No 7 UK, No 15 US). Tony, too, was a permanent fixture in the Brill building at the time, being the staff 'demo' singer. From then on the Mann/Weill team turned out hit after hit for the next ten years.

In 1973, Barry and Cynthia moved from New York to Los Angeles. Before the move they had begun to take an interest in writing for films, starting with *Wild in the Street*, which produced the hit song 'The Shape of Things to Come'. In Hollywood, Cynthia collaborated with arranger Quincy Jones to write the theme for the film *Cactus Flower*, while Barry collaborated with Al Gorgoni to score the film *I Never Sang for My Father*. One of its songs was 'Strangers', for which Cynthia wrote the lyrics. To date, five of their songs have achieved BMI certified million performance status, and with their continued writing they have proved that they are, unlike some teams, flexible enough to respond to the changing mood and requirements of the

music business. The Brill building certainly produced truly professional songwriters in the old tradition, and the Mann/Weill team are
two of the best.

In 1981 Cynthia co-wrote with Tom Snow 'He's So Shy', a big hit
for the Pointer Sisters, while together with Barry she also wrote 'Just
Once', arranged by Quincy Jones for new singer James Ingram. For a
songwriting partnership to last 20 years is unusual, but not unheard
of. For a music business marriage to do so is remarkable. To quote
Walter Carter, writing in BMI's magazine *The Many Worlds of Music*
in 1978, 'The respect that Barry and Cynthia have for each other is
evident in their conversation. Although they are both articulate they
never interrupt each other, and one never repeats what the other has
just said.' Of themselves Cynthia says: 'You realize that what you
have together transcends what each of you is separately'. Barry says
that in an intangible way that also applies to their writing of music.

Some other outstanding songs by Barry Mann and Cynthia Weill:
'Blame It on the Bossa Nova' (Eydie Gormé, 1963), 'Don't Make My
Baby Blue' (The Shadows, No 10 UK, 1962), 'He's Sure the Boy I
Love' (The Crystals, 1962), 'Hungry' (Paul Revere and The Raiders,
1966; Elvis Presley, No 6 UK, 1971), 'I'll Take You Home' (The
Drifters, 1963), 'I'm Gonna Be Strong' (Gene Pitney, No 2 UK, No
9 US, 1964), 'It's Getting Better' (Mama Cass, No 8 UK, No 30 US,
1969), 'Kicks' (Paul Revere and The Raiders, 1966), 'Looking
Through the Eyes of Love (Gene Pitney, No 3 UK, No 28 US, 1965;
The Partridge Family, No 9 UK, No 39 US, 1973), 'Love Her' (The
Righteous Brothers, 1965), 'On Broadway' (The Drifters, 1962),
'Uptown' (The Crystals, 1962), 'Walking in the Rain' (The Ronettes,
1964; The Partridge Family, 1973), 'We've Gotta Get Out of This
Place' (The Animals, No 2 UK, No 13 US, 1965), 'You've Lost That
Lovin' Feeling' (The Righteous Brothers, No 1 UK and No 1 US,
1965), 'I Just Can't Help Believin'' (B J Thomas, No 9 US, 1970; No
6 Elvis Presley, 1971), 'Sometimes When We Touch' (Barry Mann
with Dan Hill, 1977), 'Here You Come Again' (1977).

MASON, Barry, *see* Reed, Les.

MERCER, John H (Johnny), author, composer, singer.

Born Savannah, Georgia, 18 November 1909. Died Los Angeles, California, 25 June 1976. Educated Woodbury Forest School, Orange, Virginia. As explained in the introduction, Johnny Mercer is one of only three lyricists included in this book in their own right. His work has been so important to the development of the popular song lyric, that we must say a few words about him. His father was a lawyer, and Johnny received a good education until the real estate business in which his father was also involved went bankrupt in 1927. He had always shown an interest in the popular songs of his day, but it was his ability to remember all the words, including the verses, which distinguished him from other kids who would only hum or whistle the tunes. When the family fortunes failed, Mercer moved to New York in 1928, to lead a precarious existence as a bit part actor, but writing all the time.

His first break came when he was turned down for a part in a revue, *The Garrick Gaieties of 1930*, but a lyric he had written (tune by Everitt Miller), was accepted. The same show also introduced him to a dancer called Ginger Meehan, who subsequently became Mrs Mercer. At about the same time Johnny entered a singing competition organized by bandleader Paul Whiteman, and won. Paul was looking for a replacement for his highly successful vocal group, The Rhythm Boys (Bing Crosby, Harry Harris and Al Rinker), but it was to be another year before they left the band and Mercer finally was hired. Now he was at least in the music business and in a position to meet many of the great songwriters of the day, and study how they did what they did. One who was always dropping in on the Whiteman band dates was Hoagy Carmichael, and it was with a Carmichael melody that Johnny had his first real hit, 'Lazybones' in 1933.

The list of famous composers for whose melodies Johnny Mercer has provided superb lyrics reads like a 'Who's Who' of songwriters: Hoagy Carmichael, Harold Arlen, Richard Whiting, Harry Warren, Henry Mancini, Jerome Kern, Arthur Schwartz, and Jimmy van Heusen are just a few. All have their own entries in this book, and the name of Johnny Mercer is associated with many of their greatest hits. He has occasionally written music for his own songs, his first attempt being the successful 'I'm an Old Cowhand', which was given hit status when Bing Crosby sang it in the 1936 movie *Rhythm on the Range*. And there was 'Dream', for June Allyson in the 1945 film, *Her Highness and the Bellboy*, which was subsequently elevated to a hit when

Frank Sinatra recorded it. There was also 'Something's Gotta Give', a hit for Sammy Davis Jr in 1957. But by and large Johnny was a lyric writer.

In 1942 he was co-founder of Capitol Records, a company which within 10 years had become one of the most successful in the world, with an enviable roster of talent, much of it brought there by Johnny himself. He also recorded occasionally as a singer, sometimes in duet with such stars as the late Bobby Darin.

But it is the talent of Mercer the writer that will always be remembered. A man whose lyrics can range from the pure corn of 'I'm an Old Cowhand', through the moody 'Blues in the Night' (Harold Arlen), the sophisticated 'Too Marvellous for Words' (Richard Whiting), the sad 'One for My Baby' (Harold Arlen), the ingenious 'Ac-cent-tchu-ate the Positive' (Harold Arlen) to gorgeous ballads such as 'Laura' (Dave Raskin) 'Moon River' (Henry Mancini), and comedy numbers such as 'Jubilation T Cornpone' (Gene de Paul), has got to deserve a place in a book which cannot help but do less than justice to many great lyricists. Finally, here are a couple of quotes. Talking to Max Wilk for his book *They're Playing Our Song*, Mercer said, 'There are certain writers who have a great *feeling* for tunes, no matter where they come from. I think I'm one of them. I don't mean that in any egotistical way. I think Dorothy Fields is one too. She has a feel for the tune'. And Richard Whiting's daughter Margaret, also talking to Max Wilk about her father's song 'Too Marvellous for Words', said, 'My father always said the genius of Mercer really comes out in that lyric'. Johnny Mercer, lyric writer, *was* a genius at his own game.

Some other outstanding songs with Johnny Mercer lyrics:
'Pardon My Southern Accent' (Matty Malneck, 1934), 'Moon Country' (Hoagy Carmichael, 1934), 'When a Woman Loves a Man' (Bernie Hanighan, Gordon Jenkins, 1934), 'PS I Love You' (Gordon Jenkins, 1934), 'Eeny Meeny Miney Mo' (Matty Malneck, 1935), 'Goody Goody' (Matty Malneck, 1936), 'Bob White' (Bernie Hanighan, 1937), 'Jeepers Creepers' (Harry Warren, 1938), 'You Must Have Been a Beautiful Baby' (Harry Warren, 1938), 'Day In Day Out' (Rube Bloom, 1939), 'And the Angels Sing' (Ziggy Elman, 1939), 'Fools Rush In' (Rube Bloom, 1939), 'Tangerine' (Victor Schertzinger, 1942), 'Skylark' (Hoagy Carmichael, 1942), 'Dearly Beloved' (Jerome Kern, 1942), 'You Were Never Lovelier' (Jerome Kern, 1942), 'I'm Old-Fashioned' (Jerome Kern, 1942), 'That Old

Black Magic' (Harold Arlen, 1942), 'Hit the Road to Dreamland' (Harold Arlen, 1942), 'The GI Jive' (Johnny Mercer, 1944), 'How Little We Know' (Hoagy Carmichael, 1944), 'Dream' (Johnny Mercer, 1945), 'On the Atchinson, Topeka and the Santa Fe' (Harry Warren, Academy Award Winner, 1946), 'Come Rain or Come Shine' (Harold Arlen, 1946), 'Autumn Leaves' (Joseph Kosma, Jacques Prevert, 1950), 'In the Cool Cool Cool of the Evening' (Hoagy Carmichael, Academy Award Winner, 1951), 'Satin Doll' (Duke Ellington, 1953), 'Sobbin' Women' (Gene de Paul, 1953), 'The Days of Wine and Roses' (Henry Mancini, Academy Award Winner, 1962).

MERRILL, Bob, composer, author, director, producer.

Born Atlantic City, New Jersey, 17 May 1921. His family soon moved to Philadelphia, where Bob was educated at local schools. As a teenager he got the travel bug, and his mother, unlike most parents, encouraged him to see America, which he proceeded to do as a hitchhiker, earning a pittance by working in small clubs and bars as an impressionist and compère. Then his father took a hand, and young Bob found himself working in a real estate office by day, and studying in a law school by night. But in 1939 he took a humble job in the Bucks County Playhouse, gradually progressing to assistant manager, and ultimately to director.

By 1942 he was in New York, struggling in a 42nd St theatre on six dollars a week. He finally joined the army, and found himself with the Cavalry at Fort Riley in Kansas, where he started writing and producing shows for the troops.

After his army service he headed for Hollywood, where he played bit parts in films, and supplemented his income by working as a porter for Columbia Pictures. A lucky break and a bagful of confidence got him a job as a writer at NBC, where he blossomed sufficiently for Columbia to want him back, this time writing for shorts and 'B' movies, from which he progressed to directing and casting for their films and TV.

But it seems that the desire to write songs was never far beneath the surface, and 1950 found him back in New York, where before long he had his first hit called 'If I Knew You Were Comin' I'd 've Baked a Cake'. He wrote this with composer Al Hoffman, and it won a gold disc with the recording by Eileen Barton. This was her only gold record, and even with it she was hardly known in the UK where the song was popularized by Bing Crosby's recording. But that was not all. In the same year he had two more songs published, 'Me and My Imagination', and 'Candy and Cake'. The latter, while not in the million-selling class, was also a sizeable hit.

From 1951 to 1953, Bob Merrill could have been described as Guy Mitchell's personal songwriter. He wrote eight songs for the singer in that period, all of which were hits, and one of which, 'My Truly Truly Fair' (1951) won a gold disc. But Guy Mitchell did not quite monopolize Merrill's talents, for in 1953 he had a big hit with the song 'How Much Is That Doggie in the Window?', via the US recording by Patti Page, and the UK recording by Lita Roza. And in 1954 his song 'Mambo Italiano' won a gold disc for Rosemary Clooney, while in 1958 Perry Como did extremely well with the song 'Love Makes the World Go Round'.

After the end of the 1950s, Bob Merrill concentrated more on directing and producing than on writing hit songs, although he also tried his hand at writing musicals. *New Girl in Town* (1957), *Take Me Along* (1959) and *Carnival* (1961), which were all his own work, were not sensationally successful and produced no memorable numbers. In 1964, however, when he returned to lyric writing only, and collaborated with composer Jule Styne on the Barbra Streisand show *Funny Girl*, success was his once again, with such hits as 'People', and 'Don't Rain on My Parade'. In 1967 he had a further attempt at a musical on his own, with the unsuccessful *Henry, Sweet Henry*, and in 1972 returned to his collaboration with Jule Styne for the show *Sugar*, but this time nothing memorable emerged.

Some other outstanding Bob Merrill songs:
'Sparrow in the Treetop' (1951), 'Belle, Belle, My Liberty Belle' (1951), 'There's Always Room at Our House' (1951), 'We Won't Live in a Castle' (1952), 'A Beggar in Love' (1952), 'There's a Pawnshop on the Corner' (1952), 'Feet Up' (1952), 'She Wears Red Feathers' (1953), 'Make Yourself Comfortable' (1955).

MONACO, James V (Jimmie), composer, pianist.

Born Fornia, Italy, 13 January 1885. Died Beverly Hills, California, 16 October 1945. His family emigrated to America in 1891, and by the age of 18 he was playing ragtime piano in the bars and cafes of Albany, New York, an art in which he was almost completely self-taught. The family soon moved to Chicago, where Monaco continued to practise his art in some of the less salubrious night spots of the town, acquiring the nickname 'Ragtime Jimmy' in the process, a name that stayed with him when he moved to New York in 1910. There he played piano at the famed Bohemia Café on West 29th St, and in the summer at Coney Island.

His first published song was 'Oh You Circus Day', which appeared in a Broadway review called *Hanky Panky* in 1911. The following year Lillian Lorraine stopped the show (*Ziegfeld Follies of 1912*) when she sang his song 'Row, Row, Row'. Later the same year he followed it up with 'You Made Me Love You', and from then on another top flight popular songwriter was born.

He only made one attempt at a complete Broadway show, *Harry Delmar's Revels of 1927*. It produced no memorable songs and ran for only 112 performances. Right through from 1912 until he went to Hollywood in 1936 at the age of 51, to work for Paramount Pictures, Jimmy Monaco presented the almost archetypal portrait of a successful Tin Pan Alley writer. Hardly one of those years passed without some major hit coming to fruition, aided as he was lyrically by such first-rate authors as Ted Koehler ('Every Night About This Time'), Edgar Leslie ('Crazy People'), and Joseph McCarthy ('What Do You Want to Make Those Eyes at Me For?').

Once in Hollywood, he was soon in the hit parade again with such songs as 'My Heart Is Taking Lessons' (lyrics by Johnny Burke, from the 1938 Bing Crosby film *Doctor Rhythm*), 'I've Got a Pocketful of Dreams' (again with Johnny Burke, from the 1938 Bing Crosby movie *Sing You Sinners*), and 'An Apple for the Teacher' (Johnny Burke and Bing Crosby once more, this time in *The Star Maker*, 1939). The same team went from success to success with hit songs in *Road to Singapore* (1940, the first of the 'Road' pictures, with Bob Hope, Dorothy Lamour and Bing Crosby), *If I Had My Way* (1940), and *Rhythm on the River* (1940). From 1942 to 1945 his lyricist was Mack Gordon, and he and Mack contributed songs for the movies *Weekend in Havana* (1941), *Stage Door Canteen* (1943), *Sweet and Lowdown* (1944), *Pin-Up Girl* (1944), and *The Dolly Sisters* (1945). Probably their biggest hit came from *The Dolly Sisters*—it was 'I Can't Begin to Tell You'. It was later that same year that Jimmy Monaco died of heart trouble. Jack Burton, in his '*Blue Book of Tin Pan Alley* (Vol 2)' reports: 'Bing Crosby, Betty Grable, Linda Darnell, June Haver and

Dorothy Lamour, who sang his songs, found a most fitting way to express their grief in the opening lines of the last hit he wrote (with Mack Gordon): "I can't begin to tell you how much you mean to me".' In truth Jimmy Monaco's life was the story of 'from rags to riches'.

Some other outstanding songs by Jimmy Monaco:
'Me and the Man in the Moon' (1928), 'Sing a Song of Sunbeams' (1939), 'That Sly Old Gentleman From Featherbed Lane' (1939), 'April Played the Fiddle' (1940), 'Only Forever' (1940), 'Six Lessons From Madame la Zonga' (1940), 'Too Romantic' (1940), 'I'm Making Believe' (1944), 'Time Alone Will Tell' (1944).

MURRAY, Mitch, composer, author, producer.

Born Hove, Sussex, 30 January 1940. **CALLANDER, Peter,** author, composer, producer. Born 10 October 1939, 'somewhere in Hampshire', England. Mitch Murray's family moved to London when he was quite small, and he was educated at a local school and Davies' College. On leaving school he had a variety of jobs, including that of junior salesman to Crosse and Blackwell Foods. But music had always interested him from the time someone gave him a ukelele, which he taught himself. He ultimately progressed to the piano. Meanwhile Peter Callander's life was developing on a roughly parallel path as he, too, moved to London at an early age, and was educated at the City of London School. Like Mitch he had a variety of jobs, one of which was that of song-plugger for Cyril Shane Music at just about the time that Mitch was busy hawking his first songs round Tin Pan Alley with little or no success.

They even had their first songs published quite independently of each other, in 1962. The Murray song was called 'Save a Dream for Me', recorded by Gary Mills, while Peter's was called 'She Came As a Stranger'. It is confusing to learn that they have written complete songs separately, as well as a team. Mitch Murray's big break came when his song 'How Do You Do It?' was accepted by Gerry and The Pacemakers in 1963, while in the same year Peter Callander had a hit with his own song 'Walking Tall', recorded by Adam Faith.

In 1963 Mitch had further successes, first with another song of his own, 'I Like It', also recorded by Gerry and The Pacemakers, which went to No 1 in the UK and to No 17 in the US, and then two hits written in collaboration with Freddie Garrity, of Freddie and The Dreamers—'I'm Telling You Now' (No 2 and No 1 in the UK and the US respectively), followed by 'You Were Made for Me', which made No 3 in the UK. Peter, meanwhile, was struggling along without too much success, until in 1965 he came up with lyrics for two good songs written by Les Reed, both for The Ryan Twins, Paul and Barry. The titles were 'Don't Bring Me Your Heartaches', and 'I Love Her'. The following year Peter also wrote the English lyric for Cilla Black's hit, 'A Fool Am I'. At that time he did rather well adapting continental songs, for he followed Cilla's record with another, 'Don't Answer Me', which she took to the No 3 spot in 1966. There was also a further adaptation, this time for Dusty Springfield in 1967, called 'Give Me the Time'.

It was during these years that Murray and Callander first met and started their now famous collaboration, which culminated in their huge hit for Georgie Fame in 1967, 'The Ballad of Bonnie and Clyde'. It went to No 1 in the UK and No 7 in the US. Between then and the mid-1970s, the team welded themselves into another of the great British songwriting partnerships. There was 'Hush, Not a Word to Mary' in 1968 for John Rowles; 'Hitchin' a Ride' in 1969 for Vanity Fair; 'Ragamuffin Man' for Manfred Mann in the same year; 'Goodbye Sam, Hello Samantha' (in collaboration with Geoff Stephens, 1970), which Cliff Richard took to No 6 in the charts; 'I Did What I Did for Maria' in 1971 for Tony Christie; and in 1974 'The Night Chicago Died', which a new group, Paper Lace, took to No 1 in both the US and the UK. It was the most impressive of several big hits that Murray and Callander continued to write for Paper Lace, among the others being 'Billy Don't Be a Hero', and 'The Black-Eyed Boys'.

The last half of the 1970s saw a falling off in the popularity of the Mitch Murray/Peter Callander output. As so often happens in the songwriting business, fads and gimmicks in the style and presentation of popular music occur, and established writers frequently find their wares less and less in demand, even though the quality of their work is still of a very high standard. Peter Callander rather faded from the scene during this period, although he wrote a very successful film song, 'The Liquidator' for Shirley Bassey. Mitch Murray turned his attention to a variety of things, including writing jingles for radio and TV, and film and TV themes, among which 'Avenues and Alleyways', for the series *The Protectors*, was a notable example.

Some other outstanding songs by Mitch Murray and Peter Callander:
'Even the Bad Times Are Good' (Mitch Murray with Geoff Stephens
for The Tremeloes, 1967), 'Las Vegas' (Mitch Murray only, 1970),
'Come Back Billie Jo' (Mitch Murray and Tony Macaulay, 1973).
'Down Came the Rain' (1966), 'Turn on the Sun' (1969), 'To Make a
Big Man Cry' (Peter Callander and Les Reed, for Tom Jones, 1965),
'Leave a Little Love' (Peter Callander and Les Reed for Lulu, 1965),
'Monsieur Dupont' (Peter Callander, English lyric for Sandie Shaw,
1969), 'Suddenly You Love Me' (Peter Callander, English lyric for
The Tremeloes, 1968), 'Daddy Don't You Walk So Fast' (Peter
Callander with Geoff Stephens, a No 1 in the US for Wayne Newton,
in 1971).

NEWLEY, Anthony, composer, author, actor, director.

Born Hackney, London, 24 September 1931. Educated Oswald Street
School, Clapton, London.

After leaving school, he trained at the Italia Conti stage academy,
his first part as an actor being at the Colchester Repertory Theatre in
1946. His London debut was at the New Westgate Theatre in 1955
in the revue *Cranks*. The following year he appeared on Broadway
with the same show. All this had been preceded by his playing the
part of the Artful Dodger in David Lean's film production of *Oliver
Twist*, as well as several other films. After military service another
screen role followed in *Idle on Parade*, and it was here that his
subsequent talent as a songwriter first showed itself, when he wrote
the lyrics for four of its songs to music by Joe Henderson.

In 1960 he first met fellow-songwriter Leslie Bricusse, and the
following year they teamed up to write the score and lyrics for *Stop
the World, I Want to Get Off!*, in which Newley not only starred, but
directed as well. Three songs in particular were standouts: 'Gonna
Build a Mountain', 'Once in a Lifetime', and 'What Kind of Fool Am
I?', which won a Grammy Award in 1962. But prior to these songs,
Newley had had a taste of record success with his 1959 version of the
Peter de Angelis song 'Why?', which made No 12 in the Top Twenty
in January 1960. That same year he had another hit with his version

of the old nursery rhyme, 'Pop Goes the Weasel', and another with the Lionel Bart song 'Do You Mind'.

In 1964, Newley again collaborated with Leslie Bricusse on the score and lyrics of *The Roar of the Greasepaint, The Smell of the Crowd*. The show had considerable success both in London and New York, with Newley starring again, but in spite of a score containing a number of good songs, only one, 'Who Can I Turn To?' really captured the public imagination. In 1964 he had a hit with The Hollies' recording of his song 'Candy Man'—later to win a gold disc for Sammy Davis Jr—and in the same year with Leslie Bricusse and John Barry he wrote the James Bond song 'Goldfinger'.

After the mid-1960s, Anthony Newley concentrated more and more on acting, directing and producing, in theatre, films and television, and less and less on songwriting. But in 1970 he renewed his association with Leslie Bricusse to co-write the score for the film *Willie Wonka and the Chocolate Factory*, (which contained the song 'Candy Man'), and a year later they also wrote the score for the show *The Good Old Bad Old Days*—'The People Tree' being its most outstanding song. About the same time both men were also engaged on the score for the major TV version of *Peter Pan* in the States.

In the 1970s and 1980s cabaret and TV appearances continued to keep Newley busy, and in 1977 he began making records of his own compositions again, this time for United Artists. He has lived in Los Angeles since the early 1970s, and no new songs have emerged.

Anthony Newley's main compositions have been referred to in the text, so no further listing is needed here.

NICHOLLS, Horatio (Lawrence Wright), composer, author, publisher.

Born Leicester, England, 15 February 1888. Died London, 19 May 1964. Horatio Nicholls was the pseudonym Lawrence Wright took for himself about 1911, because he thought it sounded better for a songwriter. There are in this book examples of 'the archetypal Tin Pan Alley songwriter' such as, Sammy Cahn, one from across the Atlantic. On the English side that description precisely fits Lawrence Wright. It is also important to distinguish between Lawrence Wright the composer/author (Horatio Nicholls), and Lawrence Wright who founded a publishing empire, and might almost be said to have founded England's Tin Pan Alley, in Denmark Street, London. Other publishing houses were already in existence (Chappells as early as 1811), but it was Lawrence Wright who made Denmark Street the mecca of British songwriters.

Lawrence Wright was born into the music business. His father was a violin teacher who also ran a music shop, and Lawrie was born above it. Dad taught his son, who was reasonably proficient by the age of 10 not only on the violin, but also on piano and banjo. He was educated at a local school in Leicester, but would be up by six each morning to do a paper round before school, and in the evenings would help his father at his music stall in Leicester market. He left school by the time he was 12, and was apprenticed to a printing firm. At 14 he quit to join a concert party, where he learned the art of performing in public, something he never forgot. But after four years he decided he wanted to set up a music business of his own, for at 17 he had already written his first song, 'Down by the Stream'. So, with £18 borrowed from his mother, he too hired a stall in Leicester market. Demonstrating his wares by playing and singing, he sold not only his own songs but also those he bought from other people. That is why it is important to distinguish between Wright the composer and Wright the publisher, for as early as 1906 he had bought for £5 the rights to a song he heard performed by a local street singer, 'Don't Go Down the Mine Daddy'. It sold over a million copies of sheet music, helped by a pit disaster in the year it was published.

But that sort of luck, coupled with boundless energy and a natural instinct for promotion, was just what made Lawrence Wright the sort of man he was. It was what made him set out for London in 1911, and hire a damp basement in Denmark Street for £1 per week. It really was a one-man business. He started by scrubbing the floor, then proceeded to be his own buyer, writer, parcel packer, and copier of orchestral parts. Small wonder that such energy and dedication ultimately led to his occupying the whole of No 8 Denmark Street, then selling it, and building No 19, which naturally became 'Wright House'. It could also perhaps have contributed to the severe stroke he suffered in 1943 and which almost killed him, keeping him confined to a wheelchair for the rest of his life.

But we must concern ourselves with Lawrence Wright as Horatio Nicholls the composer. Within five years of his move to London, he had a huge hit with 'Blue Eyes', to be followed in 1919 by 'That Old-Fashioned Mother of Mine', 'Wyoming Lullaby' (1920), and 'Silver Star' (1921). The 1920s and 1930s were the really great years for his big hits. His biggest of all was 'Among My Souvenirs', published in 1927, a song which has since been recorded and sung by just about every top artist in the field of popular music. Among them were Bing Crosby and Frank Sinatra. It was also featured by Hoagy Carmichael in the film *The Best Years of Our Lives*, and was a million-seller for Connie Francis, 30-odd years later in 1959. In 1930 there was 'Amy, Wonderful Amy', dedicated to Amy Johnson, the pioneer aviator. There were also 'Babette' (1925), 'The Toy Drum Major' (1925), 'I Never See Maggie Alone' (1926), 'Mistakes' (1927), 'Shepherd of the Hills' (1927), 'Just a Little Fond Affection' (1928), 'When the Guards Are on Parade' (1931), 'We'll Be Together Again' (1932), 'Down Forget-Me-Not Lane' (1941). These are just some of Horatio Nicholls's greatest hits.

His natural flair for promotion led him to publicize his song 'Sahara' (1924) by riding a camel round Piccadilly Circus. And he telephoned the song 'Shepherd of the Hills' via transatlantic cable from his apartment in New York to bandleader Jack Hylton in London who was urgently waiting to take it down so that it could be arranged and copied for a performance that same night.

For many of his songs Lawrie Wright wrote both words and music, but he also collaborated with a number of lyric-writers, of whom the two best known are Englishman Worton David and American Edgar Leslie. It was his longstanding partnership with the latter that produced many of the most famous Nicholls hits.

He also founded a complete summer show of his own called *On With the Show* (cynics claimed that it only existed to plug Lawrence Wright copyrights, but that never stopped its success). He started it in 1924 in Douglas, Isle of Man, and the following year transferred it to Blackpool, where it ran for 32 consecutive years, a record unequalled by even such well known impresarios as Florenz Ziegfeld, George White, or C B Cochran. It also gave a start to many famous artists such as Tessie O'Shea and Hermione Gingold. The only time Lawrie ever had a flop was when he tried to bring the show to London in 1934. He couldn't find a theatre so, like Irving Berlin before him, he bought one—Prince's, for £50,000. But what was so successful in Blackpool was a terrible flop in sophisticated London, and the experiment was never repeated. Horatio Nicholls the composer could never quite separate himself from Lawrence Wright, publisher and showman. He billed himself at various times as 'The Daddy of Tin Pan Alley', 'The Prime Minister of Melody' (a twist on George Robey's billing as 'The Prime Minister of Mirth'), and 'The

King of the British Songwriters'. In spite of all this seeming immodesty, it would be hard to discover anyone who had a harsh word to say about him. Despite his stroke, he continued writing into the 1950s. Among his last compositions was 'Christine' (1952), and he never gave up personal supervision of his publishing empire. The nurse who looked after him constantly, after his illness was quoted in a 1950s broadcast in his honour as saying '... his disability often makes him frustrated. But I can say this—in all the years I've been his nurse and companion, I have never heard him grumble or complain about his misfortunes. He is only too glad that he is still alive and able to go on composing and working'. In 1962 he received an Ivor Novello Award for 'Outstanding Services to British Popular Music'.

Some other outstanding songs by Horatio Nicholls :
'Delilah' (1917), 'The Heart of a Rose' (1918), 'A Night of Romance' (1918), 'In Old Vienna' (1928), 'I'm Saving the Last Waltz for You' (1930), 'Let's All Go to the Music Hall' (1934), 'Life Begins at Oxford Circus' (1935), 'London Is Saying Goodnight' (a hit for Gracie Fields, 1938), 'Omaha' (1921), 'Playthings' (1926), 'Rock Your Care Away' (1932), 'Tell Your Father, Tell Your Mother' (1933), 'Time Alone Will Tell' (1931), 'We'll Be Together Again' (1932), 'The Festival of Britain' (1950), 'No More Goodbyes' (1943), 'My Favourite Dream' (1944).

NILSSON, Harry (Harry Edward Nelson 3rd), composer, singer, pianist, guitarist.

Born Brooklyn, New York, 15 June 1941. Harry's parents separated when he was quite young, and at about 11, his mother took him with his sister to live in San Bernardino, California, later moving to a suburb of Los Angeles where Harry was educated at the St John Vianney's School. Various odd jobs followed his leaving school, until he finally settled down in a bank in San Fernando Valley. There he did so well that by the mid-1960s he was in charge of the bank's computer centre. But music was calling, and he practised the piano, started singing at various local venues, and ultimately tried his hand at writing songs.

His job at the bank meant night work, which left him a good deal of free time to hang around various music and record companies during the day, particularly the RCA building. He made one or two records with small companies, singing his own material, but nothing significant happened until producer Phil Spector took two of his songs for the Ronettes—'Paradise' and 'Here I Sit'. Finally, in 1967 The Monkees recorded his song 'Cuddly Toy', and he decided to leave the bank and devote himself full-time to music. At no stage did he see himself as a public performer, and he doesn't to this day. He is a typical example of that modern phenomenon, the singer/songwriter, except that he likes to confine his work to the recording studio.

In many ways Harry Nilsson is a kind of anti-hero of pop. He has been seen wearing smart suits, shirts and ties, and with his hair cut. But there have been occasions when he has been asked to leave an exclusive restaurant, unless he took off the cloth cap to which he seems addicted.

In 1968 RCA expressed their faith in the budding writer by signing him to a long-term singing/writing contract, worth in the region of $75,000. His first album, *Pandemonium Shadow Show* received huge critical acclaim. John Lennon, who had been sent a copy from the States and had never met Nilsson, phoned him simply to say 'You're great!' This was partly because some Beatle tunes were featured on the album, and treated in a particularly imaginative way, Nilsson using his own voice to dub and over-dub many vocal parts. In spite of the critics, however, the album was a commercial flop.

One of the most highly regarded tracks on the LP was Paul McCartney's 'She's Leaving Home', and it is ironical that Harry Nilsson did not write either of his two biggest-selling records. These were 'Everybody's Talkin'' from the 1969 film *Midnight Cowboy* (the composer was Fred Neil), and 'Without You', written by P Hamm and T Evans, which Harry took to No 1 in both the US and UK charts in 1972. One should record that there *was* a Harry Nilsson song in *Midnight Cowboy*. It was called 'I Guess the Lord Must Be in New York City', and it brought the composer considerable success.

Nilsson is perhaps a singer's singer and a composer's composer. This may not have made him an overnight millionaire, but it does mean that his work is exceptionally highly thought of by his fellow professionals. And his second album *Aerial Ballet* did make the album charts in 1969. A year later he had a hit single, 'Waiting'.

The end of 1969 also saw the advent of the third Nilsson album, *Harry*. This contained one song that became a UK No 1 for David Cassidy, 'Puppy Song' (it was originally written for Mary Hopkin), and a variety of other items in a variety of moods, ranging from 'Nobody Cares About the Railroads Anymore', to 'Simon Smith and the Amazing Talking Bear'. Again, it earned much critical acclaim, but not many sales, although his refusal to make public appearances made promotion difficult. But his talent had already been noticed by the mighty Otto Preminger, for whom he wrote the score for the 1968 film _Skidoo_ (starring Jackie Gleason, Carol Channing and Groucho Marx), and in the same year he wrote background music for a major TV show, _The Courtship of Eddie's Father_.

By 1972 Harry Nilsson could have been said to have 'arrived', and what did it was a 60-minute animated TV programme called _The Point_. Harry contributed both the story and the music (it was a fairy tale for children, much enjoyed by grown-ups). Dustin Hoffman was the narrator, and the public loved it. It had its British showing on BBC TV in the same year. The soundtrack album made the US charts, and a single taken from it, 'Me and My Arrow', had some success.

Other good albums were soon to follow. They included _Nilsson Schmilsson_, _Aerial Pandemonium Ballet_, _Son of Schmilsson_ and _A Little Touch of Schmilsson in the Night_. There was also one on which he collaborated with John Lennon, called _Pussy Cats_, but of all his recordings, this was the one to which the critics were most unkind.

Later, on one or two rare occasions, Harry Nilsson was persuaded to overcome his dislike for performing and do a concert. But he still prefers to withdraw from the world into his apartment and concentrate on writing and composing. The 1970s saw him becoming more and more involved with film work, and after he had adapted _The Point_ for the stage of London's Mermaid Theatre, his eyes (and ears) were trained on the musical theatre.

In 1981, among other things, he started a campaign to get rid of America's 11,000 hand guns.

Some other outstanding Harry Nilsson songs:
'Coconut' (1972), 'Jump Into the Fire' (1972), 'Space Man' (1972), 'One' (1969), 'You're Breaking My Heart' (1972).

NOBLE, Stanley Raymond (Ray), composer, pianist, arranger, conductor.

Born Hove, Sussex, 17 December 1903. Died London, 3 April 1978. Apart from a few years during the 1960s when he made his home in

Jersey, in the Channel Islands, Ray lived in America from 1936 onwards.

He was educated at Dulwich College, London, originally studying to be a surgeon. But he switched his studies to the Royal Academy of Music, winning a *Melody Maker* arranging contest in 1929. This led to a job as staff arranger for HMV Records (in those days gramophone companies had 'house' orchestras, which needed 'house' arrangers), where he was soon promoted to Head of Light Music and conductor of the company's 'New Mayfair Orchestra'. He also began arranging for Jack Payne's BBC Dance Orchestra.

His first published song was written in 1928, 'Nobody's Fault but Your Own', but his first hit did not come until 1931. This was 'Goodnight Sweetheart', which also became his most famous song. 'Love Is the Sweetest Thing' and 'By the Fireside' followed in 1932, and with 'Love Locked Out' and 'Love Is a Song' in 1933, Ray Noble, already established as a successful arranger/musical director, found himself established as a successful songwriter.

Recordings of Noble's hits, both by his own orchestra and by other well known recording artists of the time, led to the offer in 1934 of a contract to lead a band at New York's new Rainbow Room, '65 floors high in the RCA building at Radio City', as the American radio announcers used to describe it. This was the band of star musicians specially picked for Noble by American trombonist/arranger Glenn Miller. The band became an immediate success with its American audiences because of its interpretations of the ballads of the day, especially Ray's own compositions. Many of them were performed by the British singer, Al Bowlly, whom Ray had taken to New York with him for the venture. The only disappointed customers might have been the jazz fans, because Miller had assembled many great names in the band, but they were seldom, if ever, allowed to play any jazz.

There were more Ray Noble hits from 1934 to 1938, and when the Rainbow Room engagement ended in 1936, Ray went to Hollywood, where he embarked on a highly successful career as musical director to George Burns and Gracie Allen. He had previously made one trip to the West Coast to appear in the film *The Big Broadcast of 1936*. It was then that he first met Burns and Allen, together with Bing Crosby and Ethel Merman, who sang his song 'Why the Stars Come Out Tonight' in the film. At about that time he also contributed songs to the Jack Buchanan picture *Brewster's Millions* (notably 'One Good Turn Deserves Another'), and several other British films.

After a return visit to England in 1938 for personal appearances in variety, he went back to Hollywood and began a 13-year association with ventriloquist Edgar Bergen of Charlie McCarthy fame, as musical director of his radio show. This subsequently transferred very satisfactorily to TV. When the series finally ended in the mid-1950s, Ray retired gracefully to his Santa Barbara home. Like one or two other songwriters in this book, Ray Noble's total output was small—perhaps no more than 50 songs—but he has been responsible for enough standards to make most writers proud. Lyrically, his main collaborators have been Jimmy Campbell and Reg Connelly, Anona Winn, and Max Kester.

Some other outstanding Ray Noble songs :
'I Found You' (1931), 'What More Can I Ask ?' (1932), 'Who's Been Polishing the Sun ?' (1934), 'The Very Thought of You' (1934), 'The Touch of Your Lips' (1936), 'I Hadn't Anyone Till You' (1938), 'Cherokee' (1938).

NOVELLO, Ivor (David Ivor Davies), composer, author, producer, actor.

Born Cardiff, 15 January 1893. Died London, 5 March 1951. He took the name Novello from his mother, Clara Novello Davies. She was both a piano teacher and the conductor of a Welsh ladies choir, so she naturally saw to it that her son received piano lessons. At the age of 10 he was sent to the Magdalen College Choir School at Oxford, the family by then having moved to London, where Clara had opened a music studio. Ivor's devotion to the theatre as opposed to a career in serious music had become evident to his parents by the time he was 10, and although they disapproved, there was little they could do about it. But to ensure the continuation of his musical education after he left Oxford, his mother used him as an accompanist for as many of her engagements as possible. He soon took to composing and had his first song, 'Spring of the Year', published when he was 17.

Four years later, after the outbreak of World War I in 1914, he found overnight fame at the age of 21 with his first big hit, 'Till the Boys Come Home' (lyric by Lena Guilbert Ford), later to become universally known as 'Keep the Home Fires Burning'. In 1916 he was commissioned as a sub-lieutenant in the Royal Naval Air Service. But within a year he was involved in two air crashes, and his superiors decided that he would be better confined to clerical duties. They posted him to the Air Ministry in London, which could not have been more convenient for the budding young composer. He continued to write and have songs published throughout the war years, including seven in 1914, with lyrics by Fred Weatherly. There were also contributions to musical comedies such as *Theodore and Co* (1916), *Arlette* (1917), *Who's Hooper?* (1919), as well as to early André Charlot revues in 1916 and 1918. In one of these called *Tabs*, he wrote a song for Bea Lillie, 'When I Said Goodbye to You'. Fourteen years later it was to become a success for Gertrude Lawrence when she recorded it. In 1918, she had been Bea Lillie's understudy.

But in spite of a prolific output during those years, Novello's next big hit did not come until 1921. Until that time Novello's songs had all been based on the tradition of operetta. But with the 1920s there began the era of George Gershwin and Vincent Youmans and many other popular American composers, who tended to write for shows that were set in New York, or London, or Paris, and not in Vienna, or indeed Ruritania. Even though 'The Golden Moth' (a show for which Ivor wrote all the music, and in which he had P G Wodehouse as lyricist) was set in a night club, its songs still had that traditional European flavour. But with his score for André Charlot's revue *A–Z*, in 1921, everything changed, and the song that did it for him was 'And Her Mother Came Too' (lyrics by Dion Titheradge), sung in the show by Jack Buchanan.

Ivor Novello's career had a great deal in common with that of Sir Nöel Coward. In addition to being songwriters, they both became playwrights, actors and producers, and they both bought houses in Jamaica. But as with Sir Nöel Coward, since this book is about songwriters, it is on that side of Novello's career that we must concentrate, mentioning only in passing that he first appeared in films in 1920 (*The Call of the Blood*), and followed it with 22 more up to 1938, including *The Vortex* (1928), *The Constant Nymph* (1928), and *Autumn Crocus* (1934). In addition there were film versions of his three biggest musicals, *Glamorous Night*, *The Dancing Years* and *King's Rhapsody*. He also appeared in no fewer than 27 plays.

The Novello musicals next highlight the career of Novello the songwriter. It was in 1935 that *Glamorous Night*, the first of the great big Novello shows, hit Drury Lane. It has been said that *Glamorous Night* was not truly a musical as we understand musicals today but rather a combination of melodrama, operetta and musical comedy. Sandy Wilson in his book *Ivor* sums it up as '... a Novello Show'. Whatever anybody likes to call it, it was a huge hit by any standards, and such songs as 'Shine Through My Dreams', 'When the Gypsy Played', 'The Singing Waltz' and the title song, 'Glamorous Night', have passed into popular music history. All lyrics for the show were written by Christopher Hassall, and the original cast included Mary Ellis, Elisabeth Welch, Olive Gilbert and Peter Graves.

This was followed in 1936 by *Careless Rapture*, which also opened at Drury Lane, and included Dorothy Dickson, Zena Dare, Olive Gilbert, Peter Graves and Walter Crisham among a star-studded cast. Lyrics were again by Christopher Hassall, and the songs included 'The Singing Lesson', 'Music in May', 'Why Is There Ever Goodbye?' and 'Love Made the Song I Sing to You'.

The next Novello spectacular was *Crest of the Wave*, again at Drury Lane (1937), again with lyrics by Christopher Hassall, and again Olive Gilbert and Walter Crisham were in the cast. In addition there were Dorothy Dickson, Marie Lohr, Peter Graves and Finlay Currie. Among the songs were 'The Haven of Your Heart', 'If You Only Knew', 'Why Isn't It You?' and 'Rose of England'.

The Dancing Years followed in 1939, still at Drury Lane, and with many of the old team—Christopher Hassall (lyrics), Mary Ellis, Olive Gilbert, Peter Graves and, for the first time, Roma Beaumont. Songs to be remembered included 'I Can Give You the Starlight', 'Waltz of My Heart' and 'My Dearest Dear'. *Arc de Triomphe*, which opened at the Phoenix Theatre in 1943, did not produce any memorable songs, but *Perchance to Dream*, presented at the Hippodrome in 1945, did.

This was also one of the few shows for which Novello wrote lyrics as well as the music. Among the stars were Roma Beaumont, Olive Gilbert, Margaret Rutherford, and Muriel Barron, and among the songs were 'Love Is My Reason', and 'We'll Gather Lilacs' which was Ivor's biggest hit since 'And Her Mother Came Too'.

In 1949 came *King's Rhapsody*, at the Palace Theatre. Lyrics were by Christopher Hassall again; Raymond Lovell, Zena Dare and Harcourt Williams were new members of the cast, among many of the old faithfuls, and among the songs were 'Someday My Heart Will Awake', 'Take Your Girl' and 'The Violin Began to Play'.

King's Rhapsody was the last of the great Novello spectaculars, but not his last show. In 1951 *Gay's the Word* opened at the Saville Theatre. It was specially written to star Cicely Courtneidge, and also in the cast were Lizbeth Webb, Thorley Walters and Maidie Andrews.

Novello himself did not appear in it as he had in all the previous shows (he was still appearing in *King's Rhapsody*), and the lyrics were by Alan Melville. It had an excellent score, but there was one final outstanding song—'Vitality'. It was Ivor Novello's last big hit and it was magnificently performed by Cicely Courtneidge.

Ivor had not been well during the run of *King's Rhapsody*, and in 1950 he left the cast and flew to Jamaica for a holiday in his home there. He returned in time for the first night of *Gay's the Word*, which he attended against his doctor's orders, and shortly afterwards insisted also on returning to the cast of *King's Rhapsody*. Less than a month later he died of thrombosis.

As a songwriter without hundreds of gigantic hits to his name, it might be said that Ivor Novello does not belong in this book. I mentioned his switching in the 1920s away from the traditional operetta/musical comedy style of writing. But most of the time he never really made the switch, which is why no more than a handful of his songs became hits in the Tin Pan Alley sense of selling millions of copies of sheet music or records. But he left behind so many songs that people still recall after hearing only the first few bars (they may not even know that they are listening to a Novello song), that in my view he more than merits his place.

The important Ivor Novello songs have been referred to in the text, so no additional listing is necessary.

O'SULLIVAN, Gilbert (Raymond O'Sullivan), composer, author, singer, pianist.

Born Waterford, Eire, 1 December 1946. He was educated at local schools until 1960, when his family moved to Swindon in England, and his education was continued at St Joseph's School, and Swindon Art College. His mother bought a piano for the family home, and, that being the era of the Beatles, a youthful Raymond continually tried to thump out Beatles hits on it, with no musical training at all.

He also acquired some drums, and played with various Swindon teenage groups, in one of which, Rick's Blues, he found a pianist who taught him the rudiments of the instrument.

At the same time he developed a teenage desire to write songs like Lennon and McCartney, and both he and his piano ended up banished to the garden shed. He started sending tapes to groups, and The

Tremeloes even included a few of his titles on an album, while producer Mike Smith of CBS Records recorded his song 'Disappear' as a single. That was in 1967, and it was the equivalent of his first published song. It turned out to be a flop, but Raymond will always be grateful to Mike Smith for re-christening him 'Gilbert O'Sullivan'.

Later that year he left Swindon for London to earn a living at various odd jobs. He continued to write songs in every spare moment, hawked them endlessly round the publishers of London's Tin Pan Alley, and showed them to every A and R man he could reach at the record companies. But it was all to no avail. In the end he decided to try and reach some of the important people in the music business by mail. Luckily, one of his packets of demo tapes was opened by pop impresario Gordon Mills, then manager of both Tom Jones and Engelbert Humperdinck.

Mills was impressed with what he heard, and later, having met the budding writer, was impressed with his personality too, But it was to be a year before Gordon Mills decided that the world was ready to have this new composer/performer launched upon it. When he did, the song he chose was 'Nothing Rhymed', which became a hit, although not a number one. It not only put Gilbert O'Sullivan on the map but added another star to the Gordon Mills stable. The outrageous dress and initial image of the new star were entirely Gilbert's own idea. The short trousers, bare knees, flat cap and large boots were partially inspired by one of his boyhood heroes, Charlie Chaplin. More importantly, he was so disillusioned by the way his songs had been rejected that he aimed to give the critics something to criticise—his personal appearance—and perhaps the resultant publicity would help his songwriting career. It certainly didn't harm it.

Between that initial success in 1970 and the end of 1974, he had big hits with such songs as 'No Matter How I Try', (1971, No 4 UK); 'Alone Again (Naturally)' (1972, No 3 UK, No 1 US); 'Ooh Wacka Doo Wacka Day' (1972, No 8 UK); 'Clair' (1972, No 1 UK, No 2 US); 'Get Down' (1973, No 7 UK, No 1 US). 'Alone Again' and 'Get Down' both earned gold discs. In 1973 he was nominated as Songwriter of the Year in the UK, and won an Ivor Novello Award. By 1972 he figured his 'Bisto Kid' image had served him well, so he discarded it, and the current Gilbert O'Sullivan personality emerged.

The 1970s brought the anti-hero to movies and TV. If there could be such a thing as the anti-songwriter of the decade, it should be Gilbert O'Sullivan. His favourite composer is Cole Porter, in an age when only rock 'n' roll seems to matter. He says of himself, 'I'm essentially a songwriter who happens to record his own work—not a pop star'. And again, 'Writing music is all I live for, and everything else comes a poor second'. He lives modestly by himself in a bungalow in Weybridge, Surrey, and he has no car—he cannot drive one. In addition to his idol Cole Porter, he also likes Rodgers and Hart, and Paul McCartney. Of Porter he says, 'Every song Cole Porter wrote is a classic—every one. If the standard of Simon and Garfunkel was up to the standard of "Bridge Over Troubled Water", it would be great. But the others are just good songs'. Although those quotes date from the early 1970s, his attitude to music remains unchanged.

Gilbert O'Sullivan's output has not been large. His biggest hits have already been mentioned, and there is a list below of some of his other best known compositions. He has earned his place here in this book because of the quality of his songs. Certainly two, 'Alone Again' and 'Clair' are already standards, and will remain so.

Some other outstanding Gilbert O'Sullivan Songs:
'No Matter How I Try' (1971), 'Underneath the Blanket Go' (1971), 'Permissive Twit' (1972), 'Matrimony' (1972), 'Ooh Baby' (1973), 'Why, Oh Why, Oh Why?' (1973), 'I Don't Love You but I Think I Like You' (1975), 'My Love and I' (1977).

PARR-DAVIES, Harry, composer, author, pianist, arranger.

Born Briton Ferry, West Glamorgan, Wales, 24 May 1914. Died London, 14 October 1955. Parr-Davies is not strictly speaking a hyphenated name, but the insertion of a hyphen has become such common practice that we have decided to adopt it rather than listing him under Davies, which is not how most people think of him. He was educated at Neath Grammar School in Wales, moving to London as a young man. He wrote his first musical at school, aged 12, and was fortunate in that in the audience was Sir Walford Davies, of Cardiff University, who was sufficiently impressed to take him as a pupil.

Harry Parr-Davies's first published song was called 'I Hate You' (1931), but success did not really come his way until 1933, when he had two songs, 'Happy Ending' and 'Mary Rose' in the movie *This Week of Grace*, starring Gracie Fields. This was followed by the title song from her 1934 film, 'Sing As We Go', and led to a lengthy friendship with this great British star of the 1930s. For many years he was her accompanist at her public performances, including those at the London Palladium. 'Sing As We Go' was based on one of the tunes he wrote as a 12-year-old for that school show. He also contributed songs to Gracie's 1938 movie *We're Going to Be Rich* ('The Sweetest Song in the World'), and the international hit 'Wish Me Luck As You Wave Me Goodbye' for her 1939 film *Shipyard Sally*. Other hits of the 1930s included 'Love Is Everywhere' (1935), 'My First Love Song' (1936) and 'Fairy on the Christmas Tree' (1937). In addition to the Gracie Fields films, Harry Parr-Davies contributed many songs to British musical pictures of the 1930s and 1940s. Among the best known of these films were *Maytime in Mayfair, Keep Smiling, Queen of Hearts* and *It's in the Air.*

During the 1940s and 1950s he was busily engaged in writing for revues and stage shows. These began in 1939 with George Black's production of *Black Velvet* at the London Hippodrome, starring Vic Oliver, Max and Harry Nesbitt, Roma Beaumont and Pat Kirkwood, among others. The best of the Harry Parr-Davies songs were 'Bubble Bubble' and 'Crash Bang I Wanna Go Home'. In the 1940s he wrote for such productions as *Top of the World* (1940, with Flanagan and Allen, Nervo and Knox, Tommy Trinder and Pat Kirkwood—the big song being 'It All Comes Back to Me Now'); *Gangway* (another George Black production at the Palladium in 1941, with Tommy Trinder, Bebé Daniels, Ben Lyon, Webster Booth and Anne Ziegler); *Jenny Jones* (1944, from which the big song was 'Where the Blue Begins'); Firth Shephard's *The Shephard Show* (1946, with Douglas Byng, Richard Hearne and Marie Burke in the cast); *Her Excellency* (1949, which gave us the song 'Sunday in England'); and his biggest success of all during the decade, the music for the 1943 production, *The Lisbon Story*, starring Jack Livesey, Patricia Burke and Noele Gordon. This gave us Harry Parr-Davies's biggest hit ever, 'Pedro the Fisherman', as well as the songs 'Never Say Goodbye' and 'Someday We Shall Meet Again'. The show was later made into a movie. The 1950s saw further contributions to such shows as *Blue for a Boy* (title song, 1950), and *Dear Miss Phoebe* (also 1950, with the songs 'I Leave My Heart in an English Garden' and 'Whisper While You Waltz').

Harry Parr-Davies's main lyricists over the years were Phil Park, Harold Purcell, and Christopher Hassall. Occasionally he wrote lyrics himself, notably for the 1942 show *Happidrome*, in which he and Phil

Park reversed their normal roles, Park contributing the music and Parr-Davies the words.

He was a prolific writer of special material for the stars, and in addition to those already referred to, Anna Neagle, Cicely Court-neidge, Beatrice Lillie, Evelyn Laye, Jessie Matthews, Fred Emney, Jack Buchanan and Hutch (Leslie Hutchinson) were all good customers. In his role as an accompanist he frequently toured the USA, Canada and South Africa. He was also a contributor to a well known 1930s radio show, *Welsh Rarebit*. During World War II he served in the Life Guards. After his death in 1955, the BBC presented a radio tribute to the man and his music, which was introduced by Anna Neagle.

Harry Parr-Davies's main hits have been referred to in the text, so no further listing is needed here.

PORTER, Cole, composer, author.

Born Peru, Indiana, 9 June 1891. Died Santa Monica, California, 15 October 1964. Educated Worcester Academy, Massachusetts, and Yale University, where he obtained a BA degree. He then went to Harvard Law School, and Harvard School of Music. It is usually said that between 1917 and 1919 Cole Porter served in the French Foreign Legion although some biographers dispute this. David Ewen, in *Great Men of American Popular Song* says, 'Porter enlisted in the "first foreign regiment", of the 32nd Field Artillery, later being transferred to the Bureau of the Military Attaché of the United States. He was really serving in the French Army as an American citizen, and for this reason was under the direct control of the Foreign Legion'.

Cole Porter is an excellent example of that comparative rarity among songwriters, a man born with a silver spoon in his mouth, without the need to rise from rags to riches. His grandfather, J O Cole, was a multi-millionaire, so even when his proposals to take up music instead of law resulted in threats to cut him off with the proverbial cent, his mother, on whom he doted, was always in the background to provide for him. Furthermore, when he eventually married in 1919 (with grandfather still refusing all co-operation), it was to a woman wealthy in her own right, for Linda Lee Thomas was a divorced American living in Paris, and one for whom money was no problem. So J O Cole's efforts to persuade his grandson to earn a living in a 'respectable' profession, and to lead the kind of life he thought fitting for a well brought-up young American, were frustrated at every turn. It seems he was never able to come to terms with the situation, even when Porter became one of the great men of American popular music.

Kate Cole, J O's daughter and Cole's mother, married Samuel Porter, a gentle and charming man, with a love for poetry, but little ambition or personality. He too was written off by J O Cole as a dead loss, and was dominated by his wife, who inherited a good deal of her father's overbearing temperament. Kate and Samuel, Cole's parents, had produced two children prior to Cole, but both had died young, leaving Cole as an only and somewhat spoiled child. An analogy between his upbringing and that of Ivor Novello is worth making, and an understanding of the family background of both men is essential to an understanding of why they wrote the kind of songs they did, though each was vastly different from the other in style. Cole was taught piano and violin from a very early age, (he was also taught to ride a horse with terrifying consequences in later life), and when he was 11 his mother paid a publisher $100 to have his tune 'The Bobolink Waltz' published.

He continued to write songs all through his school and university years, no matter how much his talents in this direction were discouraged by his family. David Ewen says of Porter during his years at Yale, 'His fellow students later remembered him as a young man who drank champagne, gin and Scotch, who smoked Fatima cigarettes, who was always meticulously groomed and socially poised, and who had a fetish for luxurious living'. Thus the Cole Porter playboy image developed at an early age, never to leave him, though when he began in later years to write songs professionally, no one could have worked harder or been more dedicated. Furthermore it was a life style that he and his wife had all the money they needed to indulge, even through the depths of the Depression of the 1930s.

In 1915 he had a song, 'Two Big Eyes', accepted for a Broadway show called *Miss Information*, for which most of the music was written by Jerome Kern, and also another, 'Esmeralda' in *Hands Up*, a show otherwise written by Sigmund Romberg. The following year he realized his ambition to write all the music for a Broadway show, when *See America First* opened at the Maxine Elliott Theater. The show was a disaster, save for one song, 'I've a Shooting Box in Scotland' and the young composer crawled away to lick his wounds.

From the time of his leaving for France during World War I, throughout most of the 1920s, Cole Porter and his wife Linda were more or less permanently based in Paris, paying only occasional visits home to the USA.

It was on one such trip that he met Raymond Hitchcock, the Broadway producer, who invited him to write the score for his revue *Hitchy-Koo of 1919*. Only one song, 'Old-Fashioned Garden', was a success but one song was all that was needed to convince the young Cole that he was going to be a professional composer. He followed up with songs for *Hitchy-Koo of 1922*, which achieved nothing, but had one good song out of the five he wrote in 1924 for the show *Greenwich Village Follies* (the song was 'I'm in Love Again', which meant nothing in the show, in spite of being sung by the then popular Dolly Sisters, but which became a classic five years later).

In 1928 he wrote the music for a Parisian revue, and again the 'I'm in Love Again' song failed, but it became a hit the following year when it turned up on Broadway sung by Clifton Webb in *Wake Up and Dream*. One or two minor hits in revues do not make a successful songwriter, and although Cole Porter had never written because he needed the money, he was nonetheless determined to succeed at his chosen profession. He needed a Broadway show of his own, and that chance came with *Paris* in 1928, which starred Irene Bordoni, and produced the song 'Let's Do It, Let's Fall in Love'. The following year came another all-Porter show, *Fifty Million Frenchmen*, starring William Gaxton and Genevieve Tobin, and this one produced from its score *You Do Something to Me*. The whole show inspired Irving Berlin to say in an advertisement: 'It's worth the price of admission to hear Cole Porter's lyrics' (right from the beginning Porter had written all the lyrics as well as the music for his songs).

Porter had a unique method of gaining inspiration for his songs and for writing his sophisticated lyrics. Frequently ideas would come from everyday incidents. For instance, according to David Ewen, ' "It's De-Lovely" was actually born when Cole Porter was taking a world cruise. Watching the sun rise over Rio from the deck, Cole remarked "It's delightful" his wife Linda responded "It's delicious"; and their friend Monty Woolley added "It's de-lovely". Cole Porter used all of that in his song. And "Well, did you evah?" was a comment Cole overheard at a 'party'. In addition to these remarkable powers of observation and recall, Porter soon became aware of the need to write a song to serve a particular purpose or person. 'Night and Day', for instance, which was introduced by Fred Astaire in *The*

Gay Divorce, was deliberately constructed with Fred's very limited vocal range in mind. 'Don't Fence Me In' was written as a send-up of all the popular cowboy ballads of the 1930s that Cole so detested—he never thought it would earn him a fortune in royalties. While his unfavourite song of all his own songs was undoubtedly 'Rosalie', which he wrote in a fit of pique when the producer of the film kept on turning down many more original ideas. Cole simply crammed every musical cliché he could think of into that number. 'The public never recognizing', says David Ewen, 'that he had written it with tongue in cheek'. Likewise, 'Miss Otis Regrets' was written for his friend Monty Woolley to perform at a party, with no thought of publication at all.

Cole and Linda Porter finally left their beloved Paris and moved back to New York in the early 1930s, but throughout his life the Porter love affair with his favourite city never left him, as the lyrics and settings of so many of his subsequent songs demonstrate. It was perhaps *Gay Divorce*, the show he wrote for Fred Astaire, which opened in New York in 1932 and moved to London in 1933, that set the seal of public approval on Cole Porter and established him as one of the top 10 all-time greats in the world of songwriting. It was also in 1933 that his show *Nymph Errant* appeared in England, starring Gertrude Lawrence and Elisabeth Welch, a splendid and regrettably unsuccessful production that was never produced in America. Certainly the 1930s and 1940s were the great Cole Porter years. *Gay Divorce* was followed in 1934 by *Anything Goes*, which starred Ethel Merman and was one of the two best Porter scores of all time. In 1935 came *Jubilee*, perhaps especially remarkable for the fact that it contained 'Begin the Beguine', a song that was totally ignored by both public and critics and which did not become a hit until resurrected and recorded as an instrumental on the B side of aspiring young bandleader Artie Shaw's first disc three years later in 1938. The A side (or so thought Shaw's record-producer) was Rudolf Friml's 'Indian Love Call'.

In 1936 came the show *Red, Hot and Blue*, with Ethel Merman, Bob Hope and Jimmy Durante in the cast. In 1938 there was *You Never Know*, with Clifton Webb and Lupe Velez (one of the few Porter shows that contained songs by other composers as well as his own). That same year saw *Leave It to Me* with Mary Martin and Sophie Tucker, and the song 'My Heart Belongs to Daddy'. In 1939 we had *Du Barry Was a Lady*, with Betty Grable, and the song (later re-introduced in the film *High Society*) 'Well, Did You Evah!'. There was *Panama Hattie* in 1940, with a big cast that included Ethel Merman, Betty Hutton and Arthur Treacher. After that came *Let's Face It* (1941), with Danny Kaye; *Something for the Boys* (1943) with Ethel Merman again; *Mexican Hayride* (1944) with June Havoc, and the song 'Count Your Blessings'; *The Seven Lively Arts* (1944), starring among others Beatrice Lillie and the entire Benny Goodman band; and *Around the World in Eighty Days* (1946). In 1948, came Cole Porter's best score since *Anything Goes*, and arguably his best score ever: *Kiss Me Kate* (based on Shakespeare's *The Taming of the Shrew*), starring Alfred Drake and Patricia Morison. There were 17 songs in the show, of which at least six are standards, and out of them all there was not a dull one. It was also the Porter musical that had the longest run and made the most money. Yet there were still two more highly acclaimed shows to come—*Can-Can* in 1953 and *Silk Stockings* in 1955, both of which had Parisian backgrounds.

While all this Broadway activity was going on, Hollywood had not been neglecting Cole Porter, nor he Hollywood. *The Gay Divorce* had been made into a film in 1934 with the title changed to *The Gay Divorcée*, and in 1936 he wrote *Born to Dance* for Eleanor Powell, James Stewart, Virginia Bruce and Una Merkel. *Anything Goes* was filmed in 1936, with Bing Crosby. In 1937 there was *Rosalie*, to which we have already referred (it had Nelson Eddy and Eleanor Powell in the cast); *Broadway Melody of 1940* with Eleanor Powell and Fred Astaire (the success of the Artie Shaw record of 'Begin the Beguine' led to the number's being re-introduced into this film); *You'll Never Get Rich* in 1941 with Fred Astaire and Rita Hayworth; *Something to Shout About* in 1943 with Don Ameche, Janet Blair and Jack Oakie; *Hollywood Canteen* in 1944 with Jack Benny, Eddie Cantor, Joan Crawford, Bette Davis, Roy Rogers, Barbara Stanwyck, Jane Wyman, The Andrews Sisters, and the complete bands of Jimmy Dorsey and Carmen Cavallaro (yet its only hit was a hitherto unused 1934 song, 'Don't Fence Me In'); *The Pirate* in 1948, starring Judy Garland and Gene Kelly; and there were two unremarkable films, *Adam's Rib* in 1949, and *Stage Fright* in 1950.

But that was not quite all. There was one more film called *Les Girls* (1956), and then, almost as if he were determined to end his film career on a high note, there was the utterly magical *High Society*, in 1957, starring Bing Crosby, Frank Sinatra, Louis Armstrong, and Grace Kelly, which brought him his last really big hit, 'True Love'. He also wrote one of the few musical TV Specials, *Aladdin*, for the CBS Network in 1958.

Aside fom the fabulous output of this remarkable man, his private life was not without incident. As far back as 1937, both legs had been shattered in a riding accident, when his horse reared and fell on top of him. Within a year he had suffered no less than seven operations on them, was in almost continuous pain, and confined to a wheelchair. Thirty more operations were to follow during the next five years, in attempts to save his legs, and sheer strength of will more than any other single thing kept him going over the next 20 years.

Slowly he started going out again, throwing his famous parties, and forcing himself to sit at the piano and compose. He even resumed his trips aboard, helped and sometimes carried by his wife and friends. But the man with everything going for him, the composer with the golden, magic touch, was never again able to enjoy the life style to which he had been accustomed, and which meant so much to him.

In 1952 his mother died. And in 1954, his wife Linda, who had not been well for some time, also died, and was buried near his mother at his birthplace, Peru, Indiana. In 1958 he was told that because of bone inflammation his right leg would have to be amputated. He appeared to accept this remarkably well, but afterwards the process of trying to walk with an artificial limb was too much for him, in spite of strenuous efforts. He finally resigned himself to being carried everywhere.

From then on Porter became more and more withdrawn, seldom going anywhere, and even refusing all attempts to persuade him to attend functions that were staged in his honour. As a result, he did not go to the splendid *Salute to Cole Porter* staged at the Metropolitan Opera House in 1960. Nor did he attend the special celebrations put on at the Orpheum Theater in New York to mark his 70th birthday. In June 1964 he went to his home in California, as he had always done at that time for many years, and in October was admitted to Santa Monica hospital for the removal of a kidney stone. Two days after the operation he died. His doctors deduced that the only reason for his death must have been his wilful decision not to live any longer. He was buried in Peru, Indiana, between the bodies of his mother and his wife.

Some other outstanding Cole Porter songs:
'What Is This Thing Called Love?' (*Wake Up and Dream*, 1929), 'Love for Sale (*The New Yorkers*, 1930), 'Experiment' (*Nymph Errant*, 1933), 'I Get a Kick Out of You' and 'You're the Top' (both from *Anything Goes*, 1934), 'Just One of Those Things' (*Jubilee*, 1935),

'Ridin' High' (*Red Hot and Blue*, 1936), 'Easy to Love' and 'I've Got You Under My Skin' (both from *Born to Dance*, 1936), 'In the Still of the Night' (*Rosalie*, 1937), 'I Concentrate on You' and 'I've Got My Eyes on You' (both from *Broadway Melody of 1940*), 'You'd Be So Nice to Come Home To' (*Something to Shout About*, 1943), 'Hey, Good Lookin'' (*Something for the Boys*, 1943), 'Ev'ry Time We Say Goodbye' (*Seven Lively Arts*, 1944), 'Be a Clown' (*The Pirate*, 1948), 'So in Love', 'Always True to You in My Fashion', and 'Why Can't You Behave?' (all from *Kiss Me Kate*, 1948), 'From This Moment On' (*Out of this World*, 1950), 'C'est Magnifique', 'I Love Paris', and 'It's All Right With Me' (all from *Can-Can*, 1953), 'I Love You Samantha', 'Who Wants to Be a Millionaire?', and 'Now You Has Jazz' (all from *High Society*, 1956).

RAINGER, Ralph, composer, pianist, arranger.

Born New York, 7 October 1901. Died Beverly Hills, California, 23 October 1942. Educated at Damrosch Conservatory where he won a scholarship, and at Brown University Law School, where he obtained his LLB. Rainger had always wanted to play music ever since having piano lessons at an early age. When he found, during his first job with a law firm, that they only paid him $25 per week, but that he could earn more than that playing in a local dance band, it was goodbye to his family's idea of taking up a secure profession. His first real job in music was playing piano in the pit orchestra at the Ambassador's Theater in New York. After hours, he spent much of his time writing songs, but none of the publishers wanted to know. When the show closed he took a job with Clifton Webb and Mary Hay as accompanist to their vaudeville act. This, in turn, led to a job as rehearsal pianist for a New York revue in which Webb had a leading role. The music had been written by Arthur Schwarz and Howard Dietz, but an extra song was needed for Webb, so Rainger came up with a tune for which Dietz wrote the lyrics. It became the first Rainger hit, called 'Moanin' Low' (1929).

From then on success came quickly. He met Leo Robin (born in Pittsburgh, Pennsylvania, 6 April 1900), and throughout the 1930s they were one of Hollywood's most successful teams of songwriters. They first wrote for Bing Crosby in *The Big Broadcast* (1932), with the song 'Please'. Five more Crosby films followed: *She Loves Me Not*

(1934, 'Love in Bloom'); *Here Is My Heart* (1934, 'June in January'); *The Big Broadcast of 1936* (1935, a film in which Rainger had hits with 'I Wished on the Moon', lyrics by Dorothy Parker, and 'Miss Brown to You', lyrics by Richard Whiting); *Waikiki Wedding* (1937, 'In a Little Hula Heaven', and 'Blue Hawaii'); and *Paris Honeymoon* (1939, 'You're a Sweet Little Headache'). During their Hollywood career they also wrote for some 42 other films, and for such stars as Fanny Brice, Maurice Chevalier, Claudette Colbert, Mae West, Cary Grant, George Raft, Shirley Temple, Ida Lupino, Carole Lombard, Jack Oakie, Genevieve Tobin, Dorothy Lamour, Frances Langford, Jack Benny, Burns and Allen, Martha Raye, Shirley Ross, Bob Hope ('Thanks for the Memory'), Joan Bennett, Betty Grable, Rita Hayworth, Ginger Rogers and many more.

Their successful career was cut short by Ralph Rainger's tragic death in an air crash in 1942. Leo Robin, however, continued to turn out lyrics as well as ever, and among his other collaborators were Vincent Youmans ('Hallelujah', 1927); Richard Whiting ('Louise', 1929, and 'Beyond the Blue Horizon', 1930); Arthur Schwarz ('A Gal in Calico', 1947); Harold Arlen ('Hooray for Love', 1948); and Jule Styne ('Diamonds Are a Girl's Best Friend', 1953).

Some other outstanding Robin and Rainger Songs:
'Here Lies Love' (1932), 'With Every Breath I Take' (1934), 'Faithful Forever' (1939), 'Give Me Liberty or Give Me Love' (1933), 'Double Trouble' (1935), 'La Bomba' (1936), 'Blossoms on Broadway' (1937), 'Ebb Tide' (1937), 'I Have Eyes' (1939).

REED, Leslie (Les), composer, arranger, pianist, conductor.

Born 24 July 1935, Woking, Surrey. Educated at local schools, and taught music by his father who, although not a musician, was a keen amateur impresario, running a troupe called The Westfield Kids. Young Les was soon absorbed into the troupe, and when it became obvious from his mostly self-taught prowess on the accordion and piano at the age of 7 that he had exceptional musical talent, dad even studied music himself so that, when he had to go into the army, he could keep his son on top of his musical tuition by sending him questions on theory and demanding the right answers. By the age of 15 Les had formed a little semi-pro band which did quite well playing for local dates, but after a few years he himself was called up for National Service, and joined the Military Band of the Royal East Kent Regiment. He was taught the clarinet, and continued his studies in theory to such good effect that when his service was finished he was able to earn a living as a professional pianist with various bands before joining the John Barry Seven full time in 1958.

Les stayed with Barry for three years, and it was then that he started writing songs and developing his talent for arranging. His first published composition was an instrumental piece called 'Speedy', which appeared in 1961, and his first hit came two years later with 'Tell Me When', for which Geoff Stephens wrote the lyrics, and which was taken into the charts by a group called The Applejacks in 1964. By that time he was already in demand as a musical director, not only for records, but on radio and TV as well. It was perhaps a chance incident on an Adam Faith recording session that convinced the aspiring conductor that he should do more writing.

Adam had arrived with no song for the B side of his record. Then and there Les Reed sat down and wrote 'While I'm Away', which subsequently became the A side. He followed this with a successful song for Lulu in 1965, 'Leave a Little Love'. At about the same time he had his first real smash, 'It's Not Unusual', which made No 1 in the UK and No 10 in the US charts. The idea was supplied by Tom Jones's manager, Gordon Mills, who worked on the song with Les until it became the one that really put not only the composer and the manager, but also the artist, Tom Jones, on the map. After 1965, Les Reed entered on his very successful partnership with lyricist Barry Mason. Barry was born at Wigan, Lancashire, 12 July 1935. He was educated at local schools, and for about three years in the USA. Returning to London, he took to lyric-writing while working at various jobs to earn a living, but it was not until he was introduced to Les Reed that he found success. The record by The Fortunes of their 1965 song, 'Here It Comes Again', was an instant hit.

In songwriting terms the years 1955 to 1969 were the epitome of the Reed/Mason partnership. During that period they also produced for Tom Jones 'I'm Coming Home' (1967, No 2 in the UK), and 'Delilah' (1968, No 2 in the UK and No 15 in the US). For Engelbert Humperdinck they wrote 'The Last Waltz' (1967, No 1 in the UK and No 25 in the US), 'Les Bicyclettes de Belsize' (1968—Les Reed wrote the entire score for the film), and 'Winter World of Love' (1969, No 7 in the UK, No 16 in the US). And they had hits with

The Dave Clark Five, including 'Everybody Knows' (1967, No 2 in the UK and No 15 in the US).

After his partnership with Les, Barry Mason went on to become a musical success in his own right. In 1976 he had a gold disc for his writing and singing effort with 'You Just Might See Me Cry' (No 1 in UK), and in 1977 he had a big hit in the US country charts with Tom Jones's recording of his song 'Say You'll Stay Until Tomorrow'. In 1979 Barry wrote a No 1 for singer Demis Roussos, 'When Forever Has Gone', and like Les Reed, he has, over the years, been a frequent and successful participant in many international song festivals. In 1980 Mason took on the dual role of composer and producer for the musical *Miranda*. His current and most ambitious project at the time of writing is the musical *American Heroes*, for which he has written music, book and lyrics in conjunction with M Heath Johnson and Don Gould. They have followed the successful Webber/Rice format of producing an album, which has had some critical acclaim, prior to any premiere presentation in the US.

It was also during the late 1960s that Les had two more big hits with lyrics by Geoff Stephens, 'There's a Kind of Hush' in 1967 for Herman's Hermits (No 7 in the UK and No 4 in the US), and 'Daughter of Darkness' for Tom Jones (1970, No 5 in the UK and No 13 in the US). By the 1970s Les Reed was firmly established as one of Britain's most successful songwriters. He had already been dubbed 'The quiet millionaire'. He has won 80 gold discs and two platinum, and he has won Ivor Novello Awards in the UK and Grammys in the USA.

With so many great hits to his credit, it is perhaps not surprising that Les Reed the musician tended to take over from Les Reed the songwriter throughout the 1970s. He is a glutton for work. He has appeared at countless international song festivals and won major prizes at these events throughout the world. His appearances as a conductor as well as working as musical director for many famous artists are too numerous to list here, and he has appeared in two Royal Command Performances. In 1975 he originated the 'International Pop Proms' for Granada TV, a series in which he was featured again in 1976 and 1977.

But he has not stopped composing, and the 1970s saw 'You Bring out the Best of the Woman in Me', recorded by Connie Francis, 'That's What Life Is All About', sadly Bing Crosby's last recording, and 'What Have I Got, I've Got You Babe', recorded by both Connie Francis, and Millican and Nesbitt. Many of his songs are now standards, and the list of internationally famous artists who have recorded them is endless. It ranges from Petula Clark, Mireille Mathieu and Shirley Bassey to Steve Lawrence, Sacha Distel and Ken Dodd. Teresa Brewer has had a No 1 hit in the US with 'Childhood Place', and The Carpenters almost took 'There's a Kind of Hush' to the top of the charts for the second time round in 1976.

Among the films for which Les Reed has supplied the scores are *Girl on a Motorcycle*, and *One More Time*, as well as supplying themes and songs for *The Lady Vanishes*, *Alfie*, *Play Misty for Me*, and the TV series *George and Mildred* and *To the Manor Born*. He also has two songs in the musical which was the brainchild of his old partner Barry Mason, called *American Heroes*.

Barry has continued to write successful songs with other composers, notably 'Love Grows Where My Rosemary Goes' with Tony Macaulay, and 'A Man Without Love', for which he supplied the English lyrics.

The Reed/Mason and the Reed/Stephens partnerships as song-writers may be over, but the music of Les Reed is certainly going to be with us into the 1980s.

Some other outstanding Les Reed songs:
'Love Is All' (1969), 'I Pretend' (1968), 'Leave a Little Love' (1965), 'Kiss Me Goodbye' (1968), 'Hello Happiness' (1967), 'Please Don't Go' (1968), 'Give Me One More Chance' (1972), 'Don't Bring Me Your Heartaches' (1965), 'Have Pity on the Boy' (1966), '24 Sycamore' (1967), 'When We Were Young' (1968), 'Baby I Won't Let You Down' (1970), 'Where Do I Go from Here?' (1969), 'Marry Me' (1968), 'To Make a Big Man Cry' (1965), 'Put Your Head on My Shoulder' (1965), 'If We Lived on the Top of a Mountain' (1965), 'Every Time You Go' (1980).

REID, William Gordon (Billy), composer, author, pianist.

Born Southampton, England, 19 September 1902. Died Southampton, 12 December 1974. He was educated at local schools in Southampton, and it was there he started work as a riveter in the docks, earning 5 shillings per week. He was a self-taught pianist, and also learned the piano accordion, which he used to play at local concerts and dances, and this gave him the idea of forming an accordion band, which he did in 1935. The band got a break when they were signed to play each week on a Radio Luxembourg programme called 'Stars of Luxembourg'. Before that Billy had had a job as the accordion player on stage in the Noël Coward show, *Bitter Sweet*. Another of his musical ventures was a tango band, which he ran jointly with violinist Eugene Pini. In 1938, a 15-year-old Welsh girl came to London to audition for the band, and got the job. Her name was Dorothy Squires, and she and Billy were later to form one of the best known double acts in show business.

His first published song was written in the late 1930s, and called, somewhat improbably, 'When the Rose of Tralee Met Danny Boy'. Just before World War II he also wrote a song called 'Out of the Blue', which was often played by some of the RAF bands. But his first big hit, a million-seller via the recording by The Ink Spots, came in 1945—'The Gypsy'. It had been written some five years earlier but had failed to find a publisher. Billy Reid was one of the few major songwriters to write both words and music for his songs, so they were totally his own, and the success of 'The Gypsy' was the signal for the start of the aforementioned Billy Reid/Dorothy Squires partnership.

By any standards, 'The Gypsy' was remarkable. Apart from the million-selling Ink Spots record, the song sat in the number one spot in the British Hit Parade for a long time, and also occupied the number one place on the American Hit Parade for five consecutive weeks—the first time a British song had achieved such a feat. Various estimates place the total sales of recordings of the song at between 7 and 11 million, and Billy Reid once estimated that in its first 10 years the song had earned him more than £24,000. Between then and 1953 Billy was to have two more of his songs winning gold discs. The first was 'A Tree in the Meadow', in 1948, Margaret Whiting's record being the million-seller. The second was 'I'm Walking Beside You', in 1953, and this time it was Eddie Fisher whose record sold a million.

In between those years such hits as 'This Is My Mother's Day' (1948), 'Anything I Dream Is Possible' (1948), 'I'll Close My Eyes' (1945), 'Coming Home' (1945), 'It's a Pity to Say Goodnight' (almost a million-seller for June Christy in 1946), and 'Bridge of Sighs' (1953), all reached better than number five on the British Hit Parade, several getting to number one, and most of them repeating their success in the American charts. Dorothy Squires recorded and performed all the Billy Reid hits, and the two of them became one of

Britain's top variety acts until they broke up in 1951. It is perhaps surprising that, in terms of recent sales, all the biggest versions of Billy's hits were by American artists.

After the break-up, Dorothy pursued a successful career as a singer, Billy Reid continued to write good songs. But something of the magic that they had both had together seemed gradually to disappear from each of them. And in spite of the vast sums of money his songs were earning him in royalties, by 1956 Billy was declared bankrupt, with debts of over £13,000. At the hearing he was quoted as saying that all he had left was £6 in cash, a piano worth £50, and a refrigerator. Like so many songwriters, the shy, softly spoken Billy Reid was a lousy businessman.

From then on his career went into a decline. The bankruptcy and the advent of rock 'n' roll depressed him enormously. Billy was a balladeer, and in no way was it possible for him to write the type of songs that were in demand in the late 1950s and 1960s, so he slipped quietly into retirement. Indeed, the only person who seemed to care about his death was Dorothy Squires. In spite of their tempestuous relationship throughout the years, it was Dorothy who hired the London Palladium on 29 December 1974 to present a tribute to her late partner. It was a sell-out. Had Billy Reid been an American, there would undoubtedly have been a networked TV spectacular in his honour.

Billy Reid's major songs have been referred to in the text, so no further list is needed here.

REVEL, Harry, composer, pianist.

Born London, 21 December 1905. Died New York, 3 November 1958. Studied piano from an early age, showing promise from the start, but the death of his German teacher seems to have upset him so much that from then on he studied only on his own. At the age of 15 he left England for Paris to join a so-called Hawaiian Band (there wasn't a Hawaiian in it) which then toured Europe. During the tour he quit to join a larger touring band, and settled for a while in Berlin. He had already had his first song, 'Oriental Eyes', published by an Italian publisher in 1922. While in Berlin, he received his first commission—to write the music for an operetta called *Was Frauen Traumen*, and this production was successful enough to bring him further commissions for productions in Paris, Copenhagen, Vienna and London.

It was then that the change from light to popular music seems to have finally taken place, for in 1927 he wrote the music for *André Charlot's Revue of 1927*. In 1929 he decided to try his luck in America, with just three newly published songs behind him ('I'm Going Back Again to Old Nebraska' written with bandleader Noble Sissle whom he met in Europe, and which had sold well in London), 'Just Give the Southland to Me', and 'Westward Bound'. That his decision to emigrate had been the right one was soon proved when in 1930 he wrote the music for the all black show *Fast and Furious*, and followed this with four songs for *Ziegfeld Follies of 1931*.(other contributors included Noël Coward and Walter Donaldson). For both these shows his lyricist was Mack Gordon, and from then until the partnership broke up in 1942, Revel and Gordon became one of the great songwriting teams of the 1930s.

Their first big hit was 'Underneath the Harlem Moon' (1932), and before joining the exodus to Hollywood in that same year, they managed to write the scores for two more Broadway shows, *Smiling Faces* and *Marching By*. Neither of these produced hit songs, however, and it was their first film, *Sitting Pretty* in 1933 (starring Jack Oakie, Jack Haley and Ginger Rogers), that gave them their real world beater, 'Did You Ever See a Dream Walking'. From then on it seemed to be hit songs throughout the 1930s, mostly from movies. *Broadway Thru a Keyhole* (1933), with Constance Cummings, Blossom Seeley and Russ Columbo in the cast, produced 'Doin' the Uptown Lowdown'; *We're Not Dressing* (1934) with Bing Crosby and Carole Lombard produced 'May I ?' and 'Love Thy Neighbour'; *Shoot the Works* (1934) with Jack Oakie amd Ben Bernie gave us 'With My Eyes Wide Open I'm Dreaming'; *College Rhythm* (1934) produced 'Stay As Sweet As You Are'; *Love in Bloom* (1935) with Burns and Allen, and Dixie Lee (later to be Mrs Bing Crosby), gave us 'Let Me Sing You to Sleep With a Love Song'; *Two for Tonight* (1935) starred Bing Crosby and Joan Bennett, and produced the beautiful title song, 'Without a Word of Warning' and 'From the Top of Your Head to the Tip of Your Toes'; *Collegiate* (1936) had Jack Oakie again, with Frances Langford and Betty Grable, and two big hits 'I Feel Like a Feather in the Breeze' and 'You Hit the Spot'; *Stowaway* (1936) had Shirley Temple, Robert Young and Alice Faye, and the song 'Goodnight My Love'; *Wake Up and Live* (1937) starred Walter Winchell, Alice Faye and Ben Bernie and the song 'Never in a

Million Years'; *My Lucky Star* (1938) with Sonja Henie, Richard Greene and Cesar Romero had the song 'I've Got a Date With a Dream'; and in 1939 there was 'Thanks for Everything' the title song for an Adolphe Menjou, Jack Oakie, Binnie Barnes picture. And those were only the important ones. Their greatest year was 1935, when ASCAP awarded them nine bonus awards for writing that same number of outstanding songs in one year.

During World War II the Revel/Gordon team started organizing troop shows as early as 1942, thus preceding the USO and the Stage Door Canteen by quite a bit. After 1942, Harry Revel continued to write, including a Broadway show *Are You With It?*, (lyrics by Arnold B Horwitt), as well as more films, such as *Ghost Catchers* (1944, lyrics by Paul Francis Webster); *The Stork Club* (1945, lyrics by Paul Francis Webster again); and *It Happened on Fifth Avenue* (1947, with more Webster lyrics). He also wrote three instrumental suites, *Music out of the Moon*, *Music for Peace of Mind*, and *Perfume Set to Music*. In the 1950s he formed his own publishing company, Realm Music Inc., for which he continued to write until his death.

Lyricist Mack Gordon, the other half of this incredibly successful team, was born in Warsaw, Poland, 21 June 1904, and died in New York, 1 March 1959. His family emigrated to New York when he was quite young, and he soon found himself involved in music, from being a boy soprano in a minstrel show to becoming a successful act as singer/comedian in vaudeville. It was while he was doing his act that he first met Harry Revel, who became his accompanist. After a few songs written together, Revel realized how well Gordon's words fitted his music, and ultimately persuaded him to give up touring and become a full-time songwriter. In spite of his long and fruitful collaboration with Harry Revel, Mack Gordon amazingly found time to write hit songs with other composers. There was 'Down Argentine Way' and 'It Happened in Sun Valley', both with Harry Warren, the two of them then going on to write all those superb tunes for the Glenn Miller picture *Orchestra Wives*. Further examples of Mack Gordon's collaboration with Harry Warren will be found under that composer's listing. He also wrote, with Joseph Myrow, the hit song 'You Make Me Feel So Young', popularized by Frank Sinatra in the 1950s, and 'I Can't Begin to Tell You', with Jimmy Monaco, as well as contributing lyrics to compositions by Jimmy Van Heusen, Vincent Youmans, and Ray Henderson. It adds up to an impressive career for a man who didn't think much to songwriting, and had to be talked into it by Harry Revel on a boat trip up the Hudson River.

Some other outstanding Harry Revel/Mack Gordon songs:
'You're My Past, Present and Future' (1933), 'Don't Let It Bother You' (1934), 'I Wish I Were Aladdin' (1935), 'A Star Fell Out of Heaven' (1936), 'There's a Lull in My Life' (1937), 'Wake Up and Live' (1937), 'Thanks for Everything' (1938).

RICE, Tim, *see* Webber, Andrew Lloyd.

RODGERS, Richard, composer, author, producer, publisher.

Born Arverne, Long Island, NY, 28 June 1902. Died New York, 30 December 1979. Educated at Columbia University where he started writing amateur musical shows. Richard Rodgers is another one of the few songwriters in this book who was born, if not into a wealthy family into one that was at the very least comfortably off. His father was a successful doctor, who loved literature and music. His mother, who shared these loves with her husband, was also a talented amateur pianist. Young Richard was therefore exposed to music and received lessons from a very early age. From his student days he was devoted to the theatre, and once said 'Life for me began on Saturdays at 2.30', a reference to the era of the matinée performance at cheap rates. He was only 14 when he saw his first musical, Jerome Kern's *Very Good Eddie*, a show that could reasonably be described as a real American musical, that is, one not based on the traditions of Vienna and operetta, which was still the dominant force behind many American productions. He was only 11 when he composed his first song. By 1917 he had contributed no fewer than seven songs to a charity production designed to raise funds for the troops, and in 1919 he contributed 20 songs to another amateur show, three of them actually being published. But the most important thing to happen to him was his introduction in 1918 to Lorenz Hart, a man seven years his senior (born New York, 2 May 1895), who had also been educated at Columbia University, who was struggling to become a writer, and who had a talent for writing verse.

Rodgers and Hart did not immediately take to each other as individuals (Rodgers was always a meticulously well-groomed, punctual person, while Hart would frequently not dress unless he had to go out, and had the playboy instinct from his earliest days). Yet after their first meeting each seemed to realize that he needed the other, and that each could supply something that the other lacked. They immediately started writing together and had their first joint effort published in 1919, a song called 'Any Old Place With You'. It was performed in a show called *A Lonely Romeo*. In 1920, while Rodgers was still at Columbia, he persuaded Hart to write songs with him for the university's annual show. Lew Fields, a Broadway producer, saw the show, liked what he heard, and asked the budding team to contribute some numbers to his forthcoming production, *Poor Little Ritz Girl*. Their work earned them their first critical acclaim in the local press, and as the other eight songs in the show had been written by Sigmund Romberg and didn't get a line, they might be said to have done well.

But the critics might as well not have bothered as far as Rodgers and Hart were concerned, because no matter how many songs they turned out during the next five years, nobody wanted to know. It was not until Rodgers was seriously considering giving up to become a salesman in children's clothes, and Hart considering returning to his literary work as a translator, that they had their big break. They were persuaded to have one last shot, and wrote seven songs for an early Theater Guild production called *The Garrick Gaieties*. One of the songs they took from a previously written but never performed show, and threw it in as a makeweight. Its title was 'Manhattan'. The date was 17 May 1925, and with it one of the all-time great teams of American songwriters was born. The pair were instantly snapped up by Max Dreyfus, the publishing genius who headed Harms music, and their future was assured.

By the end of 1925 they had a new musical, *Dearest Enemy*, on Broadway, and in 1926 they had five different shows running. Their income had risen in two years from between $50 and $80 per week to over $1,000 per week each. In *Great Men of American Popular Song*, David Ewen says 'They created a golden age of musical comedy all by themselves, and because of them, musical comedy in the 1920s was well along its way to adulthood'. Perhaps the best known of their 1920s productions, together with their biggest hit songs were *The Garrick Gaieties* (1926), with 'Mountain Greenery'; *The Girl Friend* (1926), with 'The Blue Room'; *A Connecticut Yankee* (1927), with 'My Heart Stood Still' (originally written for the London show *One Dam' Thing After Another* with Jessie Matthews); *Present Arms* (1928), with: 'You Took Advantage of Me'; *Spring Is Here* (1929), with 'With a Song in My Heart'.

There were some innovations practised by this dissimilar pair that helped to weld them into such a great team. Musically, Rodgers was doing things that had not been done before in popular song. He reversed standard practice by having 16-bar choruses and 32-bar verses, as well as using augmented 7th chords, when most popular songwriters confined everything to the major chords of C, G and F. Hart meanwhile was rhyming within his own rhymes, and writing what were clearly intended to be love songs with dashing wit thrown in, a technique he employed well before Cole Porter had the same idea. In the early 1920s nobody but Hart would have dared write lines such as 'I've got a mania for Pennsylvania', or 'I'd go to hell for ya, or Philadelphia'. And while it is always difficult with any team to give a definite answer to the old question, 'which comes first, the music or the lyrics?', it is a fairly safe bet that with Rodgers and Hart, mostly the music came first, while with Rodgers and Oscar Hammerstein it came second. Rodgers once said, 'When the lyrics are right, it's easier for me to write a tune than to bend over and tie my shoelaces'.

For Rodgers and Hart the 1930s may not perhaps have been quite so memorable as the 1920s, but they were good enough to give us nine productions, of which the significant ones were *Simple Simon* (1930), and the song 'Ten Cents a Dance'; *On Your Toes* (1936), with the song 'There's a Small Hotel'; *Babes in Arms* (1937), which had five big hits (see list below); *The Boys From Syracuse* (1938), with the song 'This Can't Be Love'; and *Too Many Girls* (1939), with the song 'I Didn't Know What Time It Was'. Lorenz Hart died 22 November 1943, from pneumonia, aggravated by over-indulgence in alcohol, and the fact that by the end of the 1930s he had, to quote David Ewen again: '... lost the zest that success had once brought him'. Before passing onto Richard Rodger's collaboration with Oscar Hammerstein, we must record the Rodgers and Hart venture into Hollywood and their final Broadway productions.

At the beginning of the 1930s top songwriters were flooding out of New York to work for the movie moguls in Los Angeles. At that time, Rodgers and Hart paid a quick visit to Hollywood and had their first taste of writing for films. The title was *The Hot Heiress*, which in spite of the songwriters and a reasonable cast (Walter Pidgeon, Ben Lyon, Thelma Todd), was a complete flop.

Back on Broadway, almost immediately, they had a flop show,

America's Sweetheart, written as a skit on the movie business and the star system in particular. It had one song which has survived, 'I've Got Five Dollars'. Perhaps it was this failure which tempted them to try Hollywood again. They went back in 1932 to work on *Love Me Tonight,* starring Maurice Chevalier and Jeanette MacDonald. This produced some fine songs, including 'Mimi' and 'Isn't It Romantic?'. Success was theirs at last, but it was only temporary because their next two films were fairly disastrous, even though one, *Hallelujah, I'm a Bum,* starred Al Jolson. The best song they wrote during their four years in Hollywood never made it in a film. This was the one that ended up as 'Blue Moon', although under different titles and with other lyrics it was continually rejected by producers.

Throughout that period Rodgers was never happy in the movie capital. The long waits between films irked him tremendously. In *They're Playing Our Song,* Max Wilk quotes Rodgers as saying, 'You found yourself working in competition with other writers. They did it to Larry Hart and to me, to everybody, even to Jerry Kern—and if they would do that to Kern, for God's sake ...' He shook his head sadly. Hart on the other hand, with his playboy attitude to life, loved it, for he was attending round after round of parties when there was no writing to be done. Finally, however, impressed by the successes on Broadway that were currently being enjoyed by such composers as Jerome Kern and George Gershwin, Rodgers and Hart returned to New York to write *Jumbo,* which opened in 1935 complete with Jimmy Durante and the entire Paul Whiteman Band. Songwise it produced 'Little Girl Blue' and 'The Most Beautiful Girl in the World' in its score. After 233 performances it faded into oblivion.

During the next six years, however, Broadway saw no fewer than nine new Rodgers and Hart musicals, including *Pal Joey* (1940, with 'Bewitched, Bothered and Bewildered').

Richard Rodgers' career took on a whole new dimension with his collaboration with his new lyricist, Oscar Hammerstein 2nd. Born 12 July 1895 in New York, Hammerstein was lyricist, author, producer and publisher over the years. His grandfather, Oscar Hammerstein 1st, was an operatic impresario and producer, and his father, William Hammerstein, was manager of the Victoria Theater in New York, which was owned by Hammerstein 1st. Like Hart, he was seven years older than Rodgers, and once convinced that by so doing he would not be taking work away from Hart, he willingly joined Rodgers to form yet another magical combination of composer and lyricist.

By a curious coincidence, Hammerstein was also a graduate of Columbia University who gave up his study of law to obtain theatrical experience in his father's theatre. It was not long before he started writing songs, and although he had one or two minor successes with various composers, he did not really make it until together with Otto Harbach he wrote for the music of Herbert Stothart and Vincent Youmans in the 1923 musical *Wildflower*. After that came *Show Boat* with Jerome Kern, *Rose-Marie* with Rudolph Friml and *The Desert Song* and *New Moon* with Sigmund Romberg.

Then suddenly and inexplicably, Hammerstein's writing went into a decline. Numerous Broadway shows for which he wrote lyrics flopped. He tried Hollywood but had no greater success there, one producer even paying him off to clear a contract. It was particularly fortunate for him, therefore, that with Hart also in a decline and becoming an increasing problem, Rodgers should seek out Hammerstein with an offer of possible collaboration. That the first result of this co-operation should be *Oklahoma!* is now a matter of history, though you could perhaps say without much exaggeration that it was also a little short of miraculous.

Historians of the musical theatre are now agreed that *Oklahoma!* changed the whole form and shape of popular musical production when it was first performed in New York in 1943. It ran on Broadway alone for 2,248 performances, and when it reached the Theatre Royal in London's Drury Lane in 1947, it again broke all records. *Oklahoma!* was produced just a few months before Lorenz Hart died. After the opening night, which Hart attended, he met Rodgers at dinner in Sardi's Restaurant. He congratulated his ex-partner, and added 'This thing of yours will run longer than *Blossom Time*', (until then a well-known record breaker). Then he disappeared into the night.

A list of the hits that *Oklahoma!* produced will be found below. From then on it seemed that Rodgers and Hammerstein could do no wrong. Hammerstein was as different from Hart as chalk from cheese. David Ewen in *Great Men of American Popular Song* says of him, 'He rose early each day, and was already at his desk hard at work by 9.30. After dinner he liked spending the evening quietly with his family and one or two friends, rather than go out to elaborate dinners or parties. By midnight he was asleep. Hammerstein's lyrics came slowly and with pain. It was not unusual for Hammerstein to spend weeks on one lyric ... the final result of this hard labour was a simplicity and grace that had the earmarks of utter spontaneity. Where Hart was volatile and quixotic, Hammerstein was always predictable. He could be counted upon to see a job through on time, to keep appointments, to be present when needed, and never to forget a promise'.

The success of *Oklahoma!* was so enormous that even before Rodgers and Hammerstein set to work on their next score which ironically, in view of the unhappy times they had both had in Hollywood, was a film starring Jeanne Crain and Dick Haymes, called *State Fair* (1945, with the songs 'It's a Grand Day for Singing' and 'It Might As Well Be Spring'), they had decided to set up a publishing company together—Williamson Music. This in turn developed into a full-scale production company for theatrical shows of all kinds, not just their own. For instance, it was responsible for Irving Berlin's *Annie Get Your Gun* (1946).

But with a hit such as *Oklahoma!* on your hands, where do you turn for inspiration for your next show? To Rodgers and Hammerstein this appeared to be no problem, for they came up with *South Pacific* (1949, 1,925 performances), *The King and I* (1951, 1,246 performances), and *The Sound of Music* (1959, 1,443 performances). These major hits take no account of *Carousel* (1945, 890 performances), *No Strings* (1962, for which Rodgers wrote his own lyrics, Oscar Hammerstein having sadly died of cancer in 1960), and *Flower Drum Song* (1958).

In fairness one must recall that they had two flops, just to prove that it can happen even to the greatest writers. These were *Me and Juliet* (1953), which ran for a mere 358 performances, and *Pipe Dream* (1955). All the most important Rodgers and Hammerstein musicals were made into movies. Such was *Oklahoma!* in 1955 with Shirley Jones and Gordon Macrae; *South Pacific* in 1958 with Mitzi Gaynor and Rossano Brazzi; *The King and I* in 1956 with Deborah Kerr and Yul Brynner; and above all, *The Sound of Music* in 1965, said to be the most successful musical film ever made, with Julie Andrews and Christopher Plummer. Success also attended Oscar Hammerstein in taking Bizet's opera *Carmen*, and turning it first into a Broadway musical, and secondly into the spectacular film, *Carmen Jones*.

After Hammerstein's death, Rodgers was, in his own words, 'inconsolable'. But he knew that he could not give up writing, nor did he want to. In addition to *No Strings*, he composed a number of other memorable scores during the remainder of the 1960s. In 1965 he worked with lyricist Stephen Sondheim on *Do I Hear a Waltz?*, and finally, in 1970 with Martin Charnin on *Two by Two*. Right up to the year before he died he was working on a musical adaptation of *I Remember Mama.*

Some other outstanding Rodgers songs:
'Thou Swell' (*A Connecticut Yankee*, 1927), 'Baby's Awake Now' (*Spring Is Here*, 1929), 'Dancing on the Ceiling' (*Evergreen*, 1930), 'Lover' (1933), 'Down by the River', and 'Easy to Remember' (both from *Mississippi*, a film starring Bing Crosby, 1935). 'On Your Toes' and 'Slaughter on 10th Avenue' (both from *On Your Toes*, 1936), 'Have You Met Miss Jones?' (*I'd Rather Be Right*, 1937), 'Where or When', 'The Lady Is a Tramp', 'Johnny One Note', 'My Funny Valentine', and 'I Wish I Were in Love Again' (all from *Babes in Arms*, 1937), 'I Could Write a Book' (*Pal Joey*, 1940).

Some other outstanding Rodgers and Hammerstein songs:
From *Oklahoma!* (1943): 'People Will Say We're in Love', 'Oh, What a Beautiful Mornin'', 'The Surrey With the Fringe on Top', 'Oklahoma', 'Out of My Dreams'. From *Carousel* (1945): 'If I Loved You', 'June Is Bustin' Out All Over', 'What's the Use of Wond'rin'', 'You'll Never Walk Alone', 'Mr Snow', 'Soliloquy'. From *Allegro* (1947): 'The Gentleman Is a Dope'. From *South Pacific* (1949): 'Some Enchanted Evening', 'Bali Ha'i', 'Younger Than Springtime', 'I'm in Love With a Wonderful Guy', 'This Nearly Was Mine', 'I'm Gonna Wash That Man Right Out of My Hair', 'Happy Talk', 'There Is Nothin' Like a Dame'. From *The King and I* (1951): 'Getting to Know You', 'Hello, Young Lovers', 'We Kiss in a Shadow', 'I Whistle a Happy Tune', 'I Have Dreamed', 'Shall We Dance?'. From *Pipe Dream* (1955): 'All at once You Love Her'. From *Flower Drum Song* (1958): 'You Are Beautiful', 'A Hundred Million Miracles', 'I Enjoy Being a Girl', 'Chop Suey', 'Grant Avenue', 'Love, Look Away', 'Sunday'. From *The Sound of Music* (1959): 'The Sound of Music', 'Do-Re-Mi', 'Climb Ev'ry Mountain', 'Edelweiss'. From *No Strings* (1962): 'The Sweetest Sounds'.

ROMBERG, Sigmund, composer, conductor.

Born Nagy Kaniza, Hungary, 29 July 1887. Died New York, 9 November 1951. Emigrated to the US in 1909, becoming an American citizen in 1912. Educated in engineering at Polytechnische Hochschule, then studied music in Vienna. Served in the Hungarian Army 1907–08. He started in New York as a pianist in cafés before forming his own orchestra in 1912. He also worked as a staff composer for the Shubert Brothers who commissioned him to write the music for their production *The Whirl of the World* in 1914. The success of this led to no fewer than 40 other productions for the House of Shubert, his songs being performed by, among others, Al Jolson, Clifton Webb, Nora Bayes, The Dolly Sisters and Peggy Wood. Lack of space has forced me to leave the composers of popular Viennese operetta out of this book, including such great names as Franz Lehar and Rudolf Friml, but I have included Romberg because although born of that tradition, he seems to have been able to fuse his background with the tradition of popular American song.

The result was not only a string of successful shows, but also a profusion of standard hit songs. Of his shows, the best known are *Maytime* (1917), *Sinbad* (1918), *Blossom Time* (1921), *The Student Prince*, (1924), *The Desert Song* (1926), and *The New Moon* (1928). As late as 1945 his show *Up in Central Park*, although it may not have produced any classic songs, was good enough to run for 504 performances. And famous lyricists who have been proud to set words to his songs have included Otto Harbach, Oscar Hammerstein, Dorothy Fields, Gus Kahn and Leo Robin. Many of his big Broadway successes were made into film musicals, and he wrote a number of scores specially for Hollywood, including *Viennese Nights* (1930), *Children of Dreams* (1931), *The Night Is Young*, starring Ramon Novarro, Evelyn Laye, Charles Butterworth, Una Merkel, Edward Everett Horton and Rosalind Russell (1935), *The Girl of the Golden West*, starring Nelson Eddy and Jeanette MacDonald (1938), and *Broadway Serenade* with Jeanette MacDonald (1939). He also toured many American cities with a 60-piece orchestra, which he featured on radio programmes such as *An Evening with Romberg*. It was once said that, because his music was so successful, he must be dead. Commenting on this, the *New York Herald Tribune* of the time wrote, 'There are a number of explanations for this phenomenon, but the most palpable one lies in the tendency of the American public to classify things. This results, in so far as composers are concerned, in the notion that any man whose works are heard with regularity is a revered man, and, more likely than not, a dead one. Accustomed to the radio habit of presenting memorial programmes for Gershwin and others, listeners who have tuned in on the Romberg show have admitted they thought it was intended to be commemorative. Another reason could be that because Romberg is a product of the Viennese or 'May Wine' school of composition, a lot of people have come to think of him as a contemporary of Johann Strauss, who founded the school, and Franz von Suppé and Victor Herbert, who nurtured it. But Strauss died in 1849; von Suppé in 1895 and Victor Herbert in 1924'.

Sigmund Romberg died in 1951. Yet he had one last show produced posthumously in 1954—*The Girl in Pink Tights* (lyrics by Leo Robin). To end on a sentimental note, Jack Burton, in his *Blue Book of Tin Pan Alley*, relates how Romberg, at the peak of his career, returned to visit his parents in Hungary after an absence of more than 20 years. For two days he resisted all their efforts to persuade him to play the piano. On the third day he took them to the town's concert hall, where they were escorted to the two best seats in an otherwise empty auditorium. On stage was a 60-piece orchestra, and following a fanfare, Romberg took the conductor's rostrum to give his audience of two a 2-hour concert of his biggest successes.

Some outstanding songs by Sigmund Romberg:
'Deep in My Heart, Dear', and 'Serenade' (both from *The Student Prince*, 1924), 'One Alone', 'The Riff Song', and 'The Desert Song' (all from *The Desert Song*, 1926), 'Lover, Come Back to Me' and 'Stout-Hearted Men' (both from *The New Moon*, 1928), 'When I Grow Too Old to Dream' (from the film *The Night Is Young*, 1935), 'Who Are We to Say?' and 'Shadows on the Moon' (both from the film *Girl of the Golden West*, 1938), 'Close As Pages in a Book' (*Up in Central Park*, 1945), 'My Heart Won't Say Goodbye' (from *The Girl in Pink Tights*, 1954).

SCHWARTZ, Arthur, composer, producer, lawyer.

Born Brooklyn, New York, 25 November 1900. Educated University of New York where he obtained his BA and LLD degrees, and Columbia Law School where he obtained an MA. The son of a successful lawyer, and with an older brother already receiving training in music, Arthur was destined to follow his father into the legal profession. While he was not discouraged from taking an interest in music, he was certainly not encouraged to devote any time to it. But like many other songwriters, he wrote for college shows, and in 1924 was lucky enough to meet lyricist Lorenz Hart while at a summer camp, in between completing his studies and joining a law firm. He persuaded Hart to write lyrics for some songs he had composed for one of the camp shows, and one, 'I Love to Lie Awake in Bed' actually became a Broadway hit some five years later. By then however, it had been retitled 'I Guess I'll Have to Change My Plan', and had acquired lyrics by Schwartz's famous partner, Howard Dietz. In 1925 he had his first song published. It was called 'Baltimore MD, You're the Only Doctor for Me', and it was one of five songs accepted by the producer of a small off-Broadway revue called *The Grand Street Follies*. He had more numbers accepted for the 1926 edition of the same show, and yet others in 1927 for a revue called *The New Yorkers*, which ran for only 50 performances, so all the indications were that law was the thing, and songwriting was out.

But Arthur Schwartz was not to be put off. He haunted Tin Pan Alley, auditioning his material to anyone who would listen (including George Gershwin, who by then was at Harms Music). The great publisher Max Dreyfus said to him, 'Mr Schwartz, go back and practise law'. In 1927 he was introduced to lyricist Howard Dietz, another New Yorker, and only two years older than himself, who was also struggling for recognition of his writing talents in the multiplicity of small revues that were appearing at the time. The two formed a songwriting partnership, but it was not until two years later, in 1929, when they wrote most of the songs for *The Little Show* at The Music Box Theater, that they had their first taste of success. The song was 'I Guess I'll Have to Change My Plan'. In the same year the pair had their first experience of writing for the English stage, when they composed the score for the show *Here Comes the Bride*, which opened in London in February 1930, with a cast that included Edmund Gwenn, Clifford Mollison and Jean Colin. By now Schwartz felt able to devote himself full time to songwriting, so he gave up his law work. In 1930 they contributed several songs to the show *Three's a Crowd*, which starred Libby Holman, Clifton Webb and Fred Allen, their best effort being 'Something to Remember You By'.

In 1931 Schwartz and Dietz for the first time wrote all the songs for a show, *The Band Wagon*, starring Fred and Adèle Astaire. Both performers and songs were a resounding success, with numbers such as 'Dancing in the Dark' (the most financially successful song they ever wrote), and 'New Sun in the Sky'. In 1932 there was another Schwartz/Dietz success, *Flying Colors*, with songs such as 'A Shine on Your Shoes, 'Louisiana Hayride' and 'Alone Together'.

Arthur Schwartz enjoyed a significant year in 1934. First he married singer Kay Carrington. Then he and Howard Dietz had a brave flop with *Revenge With Music*, based on the Spanish novel *The Three-Cornered Hat* (previously used successfully by Manuel de Falla for his ballet). It ran for only 158 performances, yet it contained two more hit songs, 'You and the Night and the Music', and 'If There Is Someone Lovelier Than You'.

In 1935 the team wrote for another show that was not a great success, in spite of a cast that included Beatrice Lillie, Ethel Waters, Eleanor Powell and Eddie Foy. It was called *At Home Abroad*. But again the show produced some classic songs, including 'Love Is a Dancing Thing' (later to be a recording success in England for Jessie Matthews), 'Got a Bran' New Suit' (a record hit for Fats Waller), and 'Get Yourself a Geisha', in which Bea Lillie used to interpolate the line: 'It's better with your shoes off', which usually stopped the show. Schwartz and Dietz used the first two of these songs again in 1936 for their London show *Follow the Sun*, which had Clare Luce, Ada Reeve and Vic Oliver in its cast.

There was another flop show, *Between the Devil*, in 1937. It ran for only 93 performances, although in its cast were Jack Buchanan, Evelyn Laye and Adèle Dixon, and in spite of its English cast it was never performed in London. This failure seemed to produce something of a rift in the partnership, and Arthur Schwartz parted company with Howard Dietz for some 10 years. He started writing instead with lyricist Dorothy Fields. The result was the 1939 show *Stars in Your Eyes*, which ran for only 127 performances, in spite of the presence in the cast of Jimmy Durante and Ethel Merman, and its only memorable song was 'Okay for Sound'.

Later that year Schwartz decided to try his luck in Hollywood. Most other songwriters of his stature had long ago made the trek from New York to Los Angeles, so he was leaving it rather late, but nevertheless he remained there until about 1946. It was during this period that he gradually switched to picture production, his most notable effort being *Cover Girl* (music by Ira Gershwin and Jerome Kern), and *Night and Day*, the Cole Porter biography. He did, however, contribute some successful songs to other movies, notably 'They're Either Too Young or Too Old', with lyrics by Frank Loesser, written for the 1943 film *Thank Your Lucky Stars*, and 'A Gal in Calico' with lyrics by Leo Robin for the 1946 film *The Time, the Place and the Girl*.

Back in New York in 1946, Schwartz and Dietz teamed up again to write a successful show, *Inside USA*, which in spite of its success didn't produce any hit songs, and their final collaborations, *The Gay*

Life in 1961 and *Jennie* in 1963 were both flops, the latter in spite of the presence of Mary Martin in the cast. Arthur Schwartz's biggest post-war Broadway successes were undoubtedly *A Tree Grows in Brooklyn* (1951, with lyrics by Dorothy Fields, and the song 'Love Is the Reason'), and *By the Beautiful Sea* (1954, also with Dorothy Fields, although it produced no hits). There was, however, to be one more Schwartz/Dietz hit, the song 'That's Entertainment', written for the 1953 film of *The Band Wagon,* starring Fred Astaire and Jack Buchanan.

In the late 1960s Schwartz retired to England to live, and in 1975 was tempted into the recording studios there by producer Alan Dell to record 14 of his songs, sung by himself. On the sleeve note of the record he writes about his association with Howard Dietz, but it is interesting that of the other lyricists with whom he worked, the only one to get a mention is Leo Robin.

Howard Dietz was a New Yorker, and only four years older than Schwartz. He had always had a talent for writing before becoming a lyricist, and in his early days had considerable success as a journalist and advertising copywriter. In 1924 he joined MGM Pictures as executive in charge of publicity, a post he retained until 1940, so that all the time he was writing successful songs with Schwartz, he was also doing a full-time job in Hollywood. It was Dietz who was credited with the idea of using Leo the Lion and the motto *Ars Gratia Artis* as the MGM trademark. In 1940 he became vice president of Loew's Inc. Apart from his association with Arthur Schwartz, he wrote lyrics for such famous composers as Jerome Kern, Jimmy McHugh, Vernon Duke and Ralph Rainger. He was, it seems, well known for his sense of humour. Arthur Schwartz quotes the lyrics Dietz wrote for his songs 'Triplets' and 'Rhode Island Is Famous for You' to prove the point. David Ewen in *Great Men of American Popular Song* quotes a conversation between Dietz and Louis B Mayer in the elevator late one morning in Loew's building. 'Do you always come to work this late', Mayer asked? 'Yes', replied Dietz, 'But I always make up for it by going home early'!

The best known of Arthur Schwartz's songs have already been referred to in the text, so no further listing is necessary here, except to include 'Then I'll Be Tired of You' (1934), 'By Myself' (1938), and 'A Rainy Night in Rio' (1946).

SEDAKA, Neil, composer, author, pianist, singer.

Born Brooklyn, New York, 13 March 1939. The family is Turkish by descent, and both his parents were amateur pianists. His grandmother was a professional concert pianist, so it seemed inevitable that Neil would somehow take up a career connected with music, although the turn that it took was certainly not the one his family expected. Educated at local schools and Lincoln High School, he went on to study classical music at Juilliard, and was selected by Arthur Rubinstein as the best high school pianist of 1956, which led to an entry in that year's Tchaikowsky piano competition. But when the officials learned that he was already involved with a school group (The Tokens), and that he had been writing pop songs, they disqualified him. In retrospect, they may have done both Neil and the world a service.

The Tokens can't have been bad for a school group. Their dates led them as far afield as the Catskill Mountains, and it was while playing a hotel date there that young Sedaka met the owner's daughter, Leba, who was later to become his wife. He already had a local reputation as a singer, with a song called 'While I Dream' (1957). But his first success as a writer came in 1958, when, with lyrics by Howard (Howie) Greenfield, Connie Francis took the song 'Stupid Cupid' to the No 1 spot in the UK and to No 17 in the US. Greenfield had also been at Lincoln High with Neil, and was to become his main lyricist for many years. They were both contemporaries of Carole King and Gerry Goffin, as well as Barry Mann and Cynthia Weill, and before they were 20 both Neil and Howie were, like the others, to find themselves part of the Don Kirshner/Al Nevins song factory, Aldon Music, in the Brill building in New York.

Their initial songwriting successes were not great, although after about a year some of their material had been recorded by such artists as Clyde McPhatter, Lavern Baker and Dinah Washington. The big break for Sedaka the singer as well as the songwriter came in 1959 when 'Oh, Carol' (dedicated, he has always said, to his first girl friend Carole King) made it to No 3 in the US charts and to No 9 in the UK. He had had one song, 'The Diary', recorded under his own name in the previous year, and although it made the No 14 spot, it was soon forgotten. Later in 1959 he won his first gold disc with his record 'I Go Ape'.

Between 1959 and 1963 there were some 14 hits for the Sedaka/

Greenfield team, among them 'Calendar Girl' (No 4 UK, No 10 US), 'Happy Birthday Sweet Sixteen' (No 4 UK, No 6 US), and 'Breaking Up Is Hard to Do' (No 1 US, No 7 UK). There was also the 1962 song 'Venus in Blue Jeans', which was co-written with Keller and Greenfield, and which became a No 7 hit in the US for Jimmy Clanton, and a No 4 in the UK for Mark Wynter. It was also in the 1960s (1960) that Sedaka and Greenfield wrote the music for the film *Where the Boys Are*, in which Connie Francis appeared. The last hit he had as a singer during that decade was 'The Answer to My Prayer'.

From the mid-1960s until the early 1970s, Neil Sedaka the singer was a forgotten man. But he never stopped writing. Over a period of some eight years many artists had hits with Sedaka songs. There was 'Is This the Way to Amarillo?' for Tony Christie in 1973; and there were others, such as 'Puppet Man', 'Working on a Groovy Thing', 'I'm a Song, Sing Me', 'Love Will Keep Us Together', 'Solitaire', and 'That's When the Music Takes Me', to name but a few. Among the artists who had major successes with such songs were Andy Williams, Donny Osmond, The Fifth Dimension, Tom Jones, David Cassidy, Petula Clark, The Carpenters, and Captain and Tenille.

What then, tempted him to go back to performing as well as writing? Partly, because it was becoming clear in the early 1970s that we were into the age of the singer/songwriter. What else was Neil Sedaka, except that he just hadn't sung for a few years? And a number of other things began to come together. In 1971 he decided to try out his re-emergence with a new album, *Emergence*, and to launch it he came to England for an English tour. He explained it this way: 'The English public are wonderful. They never forget. I was frightened, because I knew they'd come to hear "Oh, Carol" and "Happy Birthday Sweet Sixteen". I did the old songs, and then I started in on the new ones, and it went over very well'. In 1972 he had a hit with a new lyricist, Phil Cody, with the song 'Laughter in the Rain'. To quote Jacoba Atlas from the *Melody Maker* of 1974: 'England took to the new Sedaka with astonishing fervour and acceptance. His home country took a little longer, and this came about through the devotion of the man Sedaka laughingly calls "the most expensive publicist in the world"—Elton John'.

Neil had met Elton in London. They got on well together, and over a meal Elton asked him what label he was tied to in the US. When Neil said 'none', Elton couldn't believe it, and almost then and there a deal was set up for Neil Sedaka's American representation to be on Elton John's Rocket label. Polydor already had a contract with Neil for the rest of the world. In 1974–5, the album *Solitaire* became a smash hit. And his next, *Overnight Sensation* was recorded in England, with Elton John appearing as guest vocalist on the track 'Bad Blood' (lyric by Phil Cody). It shows how instant success is still possible in the field of popular music, when a disc jockey on station KHJ in Los Angleles imported a copy from England, before pressings were available in the States. His exposure of that track on his daily programme resulted in advance orders for the album that put it into the gold record category before it was even available in the stores.

Some other outstanding Neil Sedaka songs:
'Stairway to Heaven' (1960), 'You Mean Everything to Me' (1960), 'Run, Samson Run' (1960), 'Little Devil' (1961), 'King of Clowns' (1962), 'Next Door to an Angel' (1962), 'Alice in Wonderland' (1963), 'Let's Go Steady Again' (1963), 'Beautiful You' (1972), 'Standing on the Inside' (1973), 'One More Mountain to Climb' (1970), 'Love Ain't an Easy Thing' (1974), 'You Never Done It Like That' (1977), 'Should've Never Let Her Go' (1978).

SIMON, Paul, composer, author, singer, guitarist, producer.

Born Newark, New Jersey, 5 November 1942. Paul comes from a typically American middle class background, his father being a musician and also a teacher. He was educated at local schools, and is a high school graduate. Thus the typical collegiate image presented in the early days of the Simon and Garfunkel partnership was a natural one, even to the point of album sleeves showing them wearing college scarves. Art Garfunkel is only a year older than Paul Simon, and was a school friend, so that their partnership was a genuine and uncontrived one. Both Simon and Art were always interested in music, and even had a whiff of success as a sixteen-year-old duo calling themselves Tom and Jerry, when in 1957 they appeared on TV performing their song 'Hey, Schoolgirl'. This was recorded, and made the very bottom rungs of the Top 40, but could hardly be described as a hit. In those days Paul was more the hustler of the two, determined he was going to make it as a singer/songwriter. He followed the usual trail, pushing his wares round the New York publishing houses. If he'd been lucky enough to have had a hit on his own account at that time there seems little doubt that he would have gone solo, Art Garfunkel notwithstanding. But his writing efforts received continual rejection mainly because they were too derivative of the pop idols of the day.

By 1962 he had become much influenced by some of the top folk artists of the era, and was making something of a name for himself around the clubs of New York's Greenwich Village. In the mid-60s he even spent a year in England, touring the folk clubs in the north and performing his own songs, becoming quite popular in the process.

Then in 1965, back in New York, and back with Art Garfunkel, came 'The Sounds of Silence', which went to No 1 in the US charts in 1966, and the era of Simon and Garfunkel had really begun. Curiously, their recording of that song never made the UK charts. It was recorded by The Bachelors in England, who took it to No 3. They had two more big hits in 1966—'I Am a Rock', which went to No 3 in the US and No 17 in the UK, and 'Homeward Bound' (written, it is said, during his 'English' year, on the station platform at Widnes), which made No 5 in the US and No 9 in the UK.

The Simon and Garfunkel partnership continued successfully for the next four or five years. The split finally came in 1971, when Art decided he wanted to explore the film business and Paul hankered to write music that was not suitable for the singing duo. He had always been the main composing and writing force of the team, although naturally there were Garfunkel contributions to many of their big hits. The best known of these were 'The 59th St Bridge Song' (Feelin' Groovy) (1966), 'Mrs Robinson' (1968, No. 1 US, No 4 UK), 'The Boxer' (1969, No 7 US, No 6 UK), and 'Bridge Over Troubled Water' (1970, No 1 in both US and UK). In 1971 CBS records were already claiming sales of over 6 million for the *Bridge Over Troubled Water* album. At the time of writing, no one seems sure what the total sales of that one song are, but they will certainly be in excess of 10 million.

After the break with Art Garfunkel, Paul Simon could have retired in comfort had he so wished. But the split was intended to release him so that he could write as he pleased, unfettered by commercial considerations. As a result, he has been quite happy (even if his fans have not) to release just one album about every two years. There had already been some highly successful albums with Garfunkel: 'Parsley, Sage, Rosemary and Thyme' (1967), 'Bookends' (1968), and 'Wednesday Morning, 3 a.m.' (1969).

His first solo album was called simply *Paul Simon*. It was released in 1972, and was followed by *There Goes Rhymin' Simon* in 1973. In 1975 we had an album called *New Songs*. There have been others since, including one called *Still Crazy After All These Years*. Hit singles have resulted from these albums, but Paul Simon no longer thinks in terms of hit singles. The success, therefore, of such songs as 'Mother and Child Re-Union' (1972, No 4 US, No 5 UK), 'Take Me to the Mardi Gras' (1973, No 7 UK), and 'Fifty Ways to Leave Your Lover' (1975), has probably quite surprised him, although it must please him as well.

He spent the last years of the 1970s working on the challenge of a film. It was called *One Trick Pony* and, of course, there was an album of the music. Apart from its initial showing in the States, it does not seem to have been heard of since, either there or in the UK. Perhaps it was the first real Paul Simon flop.

Some other outstanding Paul Simon songs:
'Flowers Never Bend With the Rainfall' (1965), 'Red Rubber Ball' (1965), 'For Emily, Wherever I May Find Her' (1966), 'America' (1968), 'Cecilia' (1969), 'Me and Julio Down by the Schoolyard' (1972), 'Hobo's Blues' (with Stephane Grappelli, 1972), 'So Long Frank Lloyd Wright' (1969), 'Keep the Customer Satisfied' (1970), 'Kathy's Song' (1965).

SONDHEIM, Stephen Joshua, composer, author.

Born New York, 20 March 1930. Educated George School, and Williams College, where he obtained a BA in composition and music theory. In the early 1950s he contributed music to various Broadway shows, none of them famous, and made his first mark as a lyricist by writing words for some of Leonard Bernstein's songs for the revival of *Candide* in 1956. It was this introduction that led to Sondheim's first major achievement (again as lyricist), when he wrote for Leonard Bernstein's score of the hit show *West Side Story* (1957). This was followed in 1958 by a very successful collaboration, as lyricist, with Jule Styne for the show *Gypsy*, starring Ethel Merman.

The first production for which Stephen Sondheim wrote both music and lyrics was *A Funny Thing Happened on the Way to the Forum* in 1962, with Zero Mostel and Phil Silvers, but neither this show nor his next, *Anyone Can Whistle* in 1964, with Lee Remick and Angela Lansbury, produced any songs that could be described as memorable.

In 1965 he reverted briefly to lyric-writing only, in an incongruous collaboration with Richard Rodgers for the show *Do I Hear a Waltz?*, but it was a flop. He fared better in 1970 when he wrote both music and lyrics for the show *Company* with Elaine Stritch. This was judged a success in New York but produced no hit songs. Nor did his 1971 production *Follies*.

It was 1973 before a Sondheim song became an international hit, and that was 'Send in the Clowns', part of his score for *A Little Night Music*, starring Glynis Johns and Hermione Gingold. This was followed in 1976 by a disaster called *Pacific Overtures*, somewhat redeemed in the same year by a successful London presentation of *Side by Side by Sondheim*, in which Millicent Martin, Julia McKenzie, David Kernan and Ned Sherrin (whose idea it was, and who also directed it), performed selections of Sondheim's songs. The show had a successful run at The Mermaid Theatre, and then transferred to Wyndhams, but did not make New York. The latest Sondheim production is a musical version of *Sweeney Todd*.

Stephen Sondheim has become a cult figure in the world of musical theatre. He himself is less interested in his ability to write lyrics for other composers than in his desire to be a complete writer of both music and lyrics, integrated into the book or story line of a show. Clearly, in this respect he writes more in the tradition of opera than musical comedy.

With the exception of *A Little Night Music*, New York theatre critics (at least the three most important ones) have been consistently unkind to Sondheim shows. One of them simply wrote 'drop dead' of the show *Anyone Can Whistle*. The reviews of *Follies* closed it, losing its backers, it is said, some $800,000. How much money *Pacific Overtures* lost, is not revealed. On the other hand, Sondheim shows have consistently received rave reviews in London. He is, therefore, a much more respected figure in England than he is in America, in spite of the fact that *Company*, *Follies*, *A Little Night Music*, *Pacific Overtures*, and *Sweeney Todd* have all won American Tony Awards and New York Drama Critics Circle Awards.

Leonard Bernstein has said that Stephen Sondheim is 'now the most important theater man writing', and Jule Styne says: 'I adore him'. But perhaps English critic Sheridan Morley sums up best the complexity that is Sondheim when he says: '... he is first and foremost a wordsmith ... a writer who can condense the entire autobiography of an ex-Ziegfeld Follies girl into four broken lines'.

I would not necessarily take that as a recommendation—he has still only written one hit song, 'Send in the Clowns'.

STEPHENS, Geoff, *see* Macaulay, Tony.

STOLLER, Mike, *see* Leiber, Jerry.

STYNE, Jule, composer, publisher, producer, pianist.

Born London, 31 December 1905. His family emigrated to the USA in 1913. Educated Chicago College of Music (scholarship), and Northwestern University. He was a child prodigy at nine, playing solo piano with the Chicago Symphony Orchestra. As he grew older he began playing piano in local dance bands, leading his own outfit by the time he was 20. He soon moved to New York, working as an arranger and as a vocal coach for singers. Later he moved to Hollywood, where he did the same kind of work. In 1927 he had his first taste of songwriting success with 'Sunday', sharing the credit with three other people. He also earned money accompanying singers such as Harry Richman, and it was through this that he spent the first half of the 1930s coaching the stars of 20th Century Fox films in singing.

It was Daryl Zanuck of Fox who advised him to become a songwriter, and found him a job to do just that with Republic Pictures. It meant a drop in salary but it also resulted, after a lot of hard work and menial tasks, in his first collaboration with lyricist Frank Loesser, and their 1941 hit 'Since You', from the film *Sailors on Leave*, with Dorothy Lamour. In 1942 they had further success with 'I Don't Want to Walk Without You', from the film *Sweater Girl*.

Max Wilk, in his book *They're Playing Our Song*, quotes Styne as saying that Republic traded John Wayne to Paramount for a movie in return for a set of Frank Loesser lyrics to some songs Styne had written for one of their films. Loesser was so impressed with the collaboration that he then took Styne away from Republic to

Paramount, where they had some very successful films together until Loesser joined the army.

This left Styne without a writing partner, and it was at that time that one of the movie producers insisted on bringing in Sammy Cahn which, although Styne was originally against the idea, resulted in a very fruitful partnership. Their first hit was 'There Goes That Song Again', from the 1944 picture *Carolina Blues*. By then Republic had hired Styne back again from Paramount at a greatly increased fee. Although that was their first big movie hit, the first song they wrote together just a couple of years earlier also became a hit in due time— 'I've Heard That Song Before'. The 1940s saw some sensational success for the Styne/Cahn partnership, and at one point their songs occupied the first three places in the Hit Parade. Among the successful titles were 'I'll Walk Alone', 'It's Magic', 'Five Minutes More' and 'Time After Time', all written between 1944 and 1948.

But Jule Styne, who had come to songwriting late in life at 35, decided that if he didn't try to do fresh things he would be engulfed by the Hollywood songwriting machine. He and Sammy Cahn were lucky enough to be asked to write the score for a Broadway musical, *High Button Shoes*, which opened in 1947, with Phil Silvers in the cast, and such songs as 'I Still Get Jealous', and 'Papa, Won't You Dance With Me?'. It ran for over 700 performances, and Jule decided to stay in New York. Sammy Cahn, however, preferred the Hollywood scene, and for Styne's next commission, the 1949 stage version of *Gentlemen Prefer Blondes*, his lyricist was Leo Robin. Carol Channing played the part that was given to Marilyn Monroe in the film, and the top song was 'Diamonds Are a Girl's Best Friend'.

In Max Wilk's book *They're Playing Our Song*, Jule Styne says: 'It was during the McCarthy witch hunt, when the writers in Hollywood, all those talented guys, were blacklisted, not allowed to work or write, that I did *Pal Joey*. That was the first time *I produced* a show. Won the Drama Critic's award—and this is what made me. Now, on top of two hits, this happened'. The date was 1950, and he was referring to the revival version of the Rodgers and Hart stage musical originally produced in 1940. The 1950 show had no Styne music in it, and retained all the Rodgers and Hart songs, although changes in casting included Lionel Stander's replacing Jack Durant. Jule Styne's other major show as producer was the 1956 musical *Mr Wonderful*, which had music by Jerry Bock, and put Sammy Davis Jr on the road to stardom.

During the 1950s Styne did write more movie songs, some with his old partner Sammy Cahn, including the monumentally successful 'Three Coins in the Fountain', but by that time he was really committed to the theatre. His next big hit was in collaboration with lyricists Betty Comden and Adolph Green, the score for the 1956 show *Bells Are Ringing*, which starred Judy Holliday and Sydney Chaplin, and produced such hits as 'Just in Time', 'The Party's Over', and 'Long Before I Knew You'. The show was just as successful when it opened in London in 1957 with Janet Blair replacing Judy Holliday, and it was made into a film in 1960. In 1959 he wrote the score for *Gypsy*, his first collaboration with lyricist Stephen Sondheim, which produced another hit, 'Everything's Coming Up Roses'. In 1960, there was the show *Do Re Mi*, with the song 'Make Someone Happy', another collaboration with Comden and Green. And this was followed by other shows and occasional contributions to films until his next big musical, *Funny Girl*, in 1964. This was the show that brought stardom to Barbra Streisand, and produced the songs 'Don't Rain on My Parade' and 'People'.

Since then there have been other Jule Styne shows, and other Jule Styne songs—although no more major hits. In 1971 he said to Max Wilk, 'I'm still writing! And I have been doing a lot of bad shows because there aren't any good books around. But I still practise my art'.

Some other outstanding Jule Styne songs:
'I Fall in Love Too Easily' (1945), 'Saturday Night Is the Loneliest Night of the Week' (1944), 'It's Been a Long Long Time' (1945), 'Let It Snow! Let It Snow! Let It Snow!' (1945), 'The Things We Did Last Summer' (1946), 'A Little Girl From Little Rock' (1949), 'Stay With the Happy People' (1950).

TAUPIN, Bernie, *see* John, Elton.

TOBIAS BROTHERS, The,

Harry, author, publisher, born New York, 11 September 1895. Charles, composer, author, publisher, born New York, 15 August 1898. Henry, composer, author, painist, singer, producer, director, publisher, born Worcester, Mass, 23 April 1905. Although there are examples of the three brothers writing as a team ('Miss You', a big hit from 1929, is a good instance), they mainly wrote separately, and with the collaboration of other composers/authors (Gus Arnheim, Cliff Friend, Sammy Stept, and Lew Brown are well known names among many others).

Charles and Henry centred their lives on New York, while Harry spent most of his time in Hollywood after 1929. Among Charles's contributions to Broadway shows have been scores for *Earl Carroll's Sketch Book* (1935) and *Earl Carroll's Vanities* (1932), as well as the stage version of *Hellzapoppin*. He also founded the family music publishing firm in 1923. Among his best known songs are 'When Your Hair Has Turned to Silver', 'The Broken Record', 'Somebody Loves You', 'Little Curly Hair in a High Chair', 'Don't Sit Under the Apple Tree', 'The Old Lamplighter', 'Comes Love', 'Her Bathing Suit Never Got Wet', and 'Those Lazy Hazy Crazy Days of Summer'.

Henry Tobias, in addition to contributing to various Earl Carroll shows, developed as a writer of speciality material for a number of big stars, including Eddie Cantor, Milton Berle, Jimmy Durante, Sophie Tucker, and Jackie Gleason. He also became a TV producer for the CBS network, and a musical director. Among his best known songs have been 'Katinka', 'If I Had My Life to Live Over', 'I Remember Mama', and 'Easter Sunday With You'.

Harry Tobias contributed to many Hollywood musical movies of the 1930s. Among his best known tunes have been 'Sweet and Lovely', 'Sail Along Silvery Moon', 'No Regrets', 'At Your Command', 'Goodnight My Love', 'The Daughter of Peggy O'Neill', 'Go to Sleep Little Baby', 'Love Is All', 'Take Me Back to Those Wide Open Spaces', and 'Oh Bella Maria'.

Charles, Harry, and Henry continued their songwriting through the 1950s and 1960s, even though their main interest had become publishing and production. As the main hits of the three brothers have been referred to in the text, no additional listing is necessary.

TRENT, Jackie, *see* Hatch, Tony.

TURK, Roy, *see* Ahlert, Fred.

VAN HEUSEN, James (Jimmy) (Edward Chester Babcock), composer, publisher, pianist.

Born Syracuse, New York, 26 January 1913. Educated at Casenovia College and Syracuse University. He always showed an interest in music, especially playing the piano and attempting to write songs in high school. It was a schoolboy prank, based on a comedy song of the day, that led to his being expelled. The result was that aged 16, he found himself working as a radio announcer on station WSYR, Syracuse. This in turn led to his change of name for professional purposes from Babcock to Van Heusen. The station manager apparently feared that Babcock sounded obscene, a decision that Jimmy has had no cause to regret, although it must have been totally mystifying at the time. He has never adopted Van Heusen legally, and for official purposes is still Chester Babcock, and still called Chester by those who have known him long enough to remember the incident. One of his student friends, and occasional lyricist for early Van Heusen attempts at songwriting, was Jerry Arlen, son of Harold, and it was Harold Arlen who brought the budding composer to New York as his deputy to write for the Cotton Club Revues. One of the songs he wrote at that time was actually published—'Harlem Hospitality'. But he soon found himself without work, and had to resort to every kind of job from demo pianist in a publishing house to freight elevator operator, in order to pay the rent.

Jimmy Van Heusen's first real break came in 1938, while he was working as demo pianist for yet another publishing house, where one day he met bandleader Jimmy Dorsey. Dorsey liked one of the young Van Heusen's tunes, wrote a set of lyrics for it, and it became the very successful 'It's the Dreamer in Me'. He also met bandleader and songwriter Eddie de Lange, with whom he wrote several numbers, the most successful being 'Deep in a Dream' (1938), closely followed by 'All This and Heaven Too', and 'Heaven Can Wait', both in 1939. Together Van Heusen and De Lange also wrote the music for a Broadway show, *Swingin' the Dream*, a sort of hot version of *A Midsummer Night's Dream*. The show ran for all of 13 performances, but it did produce the song 'Darn That Dream', which was subsequently recorded by Benny Goodman's band, with vocal by the great Mildred Bailey, which made it into a hit.

At about that time Jimmy Van Heusen met two people who were to have a great influence on his future career. One was Frank Sinatra, still virtually unknown, who had just joined the Tommy Dorsey

Orchestra. The other was lyricist Johnny Burke, who was to replace Eddie de Lange. One of the earliest Van Heusen/Burke songs was 'Polka Dots and Moonbeams', made into a hit by the Tommy Dorsey Orchestra with vocal by Frank Sinatra. From then on Sinatra's enthusiastic exploitation of Van Heusen's writing talents became legendary, and contributed in a major way to the success of his compositions. It could be said with equal truth that the Van Heusen/ Burke songs, and later the Van Heusen/Cahn songs, which have become associated with the singer, contributed in just as great a measure to Frank's success as a performer. By 1941, Jimmy had reached the enviable position of having three of his songs in radio's 'The Hit Parade' in one week.

It was also at about that time that the composer was invited ('summoned' might be a better word to describe a movie mogul's invitation in those days) to Hollywood, to write the score for the Jack Benny, Mary Martin, Fred Allen film, *Love Thy Neighbour* (1940). This was closely followed by the Bing Crosby, Dorothy Lamour, Bob Hope film *Road to Zanzibar* (1941), which produced the hit 'It's Always You'. For both these movies the lyricist was Johnny Burke. From then on, in addition to other 'Road' pictures with the same team, either Van Heusen and Burke, or later Van Heusen and Cahn, wrote for some 18 films starring Bing Crosby. So, with both Bing and Frank Sinatra demanding Van Heusen songs, it is hardly surprising that Jimmy turned out to be one of the most successful composers of popular songs of all time. One only needs to recall such titles as 'Moonlight Becomes You' (from *The Road to Morocco*, 1942), 'Personality' (from *The Road to Utopia*, 1945), 'You Don't Have to Know the Language' (from *Road to Rio*, 1947), 'Swinging on a Star' (from *Going My Way*, and Van Heusen/Burke's first Oscar, 1944), 'Aren't You Glad You're You?' (from *The Bells of St Mary's*, 1945), and 'Sunshine Cake' (from *Riding High*, 1950).

A little known fact about Jimmy Van Heusen is that during World War II he had a successful career quite unrelated to songwriting. He had always been keen on flying, and as he became successful he was able to take lessons and become a qualified pilot, later buying his own aircraft. He became such a good pilot that, from before America's entry into the war until just before its conclusion, he was employed under his real name, Chester Babcock, as a test pilot for the Lockheed Corporation. His fellow employees at Lockheed had no idea that flying with them was the man whose songs they were singing and humming as they worked. Equally, his bosses in Hollywood for whom he was writing, were kept in total ignorance of his flying activities. As Johnny Burke, who did know, pointed out, 'Who wants to hire a guy to write a picture knowing he might get killed in a crash before he's finished it?'.

In 1954 Johnny Burke became seriously ill, and was unable to work for almost two years. As the publishing house of Burke & Van Heusen Inc had contracts with each that prevented them working with other partners, a number of what we now know to be Van Heusen hits of those years were apparently written by unknown composers. 'Somewhere Along the Way', for example, was written according to the sheet music by one Ada Kurtz. Obviously a way round the contractual problem had to be found, and it was precisely at that time that Sammy Cahn first began to write lyrics for Jimmy Van Heusen songs. Sammy was in the process of dissolving his very successful partnership with Jule Styne, and was introduced to Jimmy Van Heusen by Bing Crosby, who needed four extra numbers for the 1956 remake movie of Cole Porter's *Anything Goes*, in which he was currently involved.

But the team's big assignment was the score for the Frank Sinatra film *The Tender Trap* (title song, 1955), closely followed by the song 'Love and Marriage', which originated in a TV show, became a huge hit as a result of a Sinatra performance, and was their first song to receive an Emmy award. The Van Heusen/Cahn team received three Oscars for songs they wrote for Frank Sinatra. There was 'All the Way' from the movie *The Joker Is Wild* (1957), 'High Hopes' from the movie *A Hole in the Head* (1959), a song which Cahn parodied as a campaign song for John F Kennedy, and thirdly 'Call Me Irresponsible', from a film which fortunately has disappeared into oblivion, called *Papa's Delicate Condition* (1963).

The last song had been written several years earlier when it was planned that Fred Astaire should star in the same film. But the project was abandoned, and when it was revived in 1963 comedian Jackie Gleason took the role. If the film is best forgotten, at least the song will be forever memorable for recordings by artists such as Frank Sinatra and Andy Williams, and it took on a whole new lease of life again in 1972 when it was recorded by Jack Jones. The song won its composers an Academy Award.

Other memorable Van Heusen/Cahn songs for whose success Sinatra was largely responsible are 'Pocketful of Miracles' (1961), 'My Kind of Town' (1964), and 'The September of My Years' (1965), which won a Grammy Award.

In 1968 the team wrote the title song for the film *Star!*, featuring Julie Andrews, and based on the life story of Gertrude Lawrence. The producer was Saul Chaplin, who many years before had been one of Sammy Cahn's first songwriting partners. Like all successful songwriters, the team would have loved to have had success on Broadway. They made two attempts with *Skyscraper* in 1965, and *Walking Happy* in 1966. In spite of good songs, neither show was successful.

Jimmy Van Heusen is an extrovert. He makes no secret of the fact that the most important interests in his life are 'chicks, booze, music and Sinatra'. But he is also a keen photographer, and an eminent collector of manuscripts by famous musical composers, ranging from Tchaikowsky to Gershwin. He still flies his own aeroplanes (including a helicopter). Sammy Cahn, who doesn't like flying, was once persuaded into the chopper. But his comment was 'Birds don't try to write songs, so what am I trying to fly for?'.

Johnny Burke, Van Heusen's first major partner, was born in Antioch, California, 3 October 1908. He died in New York, 25 February 1964. He was educated at Crane College, University of Wisconsin, and started his professional career on the staffs of various music publishing companies, first in Chicago, then in New York. Apart from Jimmy Van Heusen, Johnny Burke has been a prolific and very successful lyricist with other composers such as Jimmy Monaco, and Arthur Johnston, Bob Haggart ('What's New', 1939), and Erroll Garner ('Misty', 1960). Sammy Cahn is so important to the art of the popular song, that he is one of only three lyricists who have been included in their own right in this book, and so is listed under his own name.

Some other outstanding Jimmy Van Heusen songs with Johnny Burke:
'To See You Is to Love You' (1942), 'Suddenly It's Spring' (1944), 'Sunday, Monday or Always' (1943), 'Going My Way' (1944), 'It Could Happen to You' (1944), 'Sleigh Ride in July' (1944), 'Yah-Ta-Yah-Ta' (1945), 'My Heart Goes Crazy' (1946), 'Imagination' (1940), 'Road to Morocco' (1942), 'But Beautiful' (1947).

Some other outstanding Jimmy Van Heusen songs with Sammy Cahn:
'Our Town' (1955), 'The Man With the Golden Arm' (1955), 'Come Fly With Me' (1958), 'The Second Time Around' (1961).

Some other outstanding Jimmy Van Heusen songs:
'Shake Down the Stars' (1940, with Eddie de Lange), 'I Thought About You' (1939, with Johnny Mercer), 'Nancy With the Laughing Face' (1944, with Phil Silvers).

VON TILZER BROTHERS, The,

Harry, composer, publisher, producer, born Detroit, Michigan, 8 July 1872. Died New York, 10 January 1946. Albert, composer, publisher, born Indianapolis, Indiana, 29 March 1878. Died Los Angeles, California, 1 October 1956. Harry was the more important because when he founded his own publishing company on West 28th St, New York in 1902, he was, unknowingly, virtually starting what was to become popular as 'Tin Pan Alley'. He was one of the first to open his business on 28th St, and it is alleged that the phrase 'tin pan music' was coined in his offices. This phrase caught on as more and more publishing companies opened there, until it gave its name to the entire street.

Early Harry Von Tilzer songs were sold to vaudeville performers for a few dollars—Harry himself enjoying some success in the field as partner in a double act with George Sidney. But he was soon to have two hits almost simultaneously, in 1898 and 1899—'My Old New Hampshire Home' (lyrics by Andrew B Sterling), and 'I'd Leave My Happy Home for You' (lyrics by Will A Heelan). But although the first song sold some 2 million copies and the second over 1 million and they were to establish Von Tilzer as a major songwriter, they earned their composer a total of only $30. He had had to sell the copyright to a small printer, William Dunn, who was not even a publisher, and it was he who suddenly found himself a rich man. But having found himself in a business he little understood, he sold out to the already established house of Shapiro and Bernstein, who soon offered Von Tilzer a partnership in their business. For them, he wrote the classic 'A Bird in a Gilded Cage', which became a 2 million-seller in one year. With his share Von Tilzer quit his benefactors and set up his own publishing house.

Other Harry Von Tilzer hits were 'The Mansion of Aching Hearts', 'On a Sunday Afternoon', 'Down Where the Würzburger Flows' (originally performed by Nora Bayes), and 'Please Go 'Way and Let Me Sleep' (1902). By 1903 all these were in the million-seller bracket. In 1905 he added another, 'Wait till the Sun Shines Nellie'. This became a success a second time round when Bing Crosby sang it in the 1941 film *Birth of the Blues*, which co-starred Mary Martin. Many other Harry Von Tilzer successes were to follow (not forgetting the 1911 vaudeville hit, 'I Want a Girl Just Like the Girl That Married Dear Old Dad'), up to the middle of the 1920s, including his last big one, 'Just Around the Corner', in 1925. But the changing face of the music business in the late 1920s and particularly in the 1930s, was something to which he could never really adjust, and he decided to retire, living out the rest of his life in a New York hotel.

His brother Albert attempted many jobs, including working as a staff writer and song plugger in his brother's company before he achieved his first songwriting success. This did not come until after he had severed his connection with Harry and founded a publishing business of his own in conjunction with a younger brother Jack, who had no pretensions to being a writer. This was in 1903, and their first song, with lyrics by Cecil Mack, was a hit called 'Teasing'. Other hits followed: 'Honey Boy' (1907), 'Smarty' (1908), 'Take Me Out to the Ball Game' (1908), 'Put Your Arms Around Me, Honey' (1910), 'I'm the Lonesomest Gal in Town' (with Lew Brown, 1912), 'Give Me the Moonlight, Give Me the Girl' (1917, also with Lew Brown, revived by Britain's Frankie Vaughan in the 1950s), 'Oh, by Jingo' (1919), 'I'll Be with You in Apple Blossom Time' (1920), 'My Gee-Gee From the Fiji Isles' (1920, again with Lew Brown), 'Dapper Dan' (1921, another Lew Brown), 'My Cutie's Due at Two to Two Today' (1926), and 'Roll Along Prairie Moon' (1935). His last major success, while not a big hit, was a song very successfully recorded by Britain's Anne Shelton in 1953, three years before his death, 'I'm Praying to St Christopher'.

The departure of the Von Tilzers, especially Harry, marked the end of a particular era of American popular music.

The major Von Tilzer hits have been listed in the text so no further listing is necessary.

WALLER, Thomas (Fats), composer, pianist, singer, organist, band leader.

Born New York, 21 May 1904. Died Kansas City, Missouri (actually on the Santa Fe Chief train, returning to New York from California),

15 December 1943. His father was pastor of New York's Abyssinian Baptist Church, and it was there that Fats Waller learned to play the organ. Educated at De Witt Clinton High School, he won a competition for amateur pianists at the age of 15. His first job was as organist at the Lincoln Theater, where the star of the current show at the time was the great Florence Mills. He became an accompanist to many singers, including the blues artist Bessie Smith, and was soon recognized as one of the greatest jazz pianists of all time, forming his own bands and groups, and singing as well as playing. In fact, at his death, it would be true to say that he had achieved worldwide recognition as an entertainer as well as a jazz pianist, and he topped many vaudeville bills in America and Europe in the 1930s, including the London Palladium. Fortunately his many records live on as a tribute to his performing talents, and equally his songs live on and continue to be played and sung 40 years after his death.

Many of his early songs never earned him a cent in royalties, because they were sold to the nearest publisher or artist for a few dollars, either to pay the rent or to buy the next bottle of gin. His first published song was 'Squeeze Me', written in 1925 with lyrics by Clarence Williams. By 1929 he had met Andy Razaf, a lyricist with whom most of Waller's best known songs were to be written, and in that one year they published both 'Honeysuckle Rose' (Waller's most famous song) and 'Blue Turning Gray Over You'. Also in 1929 he wrote another standard, 'I've Got a Feeling I'm Falling', with lyrics by Billy Rose.

Fats wrote the scores for three Broadway shows—*Keep Shufflin'* in 1928, *Hot Chocolates* in 1929 (from which score came his second most famous song, 'Ain't Misbehavin'), and *Early to Bed* in 1943. Among his other hits which have become standards are 'What Did I Do to Be So Black and Blue?' (1929), 'Keepin' Out of Mischief Now' (1932), 'Aintcha Glad?' (1933), 'The Joint Is Jumpin' (1938), and 'I'm Crazy 'Bout My Baby' (1932). He also composed a number of famous instrumental pieces for piano, including 'Harlem Fuss', 'Viper's Drag', 'Handful of Keys' and 'Numb Fumbling'. After his death a number of manuscripts were found and published posthumously. Among these were *London Suite* (Whitechapel, Limehouse, Soho, Piccadilly, Chelsea, Bond Street).

Fats Waller's major songs are all referred to in the text, so no additional listing is necessary.

WARREN, Harry, composer, pianist.

Born Brooklyn, New York, 24 December 1893. Died Los Angeles, California, 22 September 1981. One of 11 children, his parents emigrated to the US from Italy, subsequently changing the family name from Guaragna to Warren. He was educated at public schools in New York up to the age of 15 and his only music training came when he was a choirboy at his local Catholic Church of Our Lady of Loretto. But he taught himself to play his father's accordion without any outside aid, and followed that by borrowing a set of drums and teaching himself to play well enough to earn a few dollars playing with local bands. At the age of 15 he simply walked out of the commercial high school where he was studying and joined a touring carnival show. By the time he returned to New York he had saved $70, which he spent on a second-hand piano and proceeded to teach himself how to play it. To support himself meanwhile, he worked as a stagehand at the Loew Theater on Liberty Avenue in Brooklyn.

By that time it was obvious that music, the theatre, and entertainment generally were to be Harry Warren's life from then on, although he had not yet attempted to write his first song. Numerous other jobs came and went before that happened, including a dogsbody job at the Vitagraph film studios, where he was expected to do everything from playing as an extra to playing background music on the piano, helping the stagehands, and even working as an assistant director. He added to his income by playing piano in one or other of the silent movie houses.

When America became involved in World War I, Harry Warren enlisted in the navy, but found himself posted no farther away from home than Long Island, where he was put in charge of entertainment. It was during this period that he first started improvising little tunes, and teaching them to participants in some of the shows for which he was responsible. But it was not until the war was over and he had returned to civilian life playing piano in the silent movies again, that he wrote his first real song, 'I Learned to Love You When I Learned My ABCs'. Hawking this manuscript round Tin Pan Alley did not find him a publisher, but it did find him a job, plugging songs for the publishing house of Stark and Cowan. This in turn led to his first published song, 'Rose of the Rio Grande', in 1922. It had some success, but earned him no money, because as he said to Max Wilk in

Wilk's book *They're Playing Our Song*, 'They gave me a promissory note on it, and by the time the note became due, the bank had folded.'

His next two songs were more useful for him, especially 'Back Home in Pasadena' (1924, with lyrics by Edgar Leslie), which resulted in his being given a job as staff composer at the Shapiro Bernstein publishing company. From then on his writing talents began to grow, with several more songs published, although his next big hit, 'Nagasaki' (lyrics by Mort Dixon), did not appear until 1928. He began to be asked to write songs for Broadway revues. Such were 'Cheerful Little Earful', with lyrics by Ira Gershwin, and 'Would You Like to Take a Walk?', with lyrics by Mort Dixon for *Sweet and Low* in 1930. And for Billy Rose's *Crazy Quilt* in 1931 he wrote 'I Found a Million Dollar Baby', also with Mort Dixon. This song turned out to be one of Bing Crosby's early recording hits as well. Also in 1931 he wrote the score for *The Laugh Parade*, the two biggest songs to emerge being 'Ooh That Kiss', and 'You're My Everything', which became a standard to match those of any other great composer of popular songs. Another Warren success from 1931 was 'By the River Sainte Marie', originally written in 1922, and turned down by every publisher who heard it. So it was nine years before it was bought, and then popularized on radio and records by Kate Smith.

It is as a composer of movie hits that Harry Warren will always be best remembered. His first two were 'Mi Amado' (*Wolf Song*, 1929) and 'Cryin' for the Carolines' (*Spring Is Here*, 1930). After these he returned to New York, and for a man who was to make his name as a Hollywood composer, his remarks, again to Max Wilk in *They're Playing Our Song* are interesting: 'I couldn't stand it here then. This place was nothing. I missed Lindy's' (the New York showbiz spot). 'No buildings anywhere, just fields. It was like being at an Indian outpost'.

Yet in 1932 Harry and his wife and family moved back to Hollywood, ultimately to make it their permanent home. This was brought about by Daryl Zanuck, boss of Warner Brothers, who was planning the movie *42nd Street*, which starred Dick Powell, Ruby Keeler and Bebé Daniels, and introduced Ginger Rogers to stardom with the song 'We're in the Money'. He had already engaged lyricist Al Dubin, and as Warners owned the publishing house of Remick for whom Warren had done a lot of writing, the match seemed a natural to Zanuck. How right he was is amply demonstrated by the list of Harry Warren/Al Dubin successes which seemed to pour out

of the team from that date, almost up to Dubin's untimely death in
1945.

The list of these great hit songs is simply too large to include at
this point, and will be found below. But one has only to mention the
names of Ruby Keeler, Dick Powell and Busby Berkeley, to conjure
up memories of the great days of the Hollywood musical.

From about 1939, Harry Warren had already written some other
big hits with collaborators of the calibre of Mack Gordon. They
included 'You'll Never Know' (1943), 'Chattanooga Choo-Choo'
(popularized by Glenn Miller, 1941), and 'The More I See You' (from
the film *Diamond Horseshoe*, 1945, starring Betty Grable). And these
had been preceded by two very successful collaborations with Johnny
Mercer in 1938, with 'Jeepers Creepers', for the Dick Powell film
Going Places, and 'You Must Have Been a Beautiful Baby', for the
Olivia de Haviland/Dick Powell movie *Hard to Get* (1938). He also
wrote 'On the Atchison, Topeka and the Sante Fe' with Mercer for
the 1946 Judy Garland film *The Harvey Girls*, and with Ira Gershwin
the complete score for the 1949 Fred Astaire/Ginger Rogers movie,
The Barkleys of Broadway. In *Great Men of American Popular Song* David
Ewen quotes Warren as believing this to be the best score of his
career, although none of its songs has become a standard except
'They Can't Take That Away From Me', which had been written by
George and Ira Gershwin for the 1937 Astaire/Rogers picture *Shall
We Dance*, and so was already a hit when it was reintroduced into *The
Barkleys of Broadway* in 1949.

By the end of the 1950s Harry Warren had begun to retire from
songwriting, and his last two big hits were 'That's Amore' from the
1953 film *The Caddy*, starring Dean Martin, and 'An Affair to
Remember', from the 1957 film of the same name.

Among all the major songwriters, Harry Warren remains another
typical example of the 'pro'. Harry wrote songs for specific purposes,
but above all he achieved less publicity than almost any other major
composer, and yet almost more acclaim in the professional sense of
million-sellers, and Oscars (he had three, the first coming for 'Lullaby
of Broadway' in 1935). He once said to Harold Arlen, 'From now on,
you walk two Oscars behind me!' Perhaps he has summed himself up
best. Max Wilk in *'They're Playing Our Song'* quotes him as saying:
'Well, I was never a publicity seeker. They wrote about the guys who
were publicised. Like the other day this guy comes to me and
interviews me about Burt Bacharach. He's telling me this guy's upset
the whole musical world. I said "No, he's just getting a lot of

publicity". He goes out and plays his songs with a big orchestra. Have you seen any songwriter doing that, except may be Mancini? Its like in the old days Johnny Mercer used to go on a lot of radio shows. So did Hoagy Carmichael. They got publicised'.

What other composer of Warren's stature would have learned that he had been nominated for an Oscar only by listening to the radio while out driving? Many people still say 'They don't write songs like that any more', but it can be said with truth of Harry Warren, 'They don't make songwriters like that any more.'

Many of Harry Warren's greatest hits were those he wrote in the Hollywood days with his partner Al Dubin. Al was born in Zurich, Switzerland, 10 June 1891. His father was a doctor, who emigrated to the USA when Al was only two, settling in Pennsylvania. Al was educated at Columbia University and St Lawrence University, obtaining a bachelor of law degree, as a result of which he became a practising lawyer in New York. His first published hit song came in 1916, and was called "T'was only an Irishman's Dream'. Having decided to quit the law for songwriting, he began working as a staff lyricist for a publishing house, but he had no luck with any subsequent songs, and took a job as a singing waiter in a bar in Philadelphia.

By that time America was at war. Young Dubin joined up, soon finding himself in charge of entertainment for the 77th Division of the US Army. He served overseas, and it was during that time that he was also able to continue his songwriting, with special material for the army shows for which he was responsible. After the war he rejoined the hopefuls looking for a break in Tin Pan Alley, and ultimately found it in 1925, with a song called 'A Cup of Coffee, a Sandwich and You', which, with music by Joseph Meyer and help from Billy Rose as co-lyricist, found its way into the English edition of *André Charlot's Revue of 1926*, starring, among others, Jessie Matthews and Anton Dolin. It was also popularized on records by Gertrude Lawrence, who appeared in the American edition together with Jack Buchanan. In the same year, in collaboration with composer Sammy Fain, he came up with 'Nobody Knows what a Red-Headed Mama Can Do', and in 1926 'The Lonesomest Gal in Town', for which Jimmy McHugh wrote the music.

By then Al Dubin was on his way as a lyricist, and in 1929 Warner Brothers brought him to Hollywood from New York. There Daryl Zanuck assigned him to write, with composer Joe Burke, the music for the 1929 movie *Gold Diggers of Broadway*. This produced two songs that were to become standards, 'Painting the Clouds With Sunshine', and 'Tip Toe Through the Tulips With Me'. The Burke/Dubin partnership continued to produce more successful movie hits, until in 1932 Zanuck teamed Dubin for the first time with Harry Warren for *42nd Street*. Although the partnership showed its first signs of breaking up in 1939, and Warren went on to work with other lyricists, Al Dubin was to have several more hits before his death in New York in 1945.

Notable among these were 'South American Way', with music by Jimmy McHugh, for the 1940 film *Down Argentine Way*, starring Carmen Miranda (which had originally seen the light of day as the 1939 Broadway show *Streets of Paris*). Shortly before his death he also wrote with Burton Lane 'Feudin' and Fightin'', which was featured in the 1944 show *Laffing Room Only*, starring Olsen and Johnson. But because of a dispute between the Shuberts, who were the producers of the show, and ASCAP, broadcasting and recording rights were not released until long after the show folded in 1947. So as far as Al Dubin was concerned, his last hit was a posthumous one. Its breakthrough came when it was sung by Dorothy Shay on a Bing Crosby radio programme. In 1940 he also wrote the lyrics for Victor Herbert's 1920 instrumental hit, 'Indian Summer', and the immortal 'Anniversary Waltz', dating from 1942, for which Dave Franklin wrote the music.

But it is the team of Dubin and Warren that will go down in musical history as one of the top examples of collaborative songwriting, alongside DeSylva, Brown and Henderson, or Rodgers and Hart.

Some other outstanding Harry Warren/Al Dubin songs:
'Keep Young and Beautiful' (*Roman Scandals*, 1933, starring Eddie Cantor and Ruth Etting), 'The Shadow Waltz', 'I've Got to Sing a Torch Song' and 'Remember My Forgotten Man' (*Gold Diggers of 1933*, starring Ruby Keeler, Dick Powell and Joan Blondell), 'Shanghai Lil' (*Footlight Parade*, 1933, starring James Cagney), '42nd Street', 'Shuffle Off to Buffalo', 'Young and Healthy' and 'You're Getting to Be a Habit With Me' (*42nd Street*, 1933, for cast see text), 'The Boulevard of Broken Dreams' (*Moulin Rouge*, 1934, starring Constance Bennett and Franchot Tone), 'I'll String Along With You' (*Twenty Million Sweethearts*, 1934, starring Ruby Keeler, Dick Powell and Joan Blondell), 'I Only Have Eyes for You' (*Dames*, 1934, starring Keeler/Powell/Blondell), 'About a Quarter to Nine' and 'She's a

Latin From Manhattan' (*Go Into Your Dance*, 1935, with Ruby Keeler and Glenda Farrell), 'Lullaby of Broadway' (*Gold Diggers of 1935*, with Adolphe Menjou, Glenda Farrell and Hugh Herbert), 'Lulu's Back in Town' (*Broadway Gondolier*, 1935, with Adolphe Menjou, Dick Powell and Joan Blondell), 'With Plenty of Money and You' (*Gold Diggers of 1937*, with Powell/Blondell/Farrell), 'September in the Rain' (*Melody for Two*, 1937), 'The Girl Friend of a Whirling Dervish' (*Garden of the Moon*, 1938), 'I Yi Yi Yi Yi' (*That Night in Rio*, 1941, with Carmen Miranda, Alice Faye and Don Ameche), 'I Know Why', and 'It Happened in Sun Valley' (*Sun Valley Serenade*, 1941, featuring the Glenn Miller Orchestra), 'I Had the Craziest Dream' (*Springtime in the Rockies*, 1942, with Betty Grable, Harry James, Carmen Miranda and Cesar Romero), 'Serenade in Blue' and 'I've Got a Gal in Kalamazoo' (*Orchestra Wives*, 1942, featuring the Glenn Miller Orchestra).

Harry Warren with Mack Gordon:
'You Say the Sweetest Things, Baby' (*Tin Pan Alley*, 1940), 'There Will Never Be Another You' (*Iceland*, 1942).

With Leo Robin:
'Zing a Little Zong' (*Just for You*, 1952, with Bing Crosby and Jane Wyman).

WEILL, Cynthia, *see* Mann, Barry.

WEBB, Jim, composer, author, pianist, arranger, producer.

Born Elk City, Oklahoma, 15 August 1946. His father was a Baptist minister, and the church had a good organist who taught the youngster to play piano from about the age of six. He was educated at the local school until, at the age of 18, the whole family moved to San Bernardino, California, where Jim joined the San Bernardino Valley College. That year his mother died suddenly of a brain tumour at the age of 36. His father soon felt he wanted to go back to Oklahoma, and did so, taking the entire family except Jim. Jim had been writing songs since he was 13, and suddenly found in California the possibility of getting close to the music that interested him and away from the strict family atmosphere in which he had been brought up.

He moved to a one-room apartment in Hollywood with nothing but a mattress on the floor, and finally took a job at $50 per week as dogsbody for a music publishing company. Thanks to his musical training he was able to earn a few supplementary dollars writing out musical lead sheets for bands and singers, for their recording sessions. In this way he met people in music, one of whom was a recording executive, Johnny Rivers, who liked Jimmy's song 'By the Time I Get to Phoenix'. He recorded it with conspicuous lack of success, and it was not until later that it was taken up first by Glen Campbell then by many other major artists, and developed into a standard. The year was 1967, and Jim Webb was not quite 21. By the time he was, he was already a millionaire.

Rivers had not lost faith in his protegé, and teamed him as writer for a group called The Fifth Dimension. That year they took Jim Webb's song 'Up, Up and Away' to No 7 in the US charts. Their record meant nothing in the UK, where at the same time the recording of the song by the Johnny Mann Singers shot to No 6 in the UK charts. Jim said later that the song took him all of 35 minutes to write. With it, he had arrived on the scene in a big way, and when 'By the Time I Get to Phoenix' was picked up by Glen Campbell, the second Webb hit had arrived, even though it had been written first.

In 1968 the now classic Richard Harris recording of 'MacArthur Park' made No 4 in the UK and No 2 in the US, followed by two more big hits for Glen Campbell in 1969. These were 'Wichita Lineman' (No 7 UK, No 3 US), and 'Galveston' (No 14 UK, No 4 US). There had also been a fair hit in 1968 with a song called 'The Worst That Could Happen', by a group called The Brooklyn Bridge. Yet in spite of all this success, journalist Janet Maslin, in *Newsweek* said 'by 1969 it was all over'. So, what went wrong?

To find an answer one must examine the person, and Jim Webb is, on his own admission, a very complex character. Talking to Edwin Miller for the magazine *Seventeen*, he once said of his early and very religious upbringing, 'I had a pretty unhappy time in my teens. We moved to San Bernardino because of a dream my father always had of going to California, and that cultural shock was something unimaginable. At eighteen I had never had any experience with sex; I had never tasted beer'. Later he said: 'Here for the first time I had stood on a mountain, I had seen the ocean, I had driven a fast car. I had all these dramatic experiences, and I could never go back where I had come from'.

In 1968, talking to Philip Norman of *The Sunday Times*, he admitted that many of his much admired lyrics were to a large extent autobiographical. Of 'By the Time I Get to Phoenix', he said it was all based on a girl named Susan whom he met at high school. 'I did get in my car and try to leave. I left her a note, and got in my car. I got as far as maybe Barstow before turning round.' The lyrics of 'MacArthur Park' have caused controversy ever since the song was first heard. They have been variously described as having the ability 'to juxtapose images to evoke dream things which cannot be put into words' and 'meaningless surrealistic rubbish—a giant con'. Jim himself says: 'My lyrics are emotional, while my arrangements give me intellectual satisfaction'. 'MacArthur Park' was written after a final parting from Susan, and recorded by Richard Harris just when the latter's marriage was breaking down. Perhaps the combined chemistry produced these curiously obscure lyrics. Webb himself has said, 'This was the symbol, a big beautiful cake with a man and woman standing on the top. What happens if you leave it in the rain? You not only lose it, you lose the memory of it'.

But by the end of 1969, there was another thought nagging at Jim Webb with ever increasing frequency. It stemmed from the fact that not only were his songs being recorded by artists such as Glen Campbell, and covered by others such as Frank Sinatra, Barbra Streisand, Andy Williams, and Henry Mancini. These artists were actually queueing up, asking for Jim Webb songs to be written for them. Here was this twenty-one-year-old, becoming idolized by a generation, not only of artists, but of audiences too, who were old enough to be his parents—and then some.

Correspondingly, his music was instantly rejected by those of his own age, and that hurt. He himself summed it up well in *Newsweek* when he said, 'You couldn't play both Vegas and Woodstock. I saw all my peers looking at me and saying "You're just sitting there making money and having a good time. We're wearing buckskin jackets and trying to stop the war"'.

With money no longer any object, he decided to switch his talents to other kinds of writing. He rejected the opportunity of earning $40,000 per week for a Las Vegas engagement, and toured local folk clubs, singing new songs of his own. The critics were cruel. In 1970 he released an album of new songs, sung by himself, called *Jim Webb: Words and Music*. To promote it, he played a big concert at the Los

Angeles Music Center. Critic Leonard Feather wrote, 'Webb's theory that a writer can sing his own works better than everyone else, even if he is not a real singer, was destroyed' (*Los Angeles Times*). Grandiose projects for films and musicals all fell by the wayside. But Webb kept remorselessly on.

There were more public performances from 1971 through 1974, with a gradually improving stage presence, and more albums: *Land's End* (1974), and *The Yard Went on Forever* (1968, for Richard Harris). There were also a couple of moderately successful singles, 'Crying in My Life' (1974), and a song he wrote in 1973, 'All I Know', which Art Garfunkel took high in the US charts, thus demonstrating that Webb had not lost his ability to write songs for other people.

By 1977, Jim had met George Martin, the man responsible for producing all the Beatles records. They started working together on a new Jim Webb album, to be called *El Mirage*. Talking to Monty Smith of *New Musical Express* before the album was released he said: 'If *El Mirage* doesn't make it, there may never be another one'.

Some other outstanding Jim Webb songs:

'Carpet Man' (1968), 'Didn't We' (1968), 'Gayla' (1968), 'Magic Garden' (1968), 'Paper Chase' (1968), 'A Tramp Shining' (1968), 'Watermark' (1968), 'Whatever Happened to Christmas?' (1968), 'Where's the Playground Susie?' (1968), 'Everybody Gets to Go to the Moon' (1970), 'Honey Come Back' (1970), 'The Worst That Could Happen' (1968), 'Rosencrans Boulevard' (1967), 'You're So Young' (1968), 'I'll Be Back' (1968), 'Our Time Is Running Out' (1968), 'I Can Do It on My Own' (1968).

WEBBER, Andrew Lloyd, composer, pianist, arranger.

Born London, 22 March 1948. Educated at Westminster School, Magdalen College Oxford, Guildhall School of Music, and the Royal College of Music. **RICE, Tim,** author, producer. Born Amersham, Buckinghamshire, 10 November 1944. Educated Lancing College, Sussex. Andrew Lloyd Webber's father was Director of the London College of Music, and his brother Julian Lloyd Webber is a professional cellist, so it is clear that in his early upbringing a formal musical education featured large. Tim Rice, apart from a teenage attachment to pop music and desire to become a singer, just had a feeling that he might be able to write lyrics. He started as a law student but gave this up to become a management trainee at EMI. This led to his becoming personal assistant to the well known record producer Norrie Paramor, then under contract to EMI.

The Andrew Lloyd Webber and Tim Rice partnership came about almost by chance. Tim heard through the music business grapevine that there was a budding composer writing songs with no words, and in 1965 wrote out of the blue to Andrew, suggesting a meeting with a view to collaboration. The invitation was taken up. At that time Tim had had just one song of his own published, 'That's My Story'. Andrew had had a suite of piano pieces accepted.

Their first collaboration produced a musical based on the life of Dr Barnardo. It was called *The Likes of Us*, and it has not been produced to this day, although it contained one quite good song, 'Love Is Here'. Their output was neither prodigious nor remarkable, but they kept trying, and had a song, 'Believe Me, I Will', accepted for a 1967 album by Sacha Distel. It was not until 1968 that their first successful collaboration saw the light of day, in the shape of a pop oratorio called *Joseph and the Amazing Technicolor Dreamcoat*, which was commissioned by the Colet Court School in the City of London. Enough important people went to see the one and only performance for a record company to record it, and for one of its songs, 'Any Dream Will Do' to find its way onto a recording by Max Bygraves.

Joseph achieved sufficient critical acclaim for both Andrew and Tim to decide to start writing together full time. And it was Tim who had the basic idea for their smash hit musical *Jesus Christ Superstar*, which opened in London in 1970 and in New York in 1971. It was an enormous box office success, and despite some religious objections to its theme (Cliff Richard was one who found it distasteful), the main Protestant and Catholic churches found it acceptable, and the two youthful writers were off to a great start in their careers. Of its many songs two, the title song and 'I Don't Know How to Love Him' were the big hits.

In 1975, Andrew Lloyd Webber wrote a musical called *Jeeves*, based on the P G Wodehouse character. Tim Rice started on it with him, but couldn't get along with the idea, and ultimately the book was written by Alan Ayckbourn. Regrettably it flopped.

The partnership with Rice was renewed when Tim, on returning from a visit to Argentina, proposed to Andrew a musical based on the life story of Eva Perón. They decided to follow the successful pattern they had evolved with *Superstar*, and make an album of the music before seeking backing for a stage production. The album was ready towards the end of 1976, and two songs, 'Don't Cry for Me, Argentina' sung by Julie Covington, and 'Another Suitcase in Another Hall', sung by Barbara Dickson were released as singles. Against all the odds, 'Don't Cry for Me' shot to No 1 in the charts, making an overnight star of Julie Covington in the process. Plans for the stage musical were immediately set in motion, and the show, starring Elaine Paige, opened in London in June 1978. It, too, was an overnight success, and the composers found themselves graced with all kinds of press labels, such as 'Saviours of the English Musical'.

Whether or not there will ever be another Webber/Rice musical remains to be seen. No sooner was *Evita* a success than the press was full of rumours of rifts and break-ups. Certainly Andrew Lloyd Webber's 1981 production *Cats* owed nothing to Tim Rice, because it was based on T S Eliot's poems in *Old Possum's Book of Practical Cats*.

Tim Rice, easily the more commercially minded member of the team, has written songs for the Lauren Bacall film *The Fan*, the song 'The Only Way to Go' to music by Marvin Hamlisch for the film *The Entertainer* (this was also recorded by George Burns and Bing Crosby), and has contributed songs to *Gumshoe*, starring Albert Finney, and to *The Odessa File*, starring Jon Voight (the last two have music by Andrew Lloyd Webber). Since 1972 he has won seven Ivor Novello Awards, two Tony Awards, and several gold discs. Many of these are shared with Andrew Lloyd Webber for their collaboration on *Evita*.

The main Webber/Rice songs have been referred to in the text, so no further additions are listed here.

WESTON, R P (Bob), composer, author.

Born London, 1878. Died 6 November 1936. **LEE, Bert,** composer, author. Born Ravensthorpe, Yorkshire, 11 June 1880. Died 27 January 1947.

Bob Weston was born in Islington in London, and his first job was with an engineering firm. This didn't last very long. He was dismissed when he was discovered writing songs on odd pieces of paper during the firm's time. In 1905, due to his wife's ill-health, he moved to Weston-super-Mare, where he joined a concert party and later became half of a double act called Conway and Weston. They played at circuses, galas and various small halls. From there he moved on to another concert party at Ramsgate, where he wrote songs. By that time it had probably developed into a life-long habit.

His first published song was called 'Boys of the Chelsea School'. He'd taken it to David Day of the music publishing firm of Francis, Day and Hunter who told him 'If you've got any more like this I'll have them.' And through the years Francis, Day and Hunter have published dozens of his songs. In his early days many of them were written in collaboration with Fred Murray. They wrote many of Harry Champion's hits, either together or singly, songs that are now regarded as classics of the music halls. Among them were 'I'm 'Enery the Eighth I Am', an immensely popular ditty in which Harry Champion became the latter-day namesake of the English monarch whose name was always good for a laugh. This one had the extra comic twist that it is the widow Burch, not 'Enery, who has already been married so often. Bob wrote alone 'The End of Me Old Cigar', in which Champion sang of the joys of smoking, and 'What a Mouth' which more than 50 years later Tommy Steele took to the charts for 11 weeks in 1960.

Another of Bob's collaborators was F J (Fred) Barnes. The pair produced such songs as 'When Father Papered the Parlour' (which Billy Williams made into an irresistible song), 'The Hobnailed Boots That Farver Used to Wear' as well as 'I've Got Rings on My Fingers' (for Seymour Hicks). He later worked with Herman Darewski with whom he wrote the tongue-twisting 'Sister Susie's Sewing Shirts for Soldiers', 'Where Are the Lads of the Village Tonight?' (for Whit Cuncliffe) and 'Now Are We All Here?—Yes!'.

Music was Bert Lee's main interest, and at an early age he was playing the organ at his local chapel. His first job was to do with music, not as a composer, but as a piano tuner. It proved to be good training for him because he tuned his own pianos all his life. He later joined a pierrot troupe as a pianist and did that job for several years, no doubt gaining experience that was to become such an asset in later life. Like his future partner, Bob Weston, he, too, wrote some of his early songs with other writers. In 1910, with George Arthur, he had an enormous success with 'Joshua' which Clarice Mayne first introduced. In 1913 with Worton David and Harry Fragson he had another success with 'Hello! Hello! Who's Your Lady Friend?' in which as a performer Harry Fragson made so many tactless enquiries. Bob Weston and Bert Lee first met early in 1915 and it was David Day, the music publisher, who suggested they should work together.

So began a 20-year partnership that was to write 3,000 songs, hundreds of sketches, be involved in 75 stage shows and 17 films.

Through the years they wrote material for the ever-changing scene of popular entertainment, from music hall, which later became variety, to revue, and then musical comedy. When films developed a voice in the late 1920s they became writers for the screen. Their output was enormous, and they had the good fortune to come together soon after the outbreak of World War I. As a result, they immediately wrote a string of war songs, among which were 'Any Complaints? No!', 'The Brave Old Contemptibles' and 'In a Land Fit for Heroes'. Their biggest wartime hit came about when they heard a crowd of girls from a jam-making factory shouting 'Goodbye' to a regiment of soldiers marching to the station en route for France. The scene and that one word inspired them that same afternoon to write one of the great songs of the war, 'Goodbye-ee'.

When they originally teamed up they agreed to keep office hours, meet every day and write a song every day. Soon they were doing much more than that. Apart from the songs, they wrote sketches for such stars as Fred Karno, Robb Wilton and Wee Georgie Wood. With the advent of revue they quickly became involved with productions such as *Cheep*, for the American star Lee White, and had a big hit with their song 'Where Did That One Go?'. They composed the tunes for J M Barrie's only revue, *Rosie Rapture*, starring Gaby Deslys, as well as shows such as *Rations*, *The Follies* and *Any Lady*, writing the book, music and lyrics for this Lupino Lane production. They became a sort of assembly-line production unit. Sometimes Bob would write the melody and Bert the words, or vice versa, and sometimes it would be a joint effort. To celebrate the end of the war they wrote a lovely and appropriate song called 'The Happiest Christmas of All'.

They continued their staggering output of songs through the 1920s with 'Paddy McGinty's Goat', 'Fancy Meeting You', 'The Gypsy Warned Me' (for Violet Loraine), 'Italiano' (for The Two Bobs), 'Ain't It Nice', 'My Girl's Mother' (for Randolph Sutton), 'What I Want Is a Proper Cup o' Coffee' (which over 50 years later was being used as a TV commercial jingle), 'I Might Learn to Love Him Later On' (which was sung by Violet Loraine in the Cochran revue *London, Paris and New York*) and 'While the Rich Man Rides By in His Carriage and Pair'. For the great British variety star, Gracie Fields, they provided ideal songs in 'Heaven Will Protect an Honest Girl', 'We're Living at the Cloisters' and 'A Coople o' Doors'. They were big hits, all of them. They also wrote a whole series of monologues, many of which became associated with Stanley Holloway. Among them were 'And Yet I Don't Know', 'My Word You Do Look Queer', 'The Body in the Bag', and perhaps the best known and most popular, the story of the ghost that walked the bloody tower in the Tower of London, 'With Her Head Tucked Underneath Her Arm'.

Still in the 1920s they either wrote completely, or contributed to, dozens of stage productions, including the Charlot Revue *A to Z*, which later took Gertrude Lawrence and Jack Buchanan to Broadway. *Pot Luck* with Beatrice Lillie and Jack Hulbert, *You'd Be Surprised* with George Robey, *Leap Year* and many others. When hit American shows were transferred from Broadway to London, it was Weston and Lee who adapted them for the English stage. Outstanding among these were *The Girl Friend* (Rodgers and Hart), *Hit the Deck* (Vincent Youmans) and *Hold Everything!* (DeSylva, Brown and Henderson). In the show business world they gained the reputation of being 'show doctors' (although in their vernacular they regarded themselves as being solers and heelers) because of their ability quickly to cure an ailing production.

In 1926 they began a highly successful association with Jack Waller and Joe Tunbridge, and the quartet wrote over a dozen musical comedies together. Many of them were specially designed to exploit the talents of the wistful comedian Bobby Howes, *Tell Her the Truth*, *He Wanted Adventure*, *Yes, Madam* and *Please Teacher*.

Like many of the early songwriters, when they began Weston and Lee had no radio, no films, and no television or records to promote their songs. What they did have was a flair for echoing the spirit of the times. Any new vogue or trend was marked with a song. When the Woolworth threepenny and sixpenny stores opened they came up with 'We'll Have a Woolworth Wedding' (perhaps an English counterpart of the song dedicated to the American Woolworths, Harry Warren and Billy Rose's 'I Found a Million Dollar Baby in a 5-and-10-Cent Store'). With the beginning of the Co-operative movement they suggested that the public should 'Stop and Shop at the Co-op Shop'. When women made the drastic decision to have short hair instead of the traditional long tresses, Bob Weston and Bert Lees wrote a gem of a song posing the question 'Shall I Have It Bobbed or Shingled?'. It was a little piece of social history in song.

So into the 1930s they went with songs such as 'Say to Yourself I Will Be Happy', 'The Legion of the Lost' (a hit for that fine singer

Peter Dawson), and 'Olga Pullofski the Beautiful Spy'. One of their biggest hits of the time was 'And the Great Big Saw Came Nearer and Nearer' which dates from 1936, the year in which Bob Weston died. Bert Lee continued for a time working with Harris Weston, Bob's son, who had written the music to some of their lyrics. But it could never be the same, although they did have a big success with their version of 'Knees Up Mother Brown'. So although the names Weston and Lee are perhaps unheralded to-day, their songs are by no means unsung. When cockneys end their parties, as they usually so, with a 'knees up' they are, maybe unknowingly, paying a tribute to the incredible partnership of Weston and Lee.

The most famous Weston and Lee songs have been referred to in the text, so there is no need for a further listing.

WHITING, Richard A, composer.

Born Peoria, Illinois, 12 November 1891. Died Beverly Hills, California, 10 February 1938. Educated Harvard Military School, Los Angeles, where his family sent him, although they lived by then in Detroit. He was always interested in music, and spent more time in Los Angeles with a taxi-driving buddy haunting the stage doors of the vaudeville houses for glimpses of the stars, than he did at the Academy. Finally he gave up his studies to return to Detroit and take a job with the publishing house of Remick, handing out copies of their latest songs to artists who came in looking for new material. It turned out to be a wise decision, for it was Remicks who published his first hit in 1915, called 'It's Tulip Time in Holland'. Equally, it was wise for the taxi-driving pal to stay in Los Angeles driving his taxi. He ultimately became Marshall Neilan, the film director. Jack Burton, in *The Tin Pan Alley Blue Book*, claims that Whiting never received any royalties for 'Tulip Time', signing over to Remicks all the rights in return for a Steinway grand. The song sold over $1\frac{1}{2}$ million copies in 6 months, so it was hardly a good deal.

In 1918 he had a big hit with the song 'Till We Meet Again', which was revived twice in the 1950s and 1960s in films such as *On Moonlight Bay* with Doris Day, and *The Eddie Duchin Story*. The tale of the song itself is fascinating, as told by Richard Whiting's daughter Margaret to Max Wilk, for his book *They're Playing Our Song*. It seems there was a war song contest to be held at a Michigan theatre, open to both amateur and professional writers. Richard had written a waltz, with lyrics by Raymond Egan, but decided it was not good enough, and threw it in the wastepaper basket. Margaret told Wilk: 'His secretary was dumping the basket, saw the manuscript, read it through, and then took it up to Mr Remick himself. He played it over and said: "Let's not tell Richard. Obviously he threw it away for some reason. If I know Richard, he didn't believe in it." Remick entered the tune in the war song contest. Well, it won, three nights in a row. Remick came in to see my father, and he said, "Richard, you have yourself a nice new hit song", and my father said: "But I haven't written anything for quite a while." "Yes you have", said Remick. He told him the song had won the contest, and that every day they were getting requests for five or six thousand copies, and I can't imagine how many recordings have been made of it. I suppose you could call it *the* World War I song.'

Perhaps it's surprising that Margaret Whiting did not draw a comparison between 'Till We Meet Again' and the Ross Parker/ Hugh Charles World War II song, 'We'll Meet Again'. For in addition to its European success with Vera Lynn, it was also immensely popular in America, as recorded by The Ink Spots. From then on hits began to come with regularity throughout the 1920s. Especially memorable were 'Sleepy Time Gal', with Ray Egan as lyricist (1926), 'The Japanese Sandman', also with Ray Egan (1920), and 'Ain't We Got Fun?', with Gus Kahn and Ray Egan (1921). His wife Eleanor soon took over his business affairs, at which she proved very astute, and after some argument talked him into leaving Detroit for New York in 1928. His first New York hit, in 1929, was a song for which he wrote the lyrics and not the music, called 'She's Funny That Way', which Margaret insists was dedicated to her mother. One of his biggest hits ever was soon to come—'Guilty', in 1931, which he co-wrote with Harry Askt, to lyrics by Gus Kahn.

Meanwhile he had not been without experience in contributing songs to Broadway revues, including *Toot Sweet* in 1919, *George White's Scandals* in 1919, and *Free for All* in 1931. His biggest success in this field came with *Take a Chance* in 1932, in which he collaborated with Nacio Herb Brown and Buddy DeSylva. It resulted in the standard, 'You're an Old Smoothie'.

Hollywood also called Richard Whiting in 1929, when at the insistence of publisher and impresario Max Dreyfus, he was teamed with lyricist Leo Robin for Paramount Pictures to write for the early Maurice Chevalier films. *Innocents of Paris* (1929) produced 'Louise';

Monte Carlo (1930, with Jeanette MacDonald and Jack Buchanan) produced 'Beyond the Blue Horizon'; *Playboy of Paris* (1930, with Maurice Chevalier) produced 'My Ideal'; *Take a Chance* (1933, with James Dunn and Cliff Edwards, which was the film version of the 1932 stage hit). It produced 'Eadie Was a Lady', popularized on records in the US by bandleader Cab Calloway, and in Britain by Al Bowlly. It had been a standout for Ethel Merman in the stage show, but she was not in the film. *Bright Eyes* (1934, with Shirley Temple) produced 'On the Good Ship Lollipop'; *The Big Broadcast of 1936* (with Burns and Allen, Bing Crosby, Ethel Merman and Ray Noble's Orchestra) produced 'Why Dream?'; and in 1937, *Hollywood Hotel*, with Dick Powell and Frances Langford produced 'Hooray for Hollywood', while *Ready, Willing and Able*, with Ruby Keeler and Lee Dixon gave us 'Too Marvellous for Words' (lyrics by Johnny Mercer).

Many of Richard Whiting's songs have been adopted by artists as themes or signature tunes. 'One Hour With You' was used by Eddie Cantor, 'Breezing Along With the Breeze' was used by bandleader Fred Waring. And Jack Benny used 'Hooray for Hollywood' for 20 years. A quiet, unassuming man, Richard Whiting was only 46 when he died. He was totally unchanged by his success. He once said to his daughter Margaret, according to Max Wilk, 'I hate to think of it as a craft, it's something that I love to do, but it is a job, it is work, and we work very hard to write a song and make it work. You must sing this song with great affection and feeling. It takes the men who write the lyrics a long time. Just believe in their words, do them simply and honestly. That's how a singer should interpret a song.'

Margaret Whiting certainly lived up to her father's advice. She became one of the most successful singers of the 1940s (she was only 14 when her father died), and made her name by introducing the beautiful song 'Moonlight in Vermont' in 1942 on a Capitol record. This company had just been founded by songwriter Johnny Mercer, who immediately signed Margaret for his radio series.

Some other outstanding Richard Whiting songs:
'Where the Black-Eyed Susans Grow' (1916), 'Ukelele Lady' (1925), 'My Future Just Passed' (1930), 'Gather Lip Rouge While You May' (1933), 'You've Got Something There' (1937), 'Ride, Tenderfoot, Ride' (1938).

WODEHOUSE, P G, *see* Kern, Jerome.

WONDER, Stevie (Steveland Morris, according to his birth certificate, although his father's name was Judkins, and his mother later became Mrs Hardaway), composer, author, singer, pianist, clarinetist, producer.

Born 13 May 1950, at Saginaw, Michigan. He has five brothers and sisters, and before he was of school age the family moved to Detroit. He has been blind from birth, although he says he himself did not realize this until he was four years old, and it never seemed to stop his getting into as much trouble as other kids of his age. He always seemed keen on music, and this started to develop when he was given first a harmonica and then a set of toy drums. Later, a piano was installed in the home, and he seized on that too. He was educated at local schools in Detroit, until a series of chance introductions led to his first recording session for Tamla Motown records at the age of 12, and a live concert appearance (which Motown also recorded) at the age of 13. His first title was 'I Call It Pretty Music (but the Old People Call It the Blues)'. Marvin Gaye played drums on the session. At that time he was billed as 'Little Stevie Wonder', and his first hit stemmed from that concert recording—an item called 'Fingertips—Part 2' (a shortened version of the album track), which reached No 1 in the US charts in 1963. From then on everybody realized that something had to be done about the education of a 13-year-old star, and he was sent to The Michigan School for the Blind, in Lansing. When he was touring, a private teacher accompanied him.

The law restricted his appearances as a minor but not his ability to write songs, which resulted in 100% of his royalties going to Motown's publishing house, although he was adequately paid for his performances. Motown however, did set up a trust fund for him, which he received when he was 21, and it amounted to over £400,000. At the same time his whole recording deal was renegotiated, much to his advantage. To quote his friend and publicist, Ira Tucker, 'It's kind of awesome. I tend to think he had it all figured out from the time he was 14. Basically, God manages Stevie, and Stevie manages himself.'

Although 'Fingertips' was Stevie's first hit, it was not a song in the true sense of the word, being more an extended jazz/rock performance. His first real composition was 'Uptight (Everything's Alright)' in 1965, which reached No 3 in the US and No 14 in the UK. He had two collaborators, Sylvia Moy and Henry Cosby. In between, Motown tried every kind of approach to establish him, but none was successful, and it was really the infectious, stomping sound of 'Uptight' that set the pattern for the series of Stevie Wonder hits that was to follow. Between 1966 and 1974 these included such major successes as 'I Was Made to Love Her' (No 2 in US, No 5 in UK, 1967), 'Shoo-Be-Doo-Be-Doo-Da-Day' (No 9 in US, 1968), 'For Once in My Life' (No 2 in US, No 3 in UK, 1968), 'My Cherie Amour' (No 4 in both US and UK, 1969), 'Signed, Sealed and Delivered' (No 3 in US, No 15 in UK, 1970), 'Superstition' (No 1 in US, No 11 in UK, 1972), 'You Are the Sunshine of My Life' (probably his best known composition, which has now become a standard, No 1 in US, No 7 in UK, 1972), and 'You Haven't Done Nothing' (No 1 in US, 1974).

Also between 1963 and 1976 Stevie made about 20 albums, many of which have reached gold disc status, and from which many of his hit singles have been taken. Probably the most outstanding albums both musically and from a sales point of view have been: *I Was Made to Love Her* (the title song was written for his first wife Syreeta, a marriage which only lasted 18 months), *Stevie Wonder Live, Signed, Sealed and Delivered, Where I'm Coming From, Music of My Heart, Talking Book, Innervisions, Fullfillingness First Finale,* and *Songs in the Key of Life.*

After his 21st birthday, Stevie Wonder embarked on protracted negotiations with Tamla for his new contract. He wanted things which they had never granted to any of their other artists, before or since. The fact that the resulting compromise ended up very much in Stevie's favour is a mark of his stature and of the respect the company had for him. He is now in full artistic charge of all material he records, and decides where and how he records it. He now has his own publishing company to take care of all his composing copyrights. The total contract is said to have guaranteed him $12 million over seven years.

In 1973 Stevie Wonder was badly injured in a car crash, and for some weeks not only his future ability, but his very life was in doubt. Fortunately he made a remarkable recovery, and his playing, singing and writing seem quite unimpaired. But it did cause a layoff for some time, something which he himself feels, in retrospect, may have been no bad thing. It gave him a chance to take stock and consider the future. After his accident, Stevie was quoted as saying, 'I also see that God was telling me to slow down, to take it easy. I still feel I'm here to do something for Him, to please people, to turn my world into music for Him, to make it possible for people to communicate with each other better.' To another reporter in 1974 he said, 'Nothing is promised to any of us. The very fact that you are able to breathe is a very special gift in itself.'

After his initial burst of hits in the 1960s, and particularly following the accident in 1973, Stevie has taken more and more time over his composing, and his public even get a bit edgy occasionally because it has sometimes been years between the release of one album of Stevie Wonder songs and the next. Nowadays, one album per year is a good rate of production for him (there was that much gap between the release of *Innervisions* and *Fullfillingness*). Nevertheless, in terms of quality, his approach would seem to be more than justified. *Innervisions* walked away with five Grammy Awards (Best Producer, Best Artist, Best Pop Vocal, Best Male R & B Vocal, and Best R & B Song). And when *Fullfillingness* made its appearance, it also won five Grammy Awards. By the same token, *Songs in the Key of Life* did not make its appearance until 1976. It was followed by *Anthology* in 1977.

Stevie Wonder's 1979 contribution was a fantastic effort for a blind man. He wrote the sound track for the Paramount film *The Secret Life of Plants*. The film was based on the book by Peter Tompkins and Christopher Bird. Naturally it was different from the kind of music that we have come to expect from him. But Stevie has not stopped writing hit singles. Remember 'Living in the City' (1974), 'Boogie on a Reggae Woman' (1975), 'I Wish' (1976), 'Send One Your Love' (1979), 'Masterblaster' (1980), and 'Happy Birthday' (1981, No 2 UK)?

Some outstanding Stevie Wonder songs:
'Ain't That Asking for Trouble' (1965), 'Sylvia' (1965), 'Everybody Needs Somebody' (1965), 'The Tears of a Clown' (1967), 'Hold Me' (1967), 'Pretty Little Angel' (1967), 'I Wanna Have Her Love Me' (1968), 'Do I Love Her?' (1968), 'Anything You Want Me to Do' (1969), 'You Can't Judge a Book by Its Cover' (1969), 'If You Really Love Me' (1971), 'Sweet Little Girl' (1971), 'Never Dreamed You'd Leave in Summer' (1971), 'To Know You Is to Love You' (1972), 'Blame It on the Sun' (1972), 'We'll Have It Made' (1972), 'He's Misstra Know It All' (1973), 'You Haven't Done Nothing' (1974), 'Please Don't Go' (1974), 'Sir Duke' (1977), 'I Can See the Sun in Late December' (1974), 'We Had a Love So Strong' (1978), 'I Can't Help It' (1978), 'Another Star' (1977), 'Melody Man' (1980), 'You're Supposed to Keep Your Love for Me' (1980), 'Don't Make Me Wait

too Long' (1980), 'Black Orchid' (1980), 'I Ain't Gonna Stand for It' (1980), 'Lately' (1980, No 2 in UK).

WOODS, Harry Macgregor, composer, author.

Born North Chelmsford, Massachusetts, 4 November 1896. Died 7 January 1970, Phoenix, Arizona. Educated at Harvard University, he received a musical education from his mother, who was a good singer. Although he had no fingers on his left hand, he still managed to play one-handed piano. He could be described as one of the mavericks among the top songwriters, for he never really seemed to take writing seriously. His first song was published in 1923, and the first to attract any attention was only his seventh, 'Paddlin' Madeline Home' published in 1925. His first big hit came in 1926 'When the Red Red Robin Comes Bob Bob Bobbin' Along', for which he wrote both words and music. He would frequently disappear, sometimes for weeks—a state of affairs that persisted in the 1930s, when he spent three years in England writing songs for Gaumont British Pictures.

A number of these were very successful, such as 'My Hat's on the Side of My Head', written for Jack Hulbert in the 1935 film *Jack Ahoy*, 'Over My Shoulder' and 'Springtime in My Heart', written for Jessie Matthews' 1935 movie *Evergreen*, as well as 'I Nearly Let Love Go Slipping Through My Fingers', for her 1936 film *It's Love Again*. Curiously, he seems to have retired from songwriting soon after 1945, and he ultimately went to live in Arizona. During the 10 years from 1926 to 1936, however, Harry Woods was responsible for a number of great songs that were to become standards as listed below.

Many of his biggest hits were written with Mort Dixon as lyricist. Mort was born in New York, 20 March 1892, and died at Bronxville, New York, 23 March 1956. He served in France in World War I, and on returning did a variety of jobs before finally settling down as a professional songwriter. His first hit 'That Old Gang of Mine, was published in 1923, to music by Ray Henderson. Apart from Harry Woods, Mort's other main collaborators have been Harry Warren, Billy Rose and Allie Wrubel. Like Harry Woods, Mort Dixon retired early from writing, to live in Westchester County, New York.

Some other outstanding Harry Woods songs :
'I'm Looking Over a Four-Leafed Clover' (1927), 'Side by Side' (1927), 'Here Comes the Sun' (1930), 'River Stay 'Way From My

Door' (1931), 'When the Moon Comes Over the Mountain' (1931), 'Just an Echo in the Valley' (1932), 'Try a Little Tenderness' (1932), 'We Just Couldn't Say Goodbye' (1932), 'What a Little Moonlight Can Do' (1934), 'I'll Never Say "Never Again" Again' (1935), 'You Ought to See Sally on Sunday' (1934).

WRIGHT, Lawrence, *see* Nicholls, Horatio.

WRUBEL, Allie, composer, author.

Born Middleton, Connecticut, 15 January 1905. Died Los Angeles, California, 13 December 1973. Educated at local schools, Wesleyan University and Columbia University.

He was one of seven brothers and sisters. The whole family were taught to play piano, and most of them learned one other instrument in addition. Allie chose woodwinds, starting off with a piccolo, and during his college days while studying medicine he played saxophone in local dance bands. He also spent a year playing in the Paul Whiteman Orchestra, and led a band touring England in 1924. His first song, 'You'll Do It Some Day', had been written for a college show, but his first professionally published song did not come until 1931 with 'Now You're in My Arms', for which singer Morton Downey wrote the lyrics. He also sang the song in a show called *The Garrick Gaieties*.

Several other hits followed during the next three years, and in 1934 he joined the flow of Tin Pan Alley composers out west to Hollywood, where he worked under contract to Warner Brothers. He contributed numerous songs to the mid-thirties Dick Powell/Ruby Keeler films, as well as to other Warner pictures that included such stars as Bette Davis, Rudy Vallee, Ann Dvorak, Glenda Farrell, Cary Grant, Jack Oakie and many others.

From his Hollywood contributions, among the best known are 'Mr and Mrs Is the Name', 'Flirtation Walk', 'Fare Thee Well Annabelle', 'The Lady in Red', and 'Goodnight Angel'. During the same period he continued to write for Tin Pan Alley, including such hits as 'Music, Maestro, Please' (1938), and 'There Goes That Song Again' (1941). During the 1940s and 1950s he divided his time between films and Tin Pan Alley, writing hits in both areas, including

'I'll Buy That Dream' (1945), 'Zip-a-Dee-Doo-Dah' (which won him an Academy Award in 1947), 'Johnny Fedora and Alice Blue Gown' (1946), and 'The Lady From 29 Palms' (1947). He retired from songwriting in the early 1960s. Among his best known collaborators of lyrics have been Herb Madgison, Ned Washington and Mort Dixon.

Allie Wrubel's best known songs are included in the text, so no further listing is necessary.

YELLEN, Jack, *see* Ager, Milton.

YOUMANS, Vincent Miller ('Millie'), composer, producer.

Born New York, 27 September 1898. Died Denver, Colorado, 5 April 1946. Educated Trinity School, Mamaroneck, New York, and Heathcote School, Rye, New York. After leaving school he worked temporarily in a humble capacity with Wall Street finance firms, then took a job as a song-plugger for Remick's, the music publishers, where an equally young George Gershwin was doing a similar job. He served in the US Navy in World War I, where he helped organize and produce naval shows. He also played piano in the accompanying band. Different sources offer widely different opinions as to Youman's ability as a pianist. One says he was 'an accomplished pianist', another that he could 'only play a rhythmic vamp on the piano, "um ta da da de dah, um to da da de dah", and he used to whistle his melodies while composing' (he must have been a good whistler, for this source insists that he had an arranger with him to copy down what he whistled, and write it out properly). Still another source indicates that he only learned to play the piano well comparatively late in life, when he studied at the Loyola School of Music in New Orleans. He was also one of the comparatively few songwriters who came from a relatively well-off family.

One of his earliest hits was written while he was still in the navy, although it did not achieve real fame until it appeared in *Hit the Deck* 10 years later. Originally it was played as a march by many naval and military bands, including that of John Philip Sousa. Its title at the time is not revealed, but we have come to know it since 1927 as 'Hallelujah'.

On leaving the navy he took a job as a song-plugger for Harms Music, and this in turn led to a job as rehearsal pianist for shows then in production with music by Victor Herbert, where he gained valuable experience from the great composer. He was also helped with introductions to important people in the world of musical theatre by George Gershwin, with whom he immediately renewed his friendship on leaving the navy. And for his first attempt at writing a Broadway show (*Two Little Girls in Blue*, 1921), he chose George's brother Ira Gershwin as his lyricist. Ira at that time was still writing under the name of Arthur Francis.

Vincent Youmans' total output must be among the smallest of all the songwriters in this book (the ASCAP Biographical Dictionary lists just over 40 songs), yet in terms of quality, every Youmans hit was so good that it became a standard. It is true that no standards emerged from *Two Little Girls in Blue*, although it did contain two pretty songs, 'Dolly', and 'Oh Me, Oh My, Oh You'. Equally, his second Broadway show, *Mary Jane McKane* (1923), was no blockbuster, and none of its songs linger in our memories today.

But later that same year Youmans really did hit the jackpot with *Wildflower* (lyrics by Otto Harbach and Oscar Hammerstein 2nd). This starred Edith Day and Guy Robertson, and ran for 477 performances. The title song, 'I Love You, I Love You, I Love You' and 'Bambalina' were perhaps the best of an excellent score. *Lollipop* (1924) and *A Night Out* (1925) were both dismal failures, and when *No, No, Nanette* appeared (also in 1925), with lyrics by Otto Harbach and Irving Caesar, it also did not appear at first as if it was going to promote the career of the budding songwriter. Fortunately a major reshuffle took place during its out-of-town performances, and by the time it reached New York, not only had five songs been replaced by new ones, so had even the principal performers, and what Broadway saw bore little resemblance to the initial try-out in Detroit. The 321-performance original run and the countless revivals over the years say all that needs to be said about a show that gave us 'I Want to Be Happy', 'The Deep Blue Sea' and 'Tea for Two' in its score.

Oh, Please! (1926) flopped, in spite of Beatrice Lillie's heading the cast, but it gave us the song 'I Know That You Know'. In 1927 Youmans became his own producer for the first time with *Hit the Deck*. The show was a resounding success, with 352 performances, but from the producer's point of view it must have been beginner's luck, because none of his subsequent attempts to produce his own shows were successful in box office terms. *Hit the Deck* had lyrics by Clifford Grey and Leo Robin, and gave us such songs as 'Sometimes I'm Happy', and 'Hallelujah'. It was made into a movie in 1930.

Vincent Youmans seems to have been choosy to the point of eccentricity about his lyricists. His list of collaborators is far longer than those of any other composer, and after his early shows he hardly ever seems to have used the same author twice. David Ewen, in *Great Men of American Popular Song* asserts that the main reason for Youman's lack of success as a producer was that 'he was assuming duties and responsibilities that belonged to professionals. He simply did not know how to be a producer.' He goes on to state that: 'Even when he worked with other producers things hardly went better. Here hard luck rather than sheer incompetence or temperament, was his worst enemy.'

So the sad story is, that of his own productions, *Great Day!* (1929) ran for only 36 performances, and *Through the Years* (1932) for only 20 performances. *Rainbow* (1929), which he did not produce, ran for 29 performances. But once again, the Youmans talent for writing excellent songs came to the fore. *Great Day!* had its title song, as well as 'Without a Song' and 'More Than You Know', all with lyrics by Billy Rose. Even *Smiles* (1930), produced by the great Florenz Ziegfeld, did not change the run of bad luck. It clocked up only 63 performances, in spite of the presence of Marilyn Miller and Fred and his sister Adèle Astaire in the cast. It did, however, give us the song 'Time on My Hands' (lyrics by Harold Adamson and Mack Gordon), while *Through the Years* (lyrics by Edward Heyman) gave us the title song (alleged to be Youman's personal favourite of all his compositions), and 'Drums in My Heart'.

After 1932 Youmans wrote no more for the Broadway theatre, but his last effort, a song he contributed to *Take a Chance*, a show otherwise written by Richard Whiting and Nacio Herb Brown, was a huge hit for him. This was 'Rise 'n' Shine', with which Ethel Merman, the star of the show, regularly brought the house down. In 1933 Vincent Youmans decided, apparently with rather bad grace, but pushed no doubt by the financial disasters of his Broadway shows, to go out West as so many other songwriters had done, and write for Hollywood. In this he was once again first time lucky, as his first commission was *Flying Down to Rio*, the debut movie of Fred Astaire and Ginger Rogers as a dance team. 'The Carioca', and 'Orchids in the Moonlight' were the outstanding songs.

From 1934 until his death, Vincent Youman's career went steadily downwards, and he wrote no more hits. In 1934 his publishing company went bankrupt, and that same year he contracted tuberculosis, which ultimately killed him. He apparently did little to preserve his health, more often than not totally disobeying his doctor's orders, or so wilfully misinterpreting them that he would rest in bed all day and then get up and spend his nights on the town, drinking in various clubs.

He spent frequent periods in various sanatoriums, especially one in Colorado, where he met and married one of his nurses, Mildred Boots. He began writing again when his health permitted, but none of his songs seems to have seen the light of day. David Ewen, in *Great Men of American Popular Song* says, 'By the time he died, he had over 150 such songs stored away, none of which had ever been heard publicly.' And Max Wilk, in *They're Playing Our Song* quotes a young writer, Ray Samuel, who met Youmans in New Orleans, as saying, 'I arranged with the band that was appearing in the Blue Room at the Roosevelt to do an evening of Youmans' tunes. Youmans sat in a corner, drinking ale, occasionally smiling at what he heard, but he wouldn't be introduced to the crowd. He stayed off in the shadows and listened.'

In 1935 he was declared bankrupt for over half a million dollars. And he still disregarded his doctors, went to parties or had friends in, entertaining them at the piano with new tunes.

For a period in 1943 his health seemed good enough to permit a brief return to New York, largely to plan and get backing for his most ambitious project ever, *The Vincent Youmans Ballet Revue*, an overwhelming combination of Latin-American music, serious music (Ravel's *Daphnis and Chloe*), and choreography by Leonide Massine.

It opened in Toronto in 1944, and to quote David Ewen again, 'The critics annihilated it, calling it a colossal bore.' It lost $4 million. Youmans retired to Hollywood, then back to the Colorado sanatorium, but it had all proved too much for his wife, who divorced him in January 1946.

Disobedient as ever, he moved out of the sanatorium into a hotel in Denver. It was there that he died in April of the same year. In spite of the relatively small output, the Vincent Youmans standards form a collection of great songs that can take its place alongside the best of Rodgers, Berlin, Gershwin, Kern or any other writer of that generation.

The main Vincent Youmans hits have been referred to in the text so no further listing is necessary.

YOUNG, Victor, composer, conductor, violinist, arranger.

Born Chicago, Illinois, 8 August 1900. Died Palm Springs, California, 11 November 1956. When he was 10, his family took him to Poland, where he was educated, and also studied classical music at Warsaw Conservatory, ultimately making his debut as a concert violinist with the Warsaw Philharmonic Orchestra. During the 1920s he returned to America, where, in addition to some classical work, he earned a living arranging music and playing the violin for dance bands, including that of Ted Fiorito. This led him into radio work, and throughout the 1930s he was musical director for various radio networks in Chicago and New York. He formed his own orchestra in 1935 and moved to Los Angeles, working in films and radio and becoming a prolific recording artist.

Although not a prolific writer of popular songs, he finds a place here because of those that he did write, many became standards of the best kind. Particularly memorable are 'Sweet Sue' (1928), 'I Don't Stand a Ghost of a Chance' (1932), 'Street of Dreams' (1933), 'Can't We Talk It Over' (1931), 'A Hundred Years From Today' (1933), 'The Old Man of the Mountain' (1933), 'Stella by Starlight' (1946), 'Golden Earrings' (1946), 'My Foolish Heart' (1949) and 'Blue Star' (1955). He also wrote a number of highly successful movie themes ('Blue Star' was originally the theme for a TV series called *The Medic*), including *For Whom the Bell Tolls, Samson and Delilah, The Greatest Show on Earth, Strategic Air Command, The Quiet Man, Shane* and *Around the World in Eighty Days*, which won an Academy Award in 1956.

His main lyricists have been Ned Washington ('Ghost of a Chance' and '100 Years From Today'), Ray Evans, Jay Livingston ('Golden Earrings') and Edward Heyman.

Appendices

The entertainment business is fond of recognizing the talents of its members with annual awards, and the music industry is no exception. Both in America and Britain there are many annual award presentations for just about everything. Since this book is about songwriters, I have selected for the following appendices the two awards commonly accepted by both British and American composers and authors as being the most prestigious for their particular art.

In the case of the American Oscar I have selected what is specifically an award for a song that has appeared in a film, thus ignoring stage musicals, million-selling records, and all kinds of other achievements. I have done so because an Oscar is the songwriter's premier award. This may be simply a hangover from the great days when the Hollywood musical virtually cornered the market in songwriting talent, but the prestige of the Oscar stays with us, even though musical films are now few and far between.

Similarly with the Ivors. Although there are many other awards presented to British songwriters, it is this category of 'most performed work of the year' that carries the most prestige. By definition, it is sometimes awarded to an instrumental work. It is also worth bearing in mind that the Ivor does not necessarily denote success in the field of million-selling records or other similar fields of songwriting.

APPENDIX 1

OSCARS
(Academy Award Winning Film Songs)

On 16 May 1929 the Academy of Motion Picture Arts and Sciences presented its first awards for what were considered to be outstanding achievements in the film industry of 1927–8. There are conflicting accounts of how the bronze statuette awarded in the various categories acquired its familiar name. The best known is that when the figure was first seen by a secretary she exclaimed, 'It reminds me of my Uncle Oscar!' So it became affectionately known as OSCAR. It was not until 1934 that it was decided that music as well as histrionic and technical ability merited recognition. Each year since then a presentation has been made for the best film song of the year.

Year	Title	Author/Composer	Film
1934	'The Continental'	Herb Magidson and Con Conrad	*The Gay Divorcée*
1935	'Lullaby of Broadway'	Al Dubin and Harry Warren	*Gold Diggers of 1935*
1936	'The Way You Look Tonight'	Dorothy Fields and Jerome Kern	*Swing Time*
1937	'Sweet Leilani'	Harry Owens	*Waikiki Wedding*
1938	'Thanks for the Memory'	Leo Robin and Ralph Rainger	*Big Broadcast of 1938*
1939	'Over the Rainbow'	E Y Harburg and Harold Arlen	*The Wizard of Oz*
1940	'When You Wish Upon a Star'	Ned Washington and Leigh Harline	*Pinocchio*
1941	'The Last Time I Saw Paris'	Oscar Hammerstein 2nd and Jerome Kern	*Lady Be Good*
1942	'White Christmas'	Irving Berlin	*Holiday Inn*
1943	'You'll Never Know'	Mack Gordon and Harry Warren	*Hello, Frisco Hello*
1944	'Swinging on a Star'	Johny Burke and J Van Heusen	*Going My Way*
1945	'It Might as Well Be Spring'	Oscar Hammerstein 2nd and Richard Rodgers	*State Fair*
1946	'On the Atchison, Topeka and the Santa Fe'	Johnny Mercer and Harry Warren	*The Harvey Girls*
1947	'Zip-A-Dee-Doo-Dah'	Ray Gilbert and Allie Wrubel	*Song of the South*
1948	'Buttons and Bows'	Jay Livingston and Ray Evans	*The Paleface*
1949	'Baby Its Cold Outside'	Frank Loesser	*Neptune's Daughter*
1950	'Mona Lisa'	Jay Livingston and Ray Evans	*Captain Carey, USA*
1951	'In the Cool, Cool, Cool of the Evening'	Johnny Mercer and Hoagy Carmichael	*Here Comes the Groom*
1952	'High Noon'	Ned Washington and Dimitri Tiomkin	*High Noon*
1953	'Secret Love'	Paul F Webster and Sammy Fain	*Calamity Jane*
1954	'Three Coins in the Fountain'	Sammy Cahn and Jule Styne	*Three Coins in the Fountain*
1955	'Love Is a Many-Splendored Thing'	Paul F Webster and Sammy Fain	*Love Is a Many-Splendored Thing*
1956	'Whatever Will Be, Will Be'	Jay Livingston and Ray Evans	*The Man Who Knew Too Much*
1957	'All the Way'	Sammy Cahn and J Van Heusen	*The Joker Is Wild*
1958	'Gigi'	A J Lerner and Frederick Loewe	*Gigi*
1959	'High Hopes'	Sammy Cahn and J Van Heusen	*A Hole in the Head*
1960	'Never on Sunday'	Billy Towne and M Hadjidakis	*Never on Sunday*
1961	'Moon River'	Johnny Mercer and Henry Mancini	*Breakfast at Tiffany's*
1962	'Days of Wine and Roses'	Johnny Mercer and Henry Mancini	*Days of Wine and Roses*
1963	'Call Me Irresponsible'	Sammy Cahn and J Van Heusen	*Papa's Delicate Condition*
1964	'Chim Chim Cher-ee'	Richard M and Robert B Sherman	*Mary Poppins*
1965	'The Shadow of Your Smile'	Paul F Webster and Johnny Mandel	*The Sandpiper*
1966	'Born Free'	Don Black and John Barry	*Born Free*
1967	'Talk to the Animals'	Leslie Bricusse	*Doctor Dolittle*
1968	'The Windmills of Your Mind'	Alan and Marilyn Bergman and Michel Legrand	*The Thomas Crown Affair*

Year	Title	Author/Composer	Film
1969	'Raindrops Keep Falling on My Head'	Hal David and Burt Bacharach	*Butch Cassidy and the Sundance Kid*
1970	'For All We Know'	Robb Wilson and Arthur James and Fred Karlin	*Lovers and Other Strangers*
1971	'Theme from Shaft'	Isaac Hayes	*Shaft*
1972	'The Morning After'	Al Kasha and Joel Kirschhorn	*The Poseidon Adventure*
1973	'The Way We Were'	Alan and Marilyn Bergman and Marvin Hamlisch	*The Way We Were*
1974	'We May Never Love like This Again'	Al Kasha and Joel Hirschhorn	*The Towering Inferno*
1975	'I'm Easy'	Keith Carradine	*Nashville*
1976	'Love Theme' ('Evergreen')	Paul Williams and Barbra Streisand	*A Star Is Born*
1977	'You Light up My Life'	Joseph Brooks	*You Light Up My Life*
1978	'Last Dance'	Paul Jabara	*Thank God It's Friday*
1979	'It Goes Like This'	David Shire and Norman Gimbal	*Norma Rae*
1980	'Fame'	Dean Pitchford and Michael Gore	*Fame*

APPENDIX 2

IVORS

(The Ivor Novello Awards)

The Ivor Novello Awards were originated by composer Bruce Sievier when he was founder chairman of the British Songwriters Protective Association (later known as the Songwriters Guild of Great Britain, and now called the British Academy of Songwriters, Composers, and Authors). He considered that annual awards of some kind would be beneficial to British songwriters if they were presented to composers, authors and publishers for works of outstanding merit. They would also encourage new popular music. It was he who, when Ivor Novello died in 1951, suggested they should be called the Ivor Novello Awards, to perpetuate the major contribution Ivor had made to British music.

The awards were first presented in 1955 by the Songwriters Guild of Great Britain to the writers and publishers of works which were regarded as being outstanding contributions to British popular and light music. The winners in each category received a bronze statuette in the form of Euterpe, the Greek Muse of Song. Since the inception of the awards the annual presentation has been televised or featured on radio and the Ivors are now regarded as the Oscars of British popular music. The following have received awards in the category 'Most Performed Work of the Year'.

Year	Title	Composer/Author
1955	'Ev'rywhere'	Tolchard Evans and Larry Kahn
1956	'My September Love'	Tolchard Evans and Richard Mullan
1957	'We Will Make Love'	Ronald Hulme
1958	'Trudie'	Joe Henderson
1959	'Side Saddle'	Trevor Stanford (Russ Conway)
1960	'As Long As He Needs Me'	Lionel Bart
1961	'My Kind of Girl'	Leslie Bricusse
1962	'Stranger on the Shore'	Acker Bilk
1963	'She Loves You'	John Lennon and Paul McCartney
1964	'Can't Buy Me Love'	John Lennon and Paul McCartney
1965	'I'll Never Find Another You'	Tom Springfield
1966	'Michelle'	John Lennon and Paul McCartney
1967	'Puppet on a String'	Bill Martin and Phil Coulter
1968	'Congratulations'	Bill Martin and Phil Coulter
1969	'Ob-La-Di Ob-La-Da'	John Lennon and Paul McCartney
1970	'Yellow River'	Jeff Christie
1971	'My Sweet Lord'	George Harrison
1972	'Beg, Steal or Borrow'	Graeme Hall and Tony Coe
1973	'Get Down'	Gilbert O'Sullivan
1974	'Wombling Song'	Mike Batt
1975	'I'm Not in Love'	Eric Stewart and Graham Gouldman
1976	'Save Your Kisses'	Tony Hiller, Martin Lee and Lee Sheridan
1977	'Don't Cry for Me Agentina'	Tim Rice and Andrew Lloyd Webber
1978	'Night Fever'	Barry, Robin and Maurice Gibb
1979	'Bright Eyes'	Mike Batt
1980	'Together We Are Beautiful'	Ken Leray

Bibliography

The *ASCAP Biographical Dictionary* (of Composers, Authors and Publishers), R R Bowker & Co, 1980

A Directory of Popular Music, Leslie Lowe, Peterson Publishing Co, 1975

The Book of Golden Discs, Joseph Murrells, Simon & Jenkins, 1978

An Encyclopaedia of Pop Rock & Soul, Irwin Stambler, St James' Press, 1974

The Country Music Encyclopaedia, Melvin Shestack, Omnibus Press, 1977

A History of Popular Music in America, Sigmund Spaeth, Phoenix House, 1960

Sixty Years of British Hits, The Songwriters Guild of Great Britain, 1968

Great Men of American Popular Song, David Ewen, Prentice Hall Inc, 1972

They're Playing Our Song, Max Wilk, Atheneum Press, 1973

The Tin Pan Alley Blue Book Vols 1 & 2, Jack Burton, Century House, 1962

The Blue Book of Broadway Musicals, Jack Burton, Century House, 1969

The Blue Book of Hollywood Musicals, Jack Burton, Century House, 1953

The Songwriters, Tony Staveacre, BBC, 1980

Baby that Was Rock 'n' Roll, Robert Palmer, Harcourt Brace Jovanovich, 1978

Rock File Editions 1–5 Eds, Charlie Gillett and Simon Frith, Panther Books, 1972/4/5/6/8

One for the Money, Dave Harker, Hutchinson, 1980

A History of Popular Music, David Ewen, Constable & Co, 1961

The World of Musical Comedy, Stanley Green, Thomas Yoseloff, 1960

The Encyclopaedia of Popular Music, Irwin Stambler, St Martin's Press

Happy With the Blues (Harold Arlen), Edward Jablonski, Doubleday, 1961

The Beatles, Hunter Davies, Heinemann, 1968

Sometimes I Wonder, Hoagy Carmichael, Alvin Redman, 1966

The Stardust Road, Hoagy Carmichael, The Musicians Press, 1946

Bob Dylan, Anthony Scaduto, W H Allen, 1972

Harry Warren and the Hollywood Musical, Tony Thomas, Citadel Press, 1975

Perchance to Dream; The World of Ivor Novello, Richard Rose, Leslie Frewin, 1974

Ivor (Ivor Novello), Sandy Wilson, Thomas Yoseff, 1974

Ain't Misbehavin' (Fats Waller), Ed Kirkeby, Peter Davies, 1966

A Talent to Amuse (Noel Coward), Sheridan Morley, W H Allen, 1972

Noel (Noel Coward), Lesley Cole, W H Allen, 1972

I'm on a See-Saw, Vivian Ellis, Michael Joseph, 1953

Elton John and Bernie Taupin, Ed. Paul Gambaccini, Flash Books, 1975

In His Own Words (Paul McCartney), Ed. Paul Gambaccini, Omnibus Press, 1976

Paul Simon, Now and Then, Spencer Leigh, Raven Books, 1973

The Father of the Blues, W C Handy, Macmillan NY, 1941

Victor Herbert, American Music Master, Claire Lee, Panther Books, 1976

The Story of Stevie Wonder, James Haskins, Panther Books, 1975

Lyrics on Several Occasions, Ira Gershwin, Elm Tree Books, 1959

I Should Care, Sammy Cahn, W H Allen, 1975

All You Need Is Love; The Story of Popular Music, Tony Palmer, Weidenfeld & Nicholson, 1976

The World of Duke Ellington, Stanley Dance, MacMillan, 1971

The Dance Band Era, Albert McCarthy, Studio Vista, 1971

All the Years of American Popular Music, David Ewen, Prentice Hall, 1962

American Popular Song, Alec Wilder, Oxford University Press, 1972

Carole King, Mitchell S Cohen, Barnes & Noble, 1976

Irving Berlin, Michael Freedland, W H Allen, 1974

Jerome Kern, Michael Freedland, Robson, 1978

Thou Swell Thou Witty (Lorenz Hart), Dorothy Hart, Elm Tree Book, 1978

The Sound of their Music (Rodgers and Hammerstein), Frederick Nolan, Dent, 1978

Musical Stages, Richard Rodgers, Random House, 1975

Cole Porter, Charles Schwarz, W H Allen, 1978

Winners Got Scars Too (Johnny Cash), Christopher Wren, Abacus, 1974

The Life and Death of Tin Pan Alley, David Ewen, Funk & Wagnall, 1964

Tin Pan Alley, Eddie Rogers, Hale, 1964

A Guide to Popular Music, Peter Gammond and Peter Clayton, Phoenix House, 1960

The Encyclopaedia of the Musical, Stanley Green, Cassell, 1977

The Street Where I Live, Alan Jay Lerner, Hodder & Stoughton, 1978

Cole (Cole Porter), Brendan Gill, Michael Joseph, 1976

Index of Song Titles

Index of Composers and Lyricists

Capital letters indicate a main entry in The Songwriters section.

Index of Performers

Index of Musical
Shows and Films